W9-DHR-519

DATE			

BAKER & TAYLOR

Charles Lathrop Pack

Charles Lathrop Pack. (Courtesy of the State University of New York College of Environmental Science and Forestry.)

Charles Lathrop Pack

TIMBERMAN, FOREST CONSERVATIONIST,

AND PIONEER IN FOREST EDUCATION

Alexandra Eyle

ESF College Foundation, Inc.
College of Environmental Science and Forestry
State University of New York, Syracuse, New York 13210
1992

This book is part of the Charles Lathrop Pack Biographical Project at the State University of New York College of Environmental Science and Forestry. This project consists of three parts: the creation of this biography, the establishment of the Charles Lathrop Pack Archival Collection out of the materials compiled for the biography, and the establishment of the Charles Lathrop Pack Fellowship Fund from the biography royalties.

Funding for the creation of the Pack biography was provided by Virginia Lathrop (Pack) Townsend, a granddaughter of Charles Lathrop Pack. The State University of New York College of Environmental Science and Forestry provided the author with office space, a personal computer, and secretarial and clerical help.

The paper for this book was generously donated by P. H. Glatfelter Company, Spring Grove, Pennsylvania 17362.

LIBRARY OF CONGRESS CATALOG CARD NUMBER: 93-073189
ISBN 0-8156-8177-8

Charles Lathrop Pack: Timberman, Forest Conservationist, and Pioneer in Forest Education was designed, produced, and typeset by Kachergis Book Design of Pittsboro, North Carolina. It was printed on 60-pound Glatfelter Natural Smooth text stock and bound in ICG Arrestox by Braun-Brumfield of Ann Arbor, Michigan

I dedicate this book to the memory of William
H. Carr, who would be amazed at how his suggestion was carried out.

> —Virginia Lathrop (Pack) Townsend
>
> October 1993

Contents

List of Illustrations

Acknowledgments

I was asked to write this book because of my experience in profile writing and historical research—and because of my ignorance of forestry. The idea was that this ignorance would enable me to focus on Charles Lathrop Pack's personality over and above forestry and forest history.

I agree that Charles's personality should be the most prominent part of this book, and hope that it is. I do not expect to hide behind my original ignorance, however. In the process of writing this book, I spent two years learning about forestry conservation and forestry history. If there are any errors of fact, I take full responsibility for them.

I am indebted to Virginia Lathrop (Pack) Townsend, who had the idea for this book, invited me to write it, and funded it, yet never tried to control my vision of Charles. Indeed, she gave me total freedom, and was always willing to answer questions and provide insights, flattering and otherwise, about Charles Lathrop Pack. Mrs. Townsend's eagerness to have a full account of her grandfather and her helpfulness in making this happen were echoed by the rest of the Pack family, who gave unstintingly of their memories, good or bad, and shared their family letters, diaries, and photos as well.

I am also profoundly indebted to the poet, writer, and editor Robert Phillips, who had enough faith in me to recommend me for this project.

My mother, the artist Mila Agnes Johnston Mitchell, of Boulder, Colorado, and my husband, Nicolas Eyle, get three cheers for always cheering me on and almost daily telling me how proud they are of me. I am also grateful for their tactful and astute editorial comments.

I am indebted to my father, John David Mitchell, a tough journalism professor at Syracuse University, whose scrutiny of this book made it better, and whose encouragement kept me going.

Important assistance regarding my understanding of forest history and practice was provided by John Tarver, Harold K. Steen, Donald Theoe, James E. Coufal, and Barry Walsh. As a neophyte in this field, I am deeply grateful for their patient guidance.

Special thanks go to the novelist Douglas Unger, who took time out from much more pressing demands to give me welcome editorial insights and personal encouragement at the start of this project.

I am indebted also to Archer H. Mayor, author of *Southern Timberman: The Legacy of William Buchanan,* for sharing business records and photographs of the Buchanan mills with me.

My graduate assistants, Jackie Burns and Shirley Duffy, must be singled out for special praise. Both cheerfully and diligently took on monumental jobs of research and organization, and produced outstanding results. In between shouldering their tasks, they provided me with much-needed relief by being there to simply listen as I expressed frustration over some research obstacle, wondered about Charles's inconsistencies of character, or shouted "Eureka!" when we at last answered another question. Their senses of humor often provided much-needed comic relief from the grind of research. Finally, both Jackie and Shirley were gracious enough to overlook my bouts of bad humor when the going was toughest.

Special thanks are due Arthur Fritz and Ralph Sanders, who gave me total artistic freedom while they administered this project. In addition, I am grateful to Donald F. Webster, director of F. Franklin Moon Library and Learning Resources Center, for giving me an office and access to his staff. The librarians Flora Nyland, Jim Williamson, and Betsey Elkins performed miracles for me. Their friendly support, as well as that of staff member Norma Taylor, brightened many long days.

Above all, I am indebted to nearly one hundred researchers, librarians, archivists, local historians, and state government clerks across the United States, Canada, and Germany. I am also deeply grateful to all of the Pack family members who gave so generously of their memories. This book could not have been written without them. Their names, and those of the researchers who assisted me, are listed below:

PACK FAMILY MEMBERS

Mark Bahti
Elizabeth M. Boggs
Joan Pack Burns
Frances White Field
Eleanor Brown Pack Hibben
Eleanor Pack Liddell
Margaret Pack Bahti McKinley

Norma Pack
Phoebe Finley Pack
Robert Pack
Virginia Lathrop (Pack)
   Townsend
Amos White

RESEARCHERS

Jan Anderson
Mary Anteaux
Paul Axel-Lute
Lisa Backman
Jean Baker
Sharon Band
Roland Baumann
Ken Beam
Claire Bey
Lawrence J. Borger
Bruce Breitmeyer
Margaret Brill
Lewis Buck
Anna Burns
Jackie Burns
Gould P. Coleman
Glenda Cooper
Sam Christopher
Richard Crawford
Mary Creech
David Crippens
Hilary Cummings
Nancy Dean

Rosemarie DeJohn
Harry Wm. Dengler
John B. Downs
Donna Ellis
Adelaide Elm
Pete Evans
Klaus C. Ewald
Madeline Felker
John Ferris
Jeff Flannery
Marylyn Fontenelli
Barbara Fritz
Alan Fusonie
Sister Mary Christina
   Geis
Bonita Grant
John A. Gustafson
Dorothea Hammond
Marylyn L. Hebner
Gene Hendrickson
Lois Hendrickson
Mary Jane Henninger
Klaus Herrmann

Marion Hirsch
Claudia C. Holland
Edith C. Holscher
Helen Huss
Beth Johnson
Greg Kinney
Peter Knapp
Sylvia Kruger
James P. Lassoie
Joyce Le Blanc
Bob Ledford
Gary Lundell
Monica Martines
Karen M. Mason
Archer H. Mayor
Ann McLay
Jane Miller
Joseph Miller
Pauline Miller
Ellen Nemhauser
Steve Nielson
Jeanne Pablo
Faye Phillips

Nancy Pope   Richard Schwab   Stanley Walsh
Gloria Rambo   Mary Jane Sharp   Winona Walsh
Bill Rooney   Ann Sindelar   Elizabeth Wells
Sister Mary Rose   Harold K. Steen   Helen Whiting
Ann Rowles   George Stevens   Gordon Whitney
Nancy Ruben   Barbara Stevenson   Stephen R. Williams
Helen Ross Russell   Don Theoe   Len Woodbury
Bruce Rutherford   Mitch Tiegel   Harlan Yenne
Volker Schafer   David Van Tassel
Judith Schiff   Barry Walsh

Introduction

When Charles Lathrop Pack died in 1937 at the age of eighty, he left behind an impressive yet contradictory legacy. One of America's great capitalists, Charles Lathrop Pack was a multimillionaire on a par with John D. Rockefeller and Jay Gould. Reportedly, he was one of the five wealthiest men in America prior to World War I.[1]

Charles Pack made his fortune by taking over the Michigan timber mills of his millionaire father and making his own savvy investments, primarily in southern timber, but also in banking and real estate. Then, during the last twenty-nine years of his life, he became a key player in a major national forest conservation movement. Ultimately, through state and national legislation, this movement preserved millions of acres of American forests. In the process, it transformed the practices of the timber industry. Rather than clear-cutting and abandoning denuded forest land, timber companies began managing their forests as renewable crops. Now, when clear-cutting is done, it is standard procedure to leave seed trees behind for natural regeneration. If no seed trees can be left behind, the land is replanted with seedlings.

Attitudes of private citizens have changed as well. Americans gradually ended a tradition of setting fire to forests to clear land for grazing or agriculture, to settle a score against a hated neighbor, or simply for the fun of it. In addition, state and national fire control systems were established, as were national and state parks.

This American forest conservation movement (forest management had been commonplace in Europe for centuries) has a history that goes back to the 1600s. It did not begin to grow cohesively until the late 1800s, however, and only gained national momentum under the leadership of President Theodore Roosevelt and Gifford Pinchot, the chief forester for the U.S. Department of Agriculture's Division of Forestry (later called the Bureau of Forestry, and, later still, the Forest Service). Pinchot was a guiding light of the movement, and Charles Pack worked closely with him before becoming a conservation leader in his own right.

Charles Pack's conservation career began in 1908, when he attended President Theodore Roosevelt's historic Conference of Governors. The conference brought state and federal officials and timbermen together for the first time to discuss the implications of forest conservation.

When Charles died, newspapers across the country heralded him as a major leader in forest conservation. He had worked for and helped fund several lobbying organizations that helped pass key timber conservation legislation. He headed a major conservation congress. For seven years he served as a controversial president of the American Forestry Association. Then, after losing a power struggle with the other AFA officers, he left that agency and launched his own conservation organizations.

His first was the American Tree Association, established in 1922 as a vehicle for promoting forest conservation through massive public-relations campaigns. Working with a staff that sometimes swelled to three hundred, Charles Pack issued national propaganda on behalf of the cause by sending beautifully designed matrices and slick proofs containing editorials, cartoons, and news and feature articles to virtually every newspaper in the country, which in turn published these materials. The result of one campaign was that American citizens planted almost thirty million trees in a two-year period. In addition, Charles also established the American Nature Association, which monthly published *Nature Magazine* and lobbied for roadside beautification programs.

Through this publicity, Charles Lathrop Pack's name and face became paired with forest conservation in headlines, articles, editorials, and cartoons. For the public, the man and the cause became virtually synonymous.

In addition, Charles Lathrop Pack kept professional foresters informed through his *Forestry News Digest,* a monthly publication that he distributed at no charge to subscribers. The *Digest* quickly became a bible for foresters and forestry professors wanting to keep current on everything from the status of forestry regulations to the latest debate among key figures in the movement.

Charles also became a pioneer in forestry research and education. He established two demonstration forests and supported three others in the country's leading forestry colleges. Today, these "show windows of forestry," as he liked to call them, continue to give both the general public and small landowners a firsthand look at forest management in action. In addition, the forests provide excellent laboratories for forest research projects.

Furthermore, Charles endowed a soil science chair at Cornell, which was the first endowed professorship in America devoted solely to researching the relationship of soils to forest growth. He later created a major forest conservation chair at the University of Michigan. In addition, he established two private forestry education and research foundations that financed innumerable forest research projects here and abroad, including groundbreaking studies of tropical rain forests.

He also personally contributed to the field by writing numerous books on the subject, including *The Forestry Primer,* five million copies of which were distributed to schools, and which was translated into Italian.

Outside of his conservation work, Charles Pack was a zealous patriot and community man. He organized, funded, and headed the National War Garden Commission, which led the hugely successful national war garden (later called victory garden) movement during World War I. Through this commission, Charles marshaled the country in planting millions of war gardens as part of the war effort. By planting their own vegetables and preserving them, Americans left commercially grown food free to be sent to soldiers overseas. The commission's work was so successful that it has been used in college-level courses as an example of a superlative public-relations campaign.

The vision that Charles had of food gardens springing up across

America touches the heart deeply and has appeal even today, in peacetime. Such gardens could benefit America's thousands of poor, who subsist on government programs that forbid their working for hire. Such gardens would feed these people and their children and brighten their communities, visually and spiritually, at minimal cost. In these days of homelessness and increasing numbers of poor people, one yearns for a leader such as Charles Lathrop Pack to bring such a program back to life and raise up the same spirit of pride and self-sufficiency that sprang, as wonderful by-products, from the produce of the war gardens.

Following World War I, Charles helped reforest the Allied countries, whose forests had been devastated.

In his own home of Cleveland, Ohio, and, later, Lakewood, New Jersey, as an active Republican Charles lobbied for various Republican politicians at both the state and national levels. Locally he was influential in civic affairs, especially in Cleveland, where he was a mayoral nominee, chamber of commerce president, and co-founder of the Cleveland Trust Company. He also helped relocate Cleveland's business district and bring the great Statler Hotel to that city.

By the end of his life, Charles Lathrop Pack had received numerous and impressive honors and awards from around the world, including honorary degrees from Oberlin College, Rutgers College, and Syracuse University; the Liberty Service Medal of the National Institute of Social Sciences; and the grand medal of honor of the Société National d'Acclimation de France.

Whether Charles was satisfied by all of his accomplishments may never be known. At some point in his adulthood he changed his name from Charles Pack to the more grandiloquent Charles Lathrop Pack—Lathrop after his paternal grandmother, Maria Lathrop—and this change may have been symbolic of a new feeling of self-importance. Not that he seemed stuffy. With his twinkling blue eyes, pointed white beard, and small but energetic stature, he appeared to some to be as gentle and open and happy as a merry little Santa Claus. But others perceived him as an insecure man who sought outside approval and could never feel satisfied with himself. If such an insecurity existed, perhaps it was based on an underlying fear that he was not, in fact, all that he seemed.

Charles Lathrop Pack misrepresented himself and his credentials in several ways. A successful timber baron, he presented himself as having studied forestry in Germany and retired from the industry to become a forest conservationist. In addition, he claimed to have proposed to President Theodore Roosevelt, along with Gifford Pinchot, that the president hold a national conference on forest conservation (later known as the Conference of Governors). He also promoted himself as "one of the pioneers of the conservation movement."[2]

My research has revealed that one of these claims is exaggerated and others are simply untrue. He never retired from the timber industry but was instead actively involved in it throughout his conservation career, and none of the timber mills with which he was involved practiced the conservation methods he preached. There is no evidence that he ever formally studied forestry in Germany—in fact, all the available evidence suggests otherwise. Similarly, the record does not support his claim that he helped suggest the Conference of Governors to Roosevelt. Finally, he was not a pioneer in the conservation movement—it had been growing for many years before he became involved with it.

He was, however, legitimately a pioneer in forest education and in publicizing conservation issues. Thanks to his magnetic personality, public-relations genius, and vast fortune, Charles did a great deal for the forest conservation movement. Yet his name is largely missing from the annals of forest and forestry history.

My objective in writing this book is threefold: to establish Charles Lathrop Pack as a significant figure in American political, economic, social, and conservation history by documenting all his achievements; to debunk the myths about the man, such as his having retired from the timber industry to become a founding father of forest conservation; and to examine the psychological workings of this extraordinary and contradictory man.

By revealing Charles Lathrop Pack's inconsistencies and psychological motivations, I hope to set the record straight in two ways: by showing all that Charles Lathrop Pack was and all that he was not.

During his lifetime, many who had once dismissed Charles Lathrop Pack would later state unequivocally that he had done more for the cause of forest conservation—in shaping public opinion and in supporting formal forestry education and forest research—than any other single person in the country.

That judgment still holds true. Much progress has been made in forest conservation since Charles first joined the cause. Yet the public-relations skills of a Charles Lathrop Pack, as well as the private financing provided by such a figure, are needed even today. Around the world, conservationists are fighting against the daily destruction of primeval rainforests and their ecosystems; in the United States, portions of national forests are being sold to real estate developers; and conservationists and timbermen continue to do battle over whether, how, and when the nation's trees should be cut and transformed into lumber or paper. With forest conservation edging once more into the national consciousness, the time is ripe for someone as dynamic and generous as Charles Lathrop Pack to become a national—even worldwide—leader in the movement, and in so doing to make forest conservation a household word once more.

It is my opinion that when Charles Pack's forest conservation accomplishments are added to his many other achievements—creating the National War Garden Commission, establishing a major bank, helping to reforest Europe—there can be no doubt that, despite his tendency to take credit where none was due and his failure to personally practice what he preached, Charles Lathrop Pack achieved more than most people dare even dream of doing in one lifetime.

Note to Readers

The reader will find that since Charles Lathrop Pack did not become active in the forest conservation movement until 1908, when he was fifty-one years old, the early part of this biography deals with Charles's nonforestry activities. Chapters 1 through 6 and 10, 11, and 16 examine Charles's family history, including his relationship with his father and his resulting need to excel; his childhood homes and education in Michigan and Ohio; his marriage; his relationship to his children, and especially his youngest son, Arthur; and his careers as a timberman, banker, real estate speculator, and society leader of Cleveland, Ohio.

Chapter 14 deals with Charles's successful efforts, during World War I, to promote the planting of war gardens, later known as victory gardens, on a national scale. His forest conservation work is covered extensively in chapters 7, 8, 9, 15, 17, 18, and 20. Chapters 12 and 13 give a detailed account of Charles Pack's seven-year term as American Forestry Association president, and the events that led to an uprising against him as AFA president. Thus, foresters, forest historians, and conservationists who are interested only in this latter part of Charles's life may focus on these chapters, which document Charles's considerable impact on the forestry conservation movement in America, from 1908 to 1937. Likewise, general readers may wish to skim chapters that may seem too concerned with the details of forestry and the politics of forest conservation.

Readers who are interested in both Charles's private life and his work in forestry conservation will find that there is much less personal information in the second half of the book than in the first. This is due to the fact that there is virtually no documentation of

Charles Lathrop Pack's personal life during his years as a forest conservationist, beyond the occasional reference he made in his business correspondence. Nevertheless, there is early documentation regarding Charles's psychological motivations, and these are explored throughout the book.

I have tried to write this book in a style that is accessible to the general reader. Scholars of forestry and conservation history, however, may want to make use of the endnotes and the list of sources, which includes bibliographic and archival materials as well as interviews and correspondence.

Charles Lathrop Pack

CHAPTER 1

A Timberman's Son

MERICA IN THE 1800s. A time of deep ambition when fortunes were made and lost all too quickly. A time of boom or bust, of heading west to stake a claim. By the late 1800s, the vast woodlands of Michigan were also drawing ambitious men, attracted not by the pull of gold mines, but by another kind of gold—green gold. Timbermen and timber speculators were dreaming of making fortunes from Michigan timber, which fairly covered the state. By the mid-1860s, Charles Pack had seen his own father build a thriving mill, Carrington, Pack & Company, and go on to open another mill soon after. Inspired by his own father's example, and perhaps even the spirit of the times, one cold winter's day Charlie decided it was time to go into business for himself. He was barely ten years old.

First he raided the family cellar, which was packed with preserves of all kinds and sacks of flour and sugar to last through the winter, as well as fruit and nuts. He took enough apples and peanuts to fill his red wagon. After loading the wagon he pulled it to the sawmill, his footsteps crunching and the wagon wheels creaking across the snow, breaking the stillness of the crisp, cold air. Entering the mill, Charlie was blasted by the sound of saws screaming through massive white pine logs, the burning smell of hot saw teeth cutting through wood, and the sight of sawdust flying.

Calmly he settled himself and his wagon in the midst of this din. Glancing up from their dirty, dangerous work, the sawyers wondered what the boss's son was doing there. One by one they left their posts and wandered over to investigate. Was he offering them treats from the Pack cellar, perhaps? No. The apples and peanuts were for sale—the apples a bargain at two for a penny.[1]

But as he happily began selling his produce, Charlie was suddenly brought up short by one worker's curt question: "Can't your father make enough money out of our wages without your selling peanuts?" For the rest of his life Charles Pack was to remember that question. How could that man not realize that he had to make his own way, just as his father and grandfather had, and stand on his own two feet?[2]

Throughout his life Charles would be constantly driven to take on new projects, from banking to conservation, just to prove to everyone—from millworkers on up to United States presidents—that he was his own man, a man of power and prestige, and not just his father's son. As a result of this drive, Charles would manage to outdo his father in terms of his life's accomplishments. Ultimately he would become nationally known as a forest conservationist, rubbing shoulders with the likes of President Teddy Roosevelt and Gifford Pinchot. Yet as a child he must have been overwhelmed at times by the thought of competing with his father, George Willis Pack, for both his father and his grandfather, George Pack, had left impressive legacies.

Charles's grandfather, George Pack, founded the Pack timber empire when he moved to Michigan in 1848. He had grown up in New Jersey and moved to upstate New York after marrying Maria Lathrop of Madison County, New York. The couple lived for a time near Maria's father, Abram Lathrop, in his "smaller house" in Madison County; they then moved twelve miles away to Peterboro, where they stayed for eleven years. In 1848, after selling a run-down farm in Watertown, New York, for the impressive sum of $13,500, George Pack loaded his wife and ten children onto an Erie Canal sidewheeler. They rode it to the end of the line at Buffalo and from there headed up Lake Erie to Lake Huron, disembarking at Lexington, on the eastern shore of the Michigan thumb, overlooking Lake Huron.[3]

The farm sale had made George a relatively rich man, but

Michigan offered greater riches. At Lexington, George settled his wife and children—Louisa M., George Willis (Charles Pack's future father), Byron, Lorinda, Angeline, Helen, Albert, Greene, Josephine, and Emma—who ranged in age from nineteen to one, on eighty acres of land he had bought on the edge of Lexington village. George and his eldest son, George Willis, then seventeen, cleared the land and planted orchards of pear, apple, and quince. They built a barn, a frame house for the family, and a plain boardinghouse for the help.[4]

Although relatively prosperous, the Packs were isolated, and the thirteen years they spent in Lexington, from 1848 until 1861, were not easy. Winters were cold and fierce, making transport and shipping difficult if not impossible at times. To survive the year, the Packs had to ship in and store large quantities of such staples as butter, flour, cornmeal, apples, pork, and sugar from Detroit.[5]

The first year may have been the hardest. In 1849, there was no school nearby, so the children studied at home under the guidance of the eldest child, nineteen-year-old Louisa. Their studies were interrupted in October when typhoid fever swept through the family, nearly killing George Willis.

"Few who saw him," his mother wrote in a letter to her father, "thought he would live." Only George the father and one daughter, twelve-year-old Angeline, were spared the fever; George nearly made himself sick from nursing the others.[6] "George watched over us day and night," wrote Maria, "as few others would. The neighbors talked of taking him from the house saying he would kill himself with over watching." But even these heroic efforts could not save the second-eldest son, fourteen-year-old Byron, who died in November.[7]

Despite this harrowing first year, the Packs stayed in Lexington. Between 1850 and 1856 three more children, Edward, Arthur, and Herbert, were born. Maria is remembered for never raising her voice to her thirteen children and for teaching them all French.[8]

George Pack made his first investment in the timber industry this first year as well, when he paid $1,600 for 720 acres of timberland near the Black River. The acreage was located ten miles north of Lexington, near a town called Farmers, now known as Carsonville.[9] Two of his sons, George Willis and Albert, worked closely with him, first clearing the land and later building and running the mills.

Michigan had so many trees of so many types that at one time 96 percent of the land mass—35.2 million acres—was dense with oak, white pine, Norway pine, jack pine, beech, tamarack, basswood, elm, and maple, as well as cherry and yellow birch. This vast, richly varied forest remained largely untouched until 1834, when Michigan was declared a state. But by 1888, enough lumber had been sawed in the mills along the Saginaw River to make a sidewalk of two-inch planks four feet wide that could wrap around the Earth four times.[10]

For the lumbermen who reaped Michigan's green gold, the stands of white and Norway pine (also called red pine) offered some of the best timbering in the state. These remarkable trees were hundreds of years old, tall and straight, knot-free, and light enough to float on the waterways the Michigan timbermen depended on for easy access to major ports of trade. Michigan's myriad rivers ran into Lake Michigan and Lake Huron, which ultimately connected to the Erie Canal and the Hudson River.[11]

Of these early timbermen, George Pack was among the first to capitalize on white and Norway pine. In 1850, of the 435 sawmills in the state, only six were cutting pine.[12] George Pack was keenly interested in the light, easily transportable, knot-free white pine. Although he was not yet cutting it, he was buying up white pine in preparation for the time when he would open his own mills. His land featured some of "the best white or cork pine in the world," ranging in age from one hundred to three hundred years old.[13]

In 1856 George began operating his first sawmill in what had been designated Washington Township the previous year.[14] The village of Applegate grew up around that mill. In 1857 he opened a second mill, also in Washington Township. The two mills created the settlement milltown of Pack's Mills.[15] As the sawmills thrived, the Packs built a grist mill along the eastern shore of the river, and later a flour mill. By 1861 they had erected a frame house, into which George moved his family that year. Although it has been renovated and remodeled over the years, the house still stands as a reminder of the industry that once thrived there.[16]

While Maria tended the children and the farm, George, George Willis, and Albert labored in and around the Black River area of Washington Township. In addition to acquiring timberland (by 1876 sixteen hundred acres would be in the Pack name), they cleared land for agricultural purposes, believing that one day the area would become a lively community. The first millowner in Washington Township, George Pack also functioned as postmaster for the southern part of the township, operating the Pack's Mills post office from his house. He carried the mail in his hat, from whence he would retrieve it and deliver it to the locals as he encountered them on the street.[17]

There is no question that as a businessman George Pack wanted to make a profit. But unlike many of his contemporaries, he did not completely exploit the land in his quest for riches. One Sanilac County resident whose grandfather knew George Pack recalled that while many of the lumber barons who harvested the great white pines along the Black River "cut recklessly and thoughtlessly, little caring what became of the remaining forests, George Pack did care about what became of the remaining forests and lands. All the trees were not cut and much land was cleared for farming."[18]

George Pack died on April 15, 1875, at the age of seventy-five. He was remembered as "a man of more than ordinary ability [who] possessed inventive genius of no common order." In addition to his business acumen, he invented a valuable stave-cutting machine. He was also known as a man who "lived a life of usefulness, and [who was] a trustworthy and enterprising citizen."[19]

Following George Pack's death his three eldest sons, George Willis, Albert, and Greene, continued to work in the lumber industry, but it was George Willis and, later, his son Charles who expanded the Pack timber empire.

As a young man, George Willis worked with his father in the timber business until 1857. In that year, at the age of twenty-six, he moved to Fort Gratiot, an old French-and-Indian War fort north of Port Huron, to work as a government surveyor. In 1860 he entered a partnership with John L. Woods to establish a mill of his own, the Carrington, Pack & Company lumber mill. This mill was located at Sand Beach, forty miles north of Lexington, near the tip of the Michigan thumb.

In the meantime, he had also started a family of his own. In 1854 George Willis married Frances "Phoebe" Farman, daughter of Captain Samuel Ward Farman. Frances met George Willis soon after she and her family had moved to Michigan from Milwaukee, Wisconsin. The couple married in Detroit but lived at first in Lexington, where Charles, their first child, was born on May 7, 1857, shortly before the move to Fort Gratiot. Mary was born in 1860, Millicent in 1865 (she died the same year), and Beulah in 1869.

George Willis moved his family to Sand Beach in 1861, when Charles was four and Mary was one. Little more than a pioneer town, Sand Beach consisted of an "uptown" district of four log cabins, the small wooden frame house that Charles and his family lived in, and the mill, dock, general store, and boardinghouse; and another district with a school, a courthouse, and a few settler shanties.[20]

The economic key to the Sand Beach community was Carrington, Pack & Company. The importance of his father to this community could not have been lost on young Charles: over the years, Carrington, Pack & Company came to own five thousand acres of timber in Huron County alone, as well as twenty-five thousand acres of pine land further west along the Pinnebog River. Charles's father, George Willis Pack, would be remembered as one of the few millionaires who had lived in Huron County.[21]

Extremely ambitious, George Willis was not satisfied with owning only one mill. Just four years after starting Carrington, Pack & Company, he decided to expand with yet another partnership. In 1864, he, John L. Woods, and Jeremiah Jenks opened another lumber business, Pack, Jenks & Company. The new firm purchased and operated a sawmill at Allen's Creek in Rock Falls, two and a half miles south of Sand Beach.[22]

In 1870, George Willis, his brother Greene, John L. Woods, and Edwin F. Holmes formed another timber mill, Woods & Company. Located at Port Crescent, Woods & Company was run by Greene Pack and Edwin Holmes. [23] Then in 1876, George Willis sold Carrington, Pack & Company and Pack, Jenks & Company to Jeremiah Jenks, who merged them to form J. Jenks & Company, based at Sand Beach.

Above, left: George Willis Pack, father of Charles Lathrop Pack, at the time he began expanding the then fledgling Pack timber empire. (Courtesy of Elizabeth Boggs.)

Above, right: Frances Farman Pack, wife of George Willis Pack and mother of Charles Lathrop Pack. (Courtesy of Elizabeth Boggs.)

That same year, George Willis, Woods, and Holmes created a new mill, Pack, Woods & Company. Operating out of Oscoda, on the northeastern coast of Michigan, Pack, Woods & Company was conveniently located on the Au Sable River near its outlet into Lake Huron. This would become George Willis's most successful mill.[24]

George Willis was the major financier of Pack, Woods & Company, and Greene Pack was vice president and manager of the firm. In 1877, the company "purchased large holdings of pine lands on the Pine and AuSable Rivers, also some 200 acres of land in what later became Oscoda village, for a site for a mill and yards, and the following year built one of the finest mills in the state at Oscoda, together with a salt block, docks, barns, shops, store buildings and two fine homes for the resident partners, Greene Pack and E. F. Holmes."[25] Formally incorporated in 1882, by 1884 Pack, Woods & Company had improved and increased the mill's capacity to the point that it was "considered one of the finest in the world. . . . No other mill anywhere had better power." The mill averaged forty million board feet a year, running day and night.[26]

The Packs—George Willis, his brothers Greene and Albert, and later Charles, when he took over his father's businesses—were among the key consumers of Michigan white pine, producing lumber out of what Charles described as "the finest pine in the world," with "trees measuring one thousand board feet."[27]

Of all of the Pack mills, Pack, Woods & Company manufactured the most timber. In 1885, just three years after incorporating, the company set a record by cutting 310,880 board feet of lumber in one day. When a neighboring mill broke that record by 39,120 board feet, Greene Pack, then superintendent of the mill, became determined to set yet another record. On November 18, 1885, Pack, Woods & Company cut 442,830 board feet of lumber in just 10.5 hours. Greene had set a new record, but apparently would have been happier had he reached the 500,000 mark: "But for an untoward accident," one newspaper reporter observed, "necessitating some delay, and the fact that the supply of selected logs was exhausted before night, the 500,000 mark undoubtedly would have been reached." All told, Pack, Woods & Company cut 1.25 billion board feet of lumber. In just one season the mill turned out 78 million board feet.[28]

Pack, Woods & Company's timber consumption would continue into the 1890s, ending with the last gasps of the great Michigan timber boom. When the mill closed, either in 1894, 1896, or 1901—accounts of the closing vary—it was one of the last mills to shut down in the Au Sable Valley.[29] The scene that the Packs and other timber barons left behind as they headed south and to the Pacific Northwest to greener pastures was ghostly in its desolation. By 1920, of the cutover land the timbermen had abandoned across the country, eighty-one million acres had become idle land, "logged and burned into barrenness."[30]

Sometime around 1924, while looking for lands to claim and preserve as a national forest, William B. Greeley, chief forester for the U.S. Forest Service, toured the Au Sable Valley. This is what he found:

Oscoda

1878-1901 (?)
Pack Woods & Co.
(GWP)

LAKE
HURON

1870-1878
Woods & Co.
(GWP) in
Port Crescent

Port
Crescent

1861-1871
GWP and family
live in Sand Beach

Sand Beach

1860-1870
Carrington, Pack & Co.
(GWP) in Sand Beach

Rock Falls

1864-1870
Pack, Jenks & Co.
(GWP) in Rock Falls

1870
Carrington, Pack & Co.
and Pack, Jenks & Co. are
sold. Became known as
Jenks & Co., with mill
operating in Sand Beach.

1861-1875
GP and family live
in Washington Township

Applegate

Washington Township

Lexington

1856 & 1857
Packs Mills established
(GP) in Applegate

1848-1861
GP and family
live in Lexington

CANADA

THE PACKS'
MICHIGAN MILLS

GP=George Pack, Charles's grandfather
GWP=George Willis Pack, Charles's father

1871
GWP moves family
to Cleveland and
establishes lumberyard.

LAKE
ST. CLAIRE

Detroit

I hiked over many miles of burnt-out pineries looking up remnants of public land that might fit into a national forest. Between repeated fires and drifting sand, even the old stumps had mostly disappeared. It was hard to find any vestige of "tall, whispering pines." Here and there we found little hard black cones of wood forming a symmetrical pattern in the sand. They were the dense cores of knots in what was once a red pine tree or log. The rest of it had burned up completely. Here and there were pathetic evidences of attempted homesteading—a cellar half filled with sand, part of a stick and mud chimney still standing, or scraps of an old stove. The "pine barrens" of Michigan were well named.[31]

It would take years for Michigan, Pennsylvania, Maine, and other states to recover from the clear-cutting method of logging. As one historian would explain, "Since the farmland in the area

The timber mill crews had to labor throughout bitter Michigan winters. By working in winter, the timbermen could use ice roads to transport felled logs to the banks of rivers and streams. Come the spring thaw, the logs would be floated downstream to the mills. *(Courtesy of Virginia Lathrop [Pack] Townsend.)*

was submarginal for the most part and other resources were limited, many decades were to pass before tourism and a rising emphasis on outdoor recreation would finally bring some economic vitality back to the cutover region."[32]

For the young Charles, the impact of his father's success in business and his position in the community made more of an impression than the aftermath of his clear-cutting practices. From his first ventures, Charles applied the business acumen learned from his father, but he only became concerned with forest conservation much later—and never practiced these techniques in his own businesses.

CHAPTER 2

Growing Up

A S A CHILD in Sand Beach, Charles lived in a clearing that faced Lake Huron. But along the shore and behind the houses (in fact, throughout Huron County) stretched "as fine a forest of pine as ever grew heavenward."[1]

To see a stand of white pine on a sunlit day is to glimpse nature's cathedral. Shafts of sunlight alternate with lean straight trunks that range from two to five feet around and soar some seventy feet before the first lower branches appear. These majestic creatures laid the foundation of the Pack timber fortune. White pine would become Charles's favorite tree.[2]

Despite the beauty of the forest, life at Sand Beach was far from idyllic. Winters were so bitter that the children had to wear three pairs of woolen stockings with their moccasins. The nearest doctor was fifty miles away and could only be reached by horse or buggy. When Charles and Mary contracted diphtheria, George Willis felt there was no time to waste trying to get the children a doctor. Instead, he dipped a silver three-cent piece and a whalebone from a lady's corset into acid and used the whalebone to run the three-cent piece down their throats and break the diphtheria membranes. The radical remedy saved the children's lives.[3]

Life at Sand Beach was a physical trial for Charles's mother as well. Frances was a city girl, accustomed to material comforts. She was not spoiled, however, and had insisted on living at Sand Beach despite her husband's protests. For six years this frail woman endured the strain of a fierce climate and remote rural life. In 1865, she gave birth to Millicent, who died nine months later. Two years later, in 1867, with her own health weakening, Frances took Charles and Mary to the town of St. Catharines in Ontario, Canada, where she could be treated by a famous physician.[4]

At the age of nine, Charles was suddenly transported from the wild Michigan woods to a city and enrolled in a military academy. This was a far cry from the simple village schoolhouse in Sand Beach. Far from intimidated by the change, however, Charles thought nothing of asserting himself. When taking a history test, for example, Charles gave two answers to a question concerning the battle of Saratoga: "Here's what Montieth's [the history book, written from the British point of view] says, and here's what I think was the truth." At first the schoolmasters were angry at Charles's impertinence, but Charles told them, "I've only tried to show you that I've read my history. I've tried to be impartial." He won not only his argument, but the school history prize as well—a copy of the history book, which he kept throughout his life.[5]

In addition to asserting himself intellectually, Charles developed what would become a lifelong interest in stamp collecting. He was introduced to this hobby by his St. Catharines classmates, who corresponded with friends in Australia and New Zealand. In collecting the unusual new stamps, Charles laid the foundation for his later prize-winning collection of stamps from Great Britain and its colonies and from Spain and Brazil. These collections earned him virtually every medal and honor in the philatelic world. Ultimately, after donating the Canadian and Brazilian collections to a stamp collectors club and "disposing" of his Uruguayan collection, he gave his remaining collections to his son Arthur. He in turn sold them for nearly $500,000 and used the money to pay for the construction of Espanola Hospital in Espanola, New Mexico.[6]

In 1869, Charles and Mary returned to Sand Beach with their mother and a new baby sister, Beulah Brewster Pack. That year Charles launched his first major business venture since selling apples at his father's sawmill. This time he went into the manufacturing business: he cut cedar posts and then hired two sons of a millworker to haul them over the frozen lake on a large sled, presumably to sell at Oscoda, which lay directly across Saginaw Bay. Charles's sister Mary recalled that it was typical of Charles to hire out the manual labor. The investment paid off—Charles bought his first watch with the proceeds from the business.[7]

In 1871, in part because of Frances Pack's continuing delicate health and in part due to George Willis Pack's expanding business, the family moved to Cleveland, where George Willis had interests in a large lumberyard and later established one of his own.[8]

George Willis built a small wooden house at 816 Bolton Avenue in East Cleveland, then just a village. Again, Charles adapted easily to his new home. At the East Cleveland Grammar School, in addition to earning good marks, he edited and wrote for the *Progressive Weekly*, a small paper started by him and his classmates. Here his humor, interest in scholarship, and love of the written word, all hallmarks of Charles's later life, first took flower.[9]

Charles began the *Progressive Weekly* at the age of fourteen. An introduction to the second issue stated that "the progressive weekly is a paper devoted to useful reading and is published every week for the very small sum of nothing at all its contents are mostly original & are furnished by scholars as wish to improve themselves in writing composition in the English Language."[10]

What Charles and his fellow editor, L. Estep, lacked in punctuation and grammar they made up for in diligence and humor. The paper was written by hand on lined paper, divided into two columns, and apparently contained whatever topics interested its editors and contributors: short stories, articles on fishing, the city of Baltimore, carrier pigeons, the trials of writing composition, and how to make gunpowder.

At least one issue contained a moralism, written by Charles, in which a newsboy is asked if he would tell a lie for $1,000 and is admonished not to, for the "money will wear out but if you never tell a lie your reward will never wear out."[11]

Through the *Progressive Weekly*, Charles established himself within his new school and showed off his flair for storytelling, a talent that made him an outstanding publicist in his later years. But the paper also became a showcase for his ignorance of grammar and spelling, as can be seen in the samples of his writing that follow. Typical of his style is "The City Boy and the Lumber Woods Boy," in which Charles described the differences between himself and his new friends:

The City Boys Like to have good clothes and have a season tickets to the rink. They try to get out of doing any hard work and are ashamed to put on old clothes and go where any body can see them. They can not chop or cut cedar fence posts, one of the lumber Woods Boys could cut down a tree and cut it most up before one of the City boys could cut a tree down. . . . When the Snows is two or three [feet] deep, The Lumber Woods Boys like to slide down hill and had rater wear old clothes for every day than nice ones. they had rather earn there own money than to ask there pa or ma first.[12]

Two years later, Charles still preferred the excitement of his wilder life in Michigan to that of civilized Cleveland. He spent summers at his father's Port Crescent mill and logging camp, which was run by his uncle Greene Pack. Here he toughened himself on long camping trips and visits to the lumbering camps, where he was baptized into the hard life of a lumberman.[13]

In the spring of 1872, Charles had an exciting initiation into lumbering, which he wrote about later in a class essay, "Riding Logs." Here Charles's once-superior tone has shifted to a more humble and humorous one:

In the Spring of 1872 I visited an Uncle of mine who lived in the Lumber Woods of Michigan.

One morning after breakfast Uncle invited me to go up the river with him where the men were working on the drive [log drive, where the cut logs are floated, or driven, downriver]. Of course I accepted. We took two long pike poles from where they hung shead and after a walk of about twenty-five minutes we arrived at the river just below the [log] *Jam.*

Uncle jumped on a good sized log and said if I would get on we would take a ride down stream. I mounted the log and in a few moments we were floating quietly down the river.

The sensation was curious. Log drivers usually have nails or spikes in their boots. I hadn't. Before long the log gave a gentle roll to one side, and then to the other, and with a strong arm I thrust my pole down deep into the dark waters of the river. Deceived as to its deapth I had kept to short a hold on the pole, and not striking the bottom, the force of the blow threw me over and before I could get my ballance I found myself in the dark elements

Fortunately the water was not deep and I was near the opposite bank, so that I soon clambered ashore, wet however from head to foot. Uncle had left me as soon as the log I got on was fairly started but he soon jumped ashore and I was soon greated with a crackling fire the genial heat of which soon made me feel quite comfortable.

Uncle now left me to go further up stream.

. . . I was dry in about an hour and by that time Uncle had made his appearance on the opposite bank and was calling for me to come.

I was tired, constitutionaly so, and the way round the bridge was a long one, so I decided to recross on the logs but not without considerable coaxing. Springing from one log to another is good work for developing the muscles. It is exilerating particularly so when the logs are small and sink 3 or 4 inches on the water when stepped on, and grows exciting when the log you chance to be on gets separated from the jam.

I got along as well as I expected until I got to the center of the stream where I stopped to catch breath on a large and barkless and innocent looking log.—I was deceived. It gave a gentle roll to one side; I streightened up and ballanced it.—fancied myself equal to the occasion. Then it gave a roll to the other side, got wet and consequently slippery. I streightend up again and smiled at the idea of that log fooling me. It rolled again—went all the way around this time and every move of my feet increased the motion.

I grew excited—anxious—now, but again fancied myself equal to the situation.

The log was now separated a considerable distance from the others, and began another series of revolutions. I grew frantic; arms and legs flew like the arms of a wind mill, and I practised what might be termed a war-dance. So the exercise went on for perhaps a minute, when behold, the dark waters closed over me.

I grappled for another log, but it slipped and turned and I spluttered and plunged until Uncle came and fished me out.

I may add that I went home looking very much like a whipped rooster, and had the pleasure of encountering the croup together with goos-oil the following night.[14]

Although the teenage Charles seemed to take pride in testing his manhood against the wilderness, deep down he was a businessman born and bred—so much so that he even honed his business skills during visits to the lumbering camps. During one visit, Charles saw a potential profit to be made in his father's barges, which ran the Pack lumber from the mills to the lumber towns. He decided to load a barge with watermelons, which he would sell in Oscoda. Charles bought enough watermelons from the commissary to fill both his and his sister Mary's staterooms. But that night a ferocious squall struck and bashed the barge about. The watermelons were smashed into a pulp, and seeds were splattered across the walls and ceiling.[15]

Charles had better luck when he was sixteen and living in Cleveland. His father had gone to Karlsbad, Germany, to be treated for gallstones and had taken Charles's mother with him. In their absence Charles stayed with his aunt, who was far from pleased when she learned that Charles had invested his childhood savings—$40—in tomato seeds. That summer tomatoes, or "love apples" as they were called, were just being discovered as an edible fruit. Previously they had been curiosities that were never eaten and were even viewed as poisonous. Seeing a great market in their new-found popularity, Charles bought all the seeds he could and hired some girls to work for a dollar a day, helping him plant and weed. His $40 investment grew to $402. From then on, he would never have less than that sum to his name.[16]

In the spring of 1874, Charles was allowed to go to Karlsbad with his father. His German was so bad, however, that his father gave him a choice: stay and study German daily, or go home. Charles stayed and studied, but does not seem to have minded the work. His diary from this trip reflects only his impressions of his travels and mentions nothing of the work he had to do to earn these experiences. There is no record of when he and his father began their tour of Europe, except that it was sometime in the spring. They spent the spring, summer, and fall touring England, Switzerland, and France before beginning the trip home on October 1, when they boarded an ocean liner in Liverpool.[17]

During his travels he was developing an awareness and appreciation of art and beauty. At Lucerne, Switzerland, he recorded, in a very grown-up tone, his impressions of the Lion of Lucerne: "It is cut out of the solid stone by Thorwadsen. The dying lion reclines in a grotto and is sheltering with its paws the Bourbon lilly. The spot and Lion are impressive, and is a proof that in true art the simplest idea carried out by a master-hand never fails in its effect."[18] Later, on a trip to the Louvre in Paris, he noted that the Venus of Milo is "*very* fine and makes all most all of the other statuary look like stone, and looks as if it could speak."[19]

On Wednesday, September 9, during his stay in Brighton, he recorded his views on the relations between men and women: "In the afternoon I went down to the ladies bathing beach, for the ladies and gentlemen do not bath together in England or France. Very silly I think for the ladies can not be so secure when alone. Those that I saw bathing did not go out but a very little way, probably because they were afraid. If Gentlemen were with them they could have no cause to fear."[20]

The entry may seem humorous to today's reader, but it shows that Charles was a man of his time. Many years later, however, he praised women and women's organizations that had promoted some of the same causes he had, noting how important their work had been and how capable they were, thus indicating that his views had altered at least somewhat.

Although he was now seventeen years old, Charles was fine-boned, thin, and short, and seemed closer to twelve. Nevertheless, he was considered emotionally mature enough to travel alone to Scotland for ten days. Charles seems to have been as chivalrous as any Edwardian gentleman of his station, but he was not about to let gallantry get in the way of a good business deal. During his stay in Edinburgh, he visited Melrose Abbey on September 23. Later that day he wrote, "A pretty girl showed me the ruins and called my attention to the finest work and most celebrated parts. I was tempted to give her a shilling but as I was about to give it to her, she said modestly 'Four pence if you please.' So thinking that she would be better pleased with a harty 'I thank you' than with a shilling I gave her four pence and passed away."[21]

Charles must have learned this frugality from his parents. After all, the gifts of money that he saved during his own childhood only amounted to forty dollars—the equivalent of four hundred dollars today—by the time he was sixteen. Considering that George Willis was one of Michigan's first millionaires, this was hardly a considerable sum.

In fact, the Packs did not seem to live like millionaires until 1875, when George Willis was near retirement. That year the family moved from the small house in East Cleveland to 694 Euclid Avenue, more commonly known as Millionaire's Row.

In that same year, at the age of eighteen, Charles entered the prestigious Brooks Military School, a private college preparatory school for boys, then called Brooks School. There Charles's enormous energy and enthusiasm, coupled with his highly inquisitive mind, made him a top student. His first report card from Brooks included this comment: "A *very fine scholar,* and above criticism in conduct and manners." Similarly, later reports were marked "excellent"; Charles maintained an average that never fell below 90. His strengths then, as they would be in his professional life, were economics and speech. He won first prize in both his junior and senior years in Brooks's annual declamation contests. Charles also shone socially as well as scholastically. In his senior year he was elected class orator, class historian, and class prophet.[22]

On June 20, 1877, at the age of twenty, Charles Pack graduated from Brooks School and gave a speech on that occasion titled "Success." The speech contained all the elements of style that were to become his trademark in life. It was flowery, slightly sentimental, scholarly, inventive, symbolic, and inspirational.

After invoking the greatness of the American nation, the Industrial Age, Napoleon, Mary Johnson (who received "the last messages of the dying and closed the eyes of the dead" during the "great pestilence of Mobile"), and God (who "placed us at the beginning, 'a little lower than the angels and within speaking distance of His throne'"), Charles Pack assured his classmates:

A broad field is yet left for us to explore. We must press onward and upward in the ascent of life, remembering that each individual may possess some triumphant superiority over his fellows. If we would become successful, if we would gain the summit and earn the honors of true Victory, let us see to it, that we faithfully do the special duties which the All Wise One has assigned to us to perform.

> Toil on, toil on, though rough the way,
> And dark it may appear
> But look ahead, and stand the storm
> And then 'twill all seem clear.
> After years of toil and strife,
> When we our work have done,
> We'll think of bygone years and say:
> "I am glad the battles' won!"[23]

But what "triumphant superiority over his fellows" did Charles possess? What, at age twenty, did he believe would be his destiny? In a second speech that day, in his role as class prophet, Charles gave humorous forecasts of his classmates' futures as doctors, musicians, statesmen—even horsemen. But for himself he said, "In my last dream a fair sibyl appeared to me. I asked her what was to become of that Pack. The answer was 'I give it up.'"[24]

In retrospect, it is interesting to note that this speech in which Charles described his classmates' futures but not his own was, in fact, his "Tree Oration," given on the occasion of the school's first tree planting. Charles had an elm planted in honor of the class of 1877, thus establishing a tradition at the school. This is the earliest known record of Charles taking any interest in tree conservation. He expressed the wish that future graduating classes would "jealously preserve" the tree-planting custom he had started.

"I think a time will come," Charles said, "when around this nucleus a whole grove will spring up, giving it beauty to the world and suggesting something of the fair fame of the men and women (now) that planted it." Further foreshadowings of Charles's tying his fame to trees continued when he said:

No matter if we sleep, the tree which we plant will still grow. We rather hope that we may not sleep, but be wide awake, that our growth may correspond to that of this tree. And in after years may we be like it, firmly grounded with roots striking into the soil of earnest conviction. . . . It is no unchanging written record of names and a date that we shall have to represent us, but a living growing tree,—a monument of strength, a sign of use, of sturdiness, a thing of beauty and a joy forever.[25]

Despite this charming speech, there is no record of Charles being concerned about forest conservation at this time. On the contrary, both while working for his father and in business for himself, he applied the clear-cutting practices then prevailing in the Michigan woods. Although there were already warnings that these forests would one day be exhausted—just as they had been in Maine and other northeastern states by the "cut-out and get-out" philosophy—that day was still two decades away.[26]

CHAPTER 3

Coming of Age

I T WOULD HAVE BEEN natural for someone of Charles's age and social standing to go to college after graduating from high school. In fact, Charles planned on going to college, but his physician recommended that he be "put to some outdoor activity instead of spending four years in the confinement of college work."[1] There is no hint of what was wrong with Charles other than the fact that he seemed underdeveloped for his age. Whatever the case, it was decided that he would work in his father's mills rather than attend college. First, however, his parents gave him a vacation in Atlantic City as a graduation present.

Intense energy drove Charles throughout his life. Even while vacationing in Atlantic City, he worked as a correspondent for the Cleveland papers, reporting on the fashionable goings-on in the resort town. His sense of humor, another notable trait of his personality, also shone through in this venture through his by-line, "Bad Axe."

Charles took this pseudonym from a camp his father had named after the broken and badly rusted ax he and a fellow surveyor found there. The name went on their surveyor's map and stuck even after the area was settled by Michigan pioneers and lumbermen. Bad Axe is a small town today.[2]

That winter, the winter of 1877–78, Charles began to work for Woods & Company, marking and scaling logs.[3] A timber marker blazed selected trees with his ax, thus signaling loggers that these trees should be cut. As a timber marker Charles had little responsibility, for a timber cruiser decided which trees were to be blazed.

Once the trees were marked, the logging crew cut them and a skidding crew—teamsters working with teams of horses or yokes of oxen—dragged, or skidded, logs to a central landing or deck in the forest. The teamsters would hitch the felled logs to their teams with chains or giant tongs similar to ice tongs. Once the skidding crew reached a deck in the forest, the logs were loaded onto sleighs or bobs, and hauled over an ice road to a river or lake, unloaded, and stockpiled until the spring thaw. With the arrival of spring, the logs were rolled into the water and floated to the mills.

After the logs were stockpiled, Charles worked as a timber scaler. With a special scale stick, he measured the diameter of a log and then, using an algebraic formula, determined the number of board feet a sawyer could cut from the log. He recorded the calculations on scale sheets, which he sent to the mill. These scale sheets were used for planning mill production. If, for instance, Charles reported that the logs could yield ten million board feet of wood and the mill's annual capacity was ten million board feet, then the logging crew could stop cutting and transporting logs. If the haul was less than the mill's capacity, the crew continued working until the quota was met.

As a scaler, Charles also marked the logs with the Woods & Company log mark, which distinguished that company's logs from those that other companies were sending downriver. To mark the logs, Charles hammered the log mark into the end of each log, using a small ax head bearing a raised reproduction of the log mark.

The workday began at first light and ended at dark. Returning to camp after working in the cold and wet woods, the men would strip off their soggy clothes and hang them over the wood stove to dry. Quickly changing into dry clothes, they headed to the mess hall for dinner.

Seated around long wooden tables, Charles most likely partook in a strangely silent meal. Many camps prohibited talking at dinner in order to prevent fights from breaking out, as well as to save time and keep the men moving through the mess hall. After dinner, though, the men were free to talk. Gathered in their bunkhouses, they swapped tales of ever-more-amazing exploits, engendering such mythic figures as Paul Bunyan.[4]

Charles earned twenty-four dollars a month with free board. Following his first winter in the camp, he received a respite from this harsh life: Frances sent him on a five-month vacation in Europe with his father to celebrate his twenty-first birthday.[5]

Both family lore and various published accounts have it that this trip to Germany in the summer of 1878 was responsible for Charles's later interest in forest conservation. The story goes that during this trip Charles was introduced to forest management by a Herr C. Katz, a member of the German parliament, and one of the largest timber producers in the Black Forest. Charles's travel diary confirms that he did indeed meet Herr Katz during his 1878 tour of Europe.

Sunday July 7, 1878

The Herr Pfarrer [Herr Stadtpfarrer Eisenhlohr, of Gernsbach] went with me to the house of Herr Katz (to whom [I had] my letter of intro-duc[tion] in case of the absence of the Herr Pfarrer.) His house [is] plain on the outside but inside almost a palace. *Herr Katz* is a member of the *German Parliament* and one of the largest lumber manufacturers in the Black Forest.[6]

This is all that Charles recorded of their first meeting. Their second meeting took place the next day. Charles wrote,

Mr. Katz sent his carriage around to day and took me to see his sawmills of which he has several. He gave me very much general [*sic*] about the lumbering. Forests belong to town and General government. Officers to look after them. Go around every so often and mark such trees as are to be cut. Sold as they stand at auction. Sometimes trees are cut and delivered on a road by Government and then sold. Bark roots and brush command a ready sale. Young trees set in place of those cut. Inventory of Forests taken every two years and consumption of timber regulated. The quantity of lumber a fixed quanty [*sic*]. Mr. K thinks there will be as much timber in the B.F. [Black Forest] 50 years hence as there is to day.[7]

The next day, Charles noted in his diary that he had written a letter home "describing Black Forest lumbering,"[8] but made no

Charles Pack, right, with unidentified companion, during his 1878 tour of Europe. Although he appears to be about sixteen years old, he is, in fact, twenty-one. (Courtesy of the Arizona Historical Society.)

mention in the diary of how he felt about these lumbering practices. The letter he wrote has been lost.

According to Charles, he stayed with the Katz family for either six or eight months—his story changed over the years—to study German forestry. As Charles later told a reporter:

[Herr Katz's] company owned 30,000 acres of *tanne* and *fichtel*, which are varieties of spruce.

The forest had been in the Katz family for more than 200 years. No more timber was cut in any year than was grown during the year, and so the forest was continuous and the reserves were always the same. Diseased trees and weaklings were pulled down. They endangered those which were in good health, and therefore had to make room for seedlings and saplings, as is the custom in all scientifically managed forests.[9]

In this same account, Charles said he stayed with the Katz family for six months following his European tour, when his father returned to America. At the end of his life, however, he said he stayed with the family for eight months. He recalled that his day began every morning at 6:00, with breakfast at 6:30, followed by a day spent with the foresters.[10]

Yet Charles's diary gives no indication that he stayed with the Katz family for an extended period of time. Rather, it shows that he resumed his tour of Europe on July 10, going first to Stuttgart, to Ulm on the eleventh, Rogätz on the twelfth, and so on, embarking on a journey that would eventually take him to St. Moritz, Pontresina, Innsbruck, Munich, Augsburg, Paris, Utrecht, London, and Liverpool, presumably returning to Cleveland in mid-September. Other than the note that he returned to Liverpool, the port where the ship would disembark for America, there is no record of his actually returning to Cleveland. It is possible, of course, that Charles simply neglected to make a note in his diary of the Katz invitation and that he returned to Germany to stay with the family after seeing his father off in Liverpool.

If this scenario is true, the extent of his German studies are still uncertain. Although he claimed to have "specialized in several subjects at a German technical school" in the year following his alleged six-month stay with the Katz family, and an article in the *Cleveland Leader* says he graduated from the school of forestry at the University of Tübingen,[11] the university has no record of his ever being a student there.

In fact, it is unlikely that Charles took any formal courses. Schools that existed in or around the Black Forest at this time have no record of a Charles Pack being enrolled in any classes, technical or otherwise, for the period 1878 through 1882 (the later years were checked under the assumption that Charles or reporters may have misreported the year of his stay and that he may actually have returned to Germany on his own at a later date).

Two months before he died, Charles claimed to have stayed with the Katz family for eight months.[12] From the various stories, Charles would have been in Germany anywhere from six months to one year and eight months.

Regardless of the length, Charles's time in Germany was influential. His sister Mary said, "The fact that he lived in the woods during an impressionable time of his life created a love of the woods that later became strengthened through his Schwarzwald [Black Forest] experience."[13]

Whatever the details of this experience—whether or not it involved actual formal study, and its duration—the story was reported in various forms over the years and was used to back Charles's claim that he was a pioneer in forestry and forest conservation. His fellow conservationist Gifford Pinchot had studied forestry in France, Switzerland, and Germany from 1889 through 1890. By saying that he had studied German forest management techniques in 1878 at the age of twenty-one, Charles could have a basis for the claim that he was one of the first Americans to be interested in forest conservation—having studied it eleven years before his friend Pinchot, who was the primary force behind the conservation movement that began to gain national proportions in the early 1900s.

If Charles was a visionary conservationist at the age of twenty-one, his 1878 diary gives no hint of it. Rather, it indicates that he had all the normal interests of a young man of his age and stature: pretty girls, beer, fine clothes. But it also hints at some self-criticism, if not insecurity.

On May 11, 1878, Charles wrote: "The 7th of May was my birthday. . . . How fast I am growing up—21 years and a man and yet of no help to my good father."[14]

Following his stay in Europe, Charles went back to work for his father. Woods & Company had closed, so he worked for his father's new, massive and modern operation at Oscoda, Pack, Woods & Company. He spent two years as a scaler and marker before being promoted to cruiser, logging boss, and walking logging boss of all the camps.[15]

As a cruiser, Charles selected the best trees for cutting. These were then marked by the marker—possibly Charles himself, since cruisers often acted as markers as well. As a logging boss, he was in charge of the entire camp operation, from the first felling of trees to the arrival of the logs at the riverbanks for stockpiling. Then as a walking boss, Charles was in charge of walking all sixteen camps along the Au Sable River, checking on the individual cutting crews, and laying out the skid roads.

Life in the logging camps was anything but luxurious, but Charles partook of civilized comforts at least once in a while by visiting his Uncle Greene Pack in Oscoda. Greene and his partner Edwin F. Holmes had each built luxurious mansions in Oscoda, where they were known to surround "their families with all the comforts and refinements that money can furnish."[16]

After two years with Pack, Woods & Company Charles returned to Cleveland, where he sawed timber in the Pack lumberyards. Unlike the common laborers sawing lumber alongside him, though, at day's end he took part in the pleasures of Cleveland's high society.

A highly eligible, wealthy bachelor, Charles was a regular at the grand balls and coaching parties—where guests traveled by horse-drawn coaches to their destination, such as a lakeside picnic— of the day. He also joined an "independent military company" known as the 1st Troop, Cleveland City Cavalry, or Troop A.[17] With a secure job in his father's firm and a solid position in society, Charles was certainly comfortable.

But he was restless. As a young boy he had wanted to be his own man, separate from his father. Now he began planning to go into business for himself.

Although the Pack, Woods & Company mill had been built at Oscoda just three years before, and other lumbermen were still building new mills along the Michigan thumb, Charles believed that Michigan would soon see the last of its white pine. Tom Gill, a conservationist who wrote an unpublished biography of Charles, put it this way:

Those two years in the woods had taught him something that no one else believed—that the white pine of Michigan and Wisconsin was almost exhausted. . . . The young man could see ahead to a rapidly approaching day when these forests would be gone, when the investments in mills in that region would be worthless.

There had been a lot of talk among lumbermen about the possibilities of southern pines, but it was nothing more than idle speculation, for everyone thought there was still an unlimited quantity of white and red [i.e., Norway] pine left, and nobody wanted to touch southern pine.[18]

Gill's claim that nobody but Charles wanted to invest in southern pine is based on an interview in which Charles told Gill that the "people didn't realize that the white pine of Michigan and Wisconsin was exhausted, but I knew it was."[19]

This claim is disproved, however, by Charles himself, as well as other documentation. In a 1913 article, Charles is quoted as saying, "The lumbermen of Michigan and Wisconsin had begun to realize that the stock of standing timber in their part of the country soon would be exhausted. . . . We had heard about the forests of Mississippi and Louisiana. I went south . . . on a journey of investigation."[20]

A statement by George Stokes shows that Charles was not alone in his thinking and is much more consistent with the facts:

Timber speculators were among the first to recognize the impending shift of lumbering to the southern states. By 1870 two-thirds of Louisiana timber was in the hands of some sixteen organizations. Nathan Bradley of Michigan bought 111,000 acres of Louisiana. C. F. Hackley of the same state bought 90,000 acres in the Calcasieu Basin. . . . A British concern, the North American Land and Timber Company, bought 960,000 acres in southwest Louisiana, helped introduce the first railroad to the area, and brought in settlers from the Midwest.[21]

Speculation in Louisiana timber was sparked not just by the knowledge that supplies of white pine in the Lake States were running out, but also by the growth of railroads, which were starting to criss-cross Louisiana. Originally, due to the lack of rail transport, Louisiana's forests had been landlocked from the major markets of the northeastern and western states: "Commerce was limited to a few rivers such as the Sabine, Calcasieu, and Red. What lumber that left the state was shipped out of the port of New Orleans."[22]

Starting in 1870, however, railroads began linking Louisiana with major northeastern and midwestern cities. As the railroad networks grew, timber could be more easily transported to major markets, and mill owners and timber speculators from the North and South began viewing Louisiana's vast blocks of pine as the answer to the white pine shortage in the Great Lakes states.[23]

By 1884, Michigan lumbermen such as Isaac Stephenson, Jr., and James D. Lacey, who would become a major timber broker and one of Charles Pack's chief contacts, had turned Calcasieu Parish into Louisiana's first great lumber center. The boom would continue through the first quarter of the twentieth century. Indeed, the "forests themselves were a logger's dream—clear and open—promising the cheapest and most rapid of logging operations. Weather rarely impeded cutting, and the flow of logs from forest to mill was limited only by the capacity of men and machines."[24] Thus, despite claims to the contrary, Charles Pack was not the first person to see the value of Louisiana woods.

Charles was twenty-four in 1881, when he announced to his family that he was going to cruise the woods of Mississippi, Arkansas, and Louisiana to see if the timber there would be a good investment. This would prove to be the most important business decision of his life.

During his tour of southern pines, Charles made a discovery that convinced him to invest in longleaf pine. "White pine," Charles told James B. Morrow, a reporter for the *Sunday Plain Dealer*, "is particularly sensitive to heat. A slight fire on the floor of a white pine forest will kill the trees, though it may scarcely scorch the trunks. I saw a quick and fierce fire burning up the needles under some long-leafed pines. When it reached the trees, however, it suddenly went out. Gas in the exuding [resin] low down near the roots, exploded and smothered the flames. At all events, that is what I thought, I tested my theory several times, then and afterward, and found that it was chemically correct."[25]

Fire is a great hazard to any forest, as well as to timbermen. Seeing that longleaf pine seemed to be fire resistant, Charles decided to invest in it. Moreover, it was going for a mere $2.50 an acre.[26]

Returning to Cleveland, Charles pulled together two million dollars in savings and loans and invested it in mixed shortleaf and longleaf pine and in hardwoods, primarily in Louisiana. He was on the road to becoming his own man. In ten years, he would be richer than his father.[27]

Charles was first and foremost a businessman. As his sister Mary once said, "From the first, Charles was out for business. . . . Charles saw an opportunity in everything."[28] Yet during his lifetime, Charles would be portrayed not as a businessman, but as a conservationist. Says the *Dictionary of American Biography*,

The [southern timber] investment quickly proved profitable; assured of an independent income, Pack was free to participate in matters of his particular interest. He served as a trustee of Western Reserve University (1893–1937) and on the Cleveland Trust Company (1894) and in 1897 headed the Cleveland delegation to the Indianapolis Monetary Convention. He was an expert philatelist. But his principal interest was in timber conservation. From his observations in Germany he knew that forests could and should be treated like crops. This viewpoint would be widely accepted in the United States many years later, but when Charles suggested it at a meeting of economists in 1885, his audience divided between those who believed that America's timber was inexhaustible and those who feared that it was so nearly exhausted that not another tree should be cut. Americans apparently found it difficult to grasp the idea of scientific forest management.[29]

This account of Charles's life, and others like it, including one in the *National Cyclopedia of American Biography* that was approved by Charles, implies that after investing in southern forest lands Charles retired from business to support the conservation cause:

For many years he was actively engaged in valuing, buying and selling timber, with offices in Cleveland, and was prominent in business and public affairs in that city. . . . In 1900 he became a resident of Lakewood, N.J. His life thereafter was mainly devoted to pioneering work in the field of forest education and the conservation of America's natural resource. . . . He won recognition as the leader in economic forestry and as an outstanding exponent of methods of scientific forestry and timber growing designed not only to avert any possible extinction of standing timber but to meet more than adequately the nation's requirements for forest products.[30]

It is true that Charles was giving at least lip service to forestry conservation between the years 1885 and 1903. In 1885, he proposed to a group of scientists and economists, meeting in Cleveland, that timber should be treated as a crop, but that "almost every delegate who spoke at all assailed the Pack theory as untenable and absurd."[31]

In the fall of 1894 Charles wrote an editorial stating that forestry can only begin when "the general and State governments can do something by way of example in care and planting on the remaining lands. Until this is done not much can be expected from private owners, whose lands are so heavily taxed, and exposed to so much danger," from such things as fire, wild hogs in the South, and disease.[32]

In 1902, due to the death of city shrubberies, he urged Clevelanders to plant "smooth-leaved trees," which could survive the coal soot that collected on "rough elm leaves," stunting their growth.[33]

And in the fall of 1903, an article featured the following statement from Charles promoting reforestation:

Trees should be planted so that a crop will be coming along to take the place of what is cut. This should be done not merely when the trees have been cut down, but in every part of the country where there is non-productive and unused lands. State Forestry Commissioners should be constituted and legislation enacted that would require owners of unused lands unfit for other uses to plant trees, the lands to be exempt from local taxation, and subject only to a small State tax. The neglect to plant trees should invite a penalty, under default and accumulations of which the State might take possession with the right of redemption during a reasonable period reserved to the original owner.[34]

But Charles did not back these words with action, except to become a life member of the American Forestry Association in 1899, which honor involved paying a fifty-dollar fee. Waiting for state and federal government to take the lead, he did not become an active player in the forest conservation movement until 1908, eight years later than is claimed in the *National Cyclopedia* account. Furthermore, although the goal of his conservation work was to "avert any possible extinction of standing timber but to meet more than adequately the nation's requirement for forest products," Charles never funded or practiced reforestation efforts involving any of his private timber investments.[35] Finally, contrary to the implication that he retired from the timber industry shortly after 1900, he actively invested in the industry until his death.

Thus, when Charles headed south in 1881, despite his knowledge that Michigan white pine stands were quickly diminishing, it was not as an early proponent of conservation and a pioneer in the movement. It was to make a killing as a timber speculator.

When northeastern timbermen began turning to the southern pine forests Charles wanted to be there, timberlands in hand, ready to cut a deal. He had no intention of seeing that the timber he sold would be treated as a crop. As a businessman, he was simply treating his forest lands like green gold—like a highly profitable investment.

At this point in time, Charles was no different from most of his contemporaries. Reforestation and forest management were practically unheard of in America. When conservationists began preaching such practices, timbermen largely ignored them.

There was a practical business reason for this. A growing sapling was taxed the same as a mature tree. This meant that if timbermen systematically reforested the lands they cut, they would pay taxes for years before seeing any profit on their timber. Thus, it was foolhardy to grow timber as a crop: the annual taxes during the growing period might bankrupt a timberman before he could even go to market. Furthermore, who could say what the market would be when the time came to cut and sell? Consequently, timbermen simply clear-cut as quickly as possible, then moved on to the next forest.[36] Reforestation was bad business.

At this stage of his life, Charles was interested not so much in reforestation as in buying low and selling high. He bought his Louisiana timberlands as cheaply as $1.25 to $2.50 an acre and started selling in the early 1890s. "I made more money out of the southern pine timber," Charles once boasted, "than anything else I have ever tackled." By 1913, he was a multimillionaire.[37]

Although Charles sold his southern holdings to a variety of buyers, his best customer was the Louisiana-Arkansas timber baron William Buchanan.[38] With seven mills to his name, Will Buchanan was one of the biggest timbermen in the South: between 1889 and 1913 he bought the Bodcaw Lumber Company in Stamps, Arkansas, and the Grant Timber & Manufacturing Company of Louisiana, Inc., in Selma, Louisiana. He also organized the Pine Woods Lumber Company in Springhill, Louisiana; the Minden Lumber Company in Minden, Louisiana; the Trout Creek Lumber Company at Trout, Louisiana; the Good Pine Lumber Company at Good Pine, Louisiana; and the Tall Timber Lumber Company, located in Arkansas, across the border from Good Pine, which was "one of the best and last large mills built in the state."[39]

Buchanan's empire was based largely on timberland purchased from Charles Pack, as well as from the financier Jay Gould who, Charles claimed, had interviewed him upon his return from the South and paid him a thousand dollars for his tip to invest in long-leaf pine. Charles later used this story to establish his credentials as a forestry expert, claiming that this was the first recorded fee paid in this country for expert forestry advice.[40]

Will Buchanan first bought land from Charles in 1906 for $14 an acre. Since Charles had paid not more than $2.50 an acre, this was already a tidy gross profit. In 1919, however, Buchanan paid $57.41 an acre for more Pack land; in 1920, he paid $80 an acre for 14,000 acres, netting Charles a profit before taxes of at least $1,085,000, assuming that each acre had cost $2.50. By this time, too, Charles and his family were stockholders in the Buchanan mills, as well as friends of the Buchanans. Charles had also helped finance the Louisiana and Arkansas Railway, which Buchanan built to transport his lumber.[41]

"All told, the Buchanan mills in Louisiana operated for 213 mill

The Minden Lumber Company, Minden, La. *(Courtesy of the Library of Congress.)*

years, probably a record sawmill operation," Ed Kerr noted in his *Tales of the Louisiana Forests.* "From 1902 until 1935, the various Buchanan companies shipped nearly seven billion [board] feet of lumber."[42]

Some of Buchanan's timber was on hilly land, which made it impossible to clear-cut, so seed trees were left behind in these areas. As for the clear-cut lands, an eyewitness account states that no seed trees were left behind. Nor did Buchanan have these lands replanted. Although clear-cut areas can reseed naturally if surrounding trees remain to seed them, this does not always result in the area being reseeded with the same type of trees that were cut. Nor does untended, unprotected natural regrowth always survive or result in healthy trees. The point of replanting clear-cut areas rather than leaving them to reseed naturally is to ensure that the same type of trees will grow back. In addition, reforestation involves tending the second growth so that it will survive such threats as fire and insects and mature into a strong, healthy crop of trees.[43]

Louisiana taxes were not high when Buchanan first started opening his mills, so taxes were not a deterrent to reforestation. Furthermore, in 1910, Louisiana passed Act 261, the Timber Conservation Contract Law, which allowed owners to contract with the state of Louisiana for a low tax rate on growing timber and pay a severance tax at the time of harvest. The new law hardly made a difference, however. Henry Hardtner, who had advocated reforestation practices, did not sign the first contract until three years after it went into effect. Few others signed contracts until the state set up an active forestry department in 1917.[44]

Buchanan never took advantage of Act 261. To begin with, he was paying high interest rates on loans taken out to pay for land from Charles. This financial situation, coupled with operating costs, meant that Buchanan would have to "pare down his operations, massively refinance, swallow several years of red ink (not to mention his pride), and rethink the philosophy of a lifetime"[45] if he wanted to reforest his lands.

When Charles began financially supporting the conservation movement, it would have been logical for him, as an investor in the Buchanan mills, to practice what he preached by financing reforestation on Buchanan's clear-cut lands. This would have allowed Charles to legitimately hold himself up as a preeminent example of a conservation-minded timberman, and an example to others.

Two of his contemporaries had done this: Hardtner had bought and naturally reforested cutover Louisiana pinelands, including some of Buchanan's; William H. Sullivan, then vice president and general manager of the Great Southern Lumber Company, had established reforestation practices at the Great Southern's operation in Bogalusa, Louisiana. The reforestation work of both men was well known to Charles. In fact, Charles was good friends with the leaders of the Great Southern.[46] However, Charles argued that he was merely a timber speculator and as such had no control over what others did with the forest land he sold them.[47]

This argument ignores the fact that the high prices Buchanan paid Charles for his land put Buchanan in a financial situation that made it nearly impossible to institute an active reforestation program. It also disregards the fact that Charles and his family had some interest and influence in how the Buchanan mills operated; they were major stockholders in the mills and had also extended loans to Will Buchanan. Still, 225,000 acres of his land remained "as bare as the floor" before they were reforested in the 1940s.[48]

As for the Michigan white pine cut by the Pack mills, Charles told a reporter, "It has been said that the pine of the northwest was chopped down with vandal and mercenary axes and much of it wasted. That statement is untrue. The trees, after a growth of two centuries, had reached their full development. Their use was quite wise under the circumstances."[49] This statement ignores the question of whether there will be new growth after cutting. As witnessed by forester William B. Greeley, this was rarely the case in Michigan.

The gap between the image Charles presented and the reality, between what he preached and what he practiced, cannot be bridged: no diary or letter has yet been found that resolves this issue in his favor. At best, one can say that Charles was acting as a man of his times: it was not unusual for a timberman to serve on conservation boards of one type or another yet not practice conservation. J. B. White, for instance, was well known for preaching but not practicing forest management.[50] Since White and Charles were friends, Charles may have felt that he was at least a better man than White in that he later poured more money into the cause and worked harder to promote it.

As for his failure to practice timber management in his own investments, it must be remembered that as the son of a millionaire timberman, Charles had a solid sense for business. A sensible businessman would not let go of future fortunes just because he was going to support a cause—especially if the profits were to go into the cause.

In 1881, however, the contrast between what Charles practiced and what he preached was still in the future. At the age of twenty-four, he was just embarking on his remarkable and contradictory life. When he returned home to Cleveland after cruising the southern timberlands, this energetic, ambitious, and wealthy young man traded in his worn and dirty brown denim cruiser's clothes for the stiff white collars, soft ties, and elegant tie pins that made up the costume of a thriving businessman. After pulling together the two million dollars to invest in Louisiana timber, he turned his attention to matters closer to home—the Cleveland business district.

CHAPTER 4

A Cleveland Capitalist

B Y THE EARLY 1880s, swept up in the modern age of
electricity and the industrial revolution, Cleveland had
become a noisy, crowded, dirty, fast-growing industrial
and commercial center bursting with all types of people:
working-class immigrants and nonimmigrants alike filled the
streets with the babble of diverse languages as they pushed
through the streets on foot or hopped street cars to get to their
work as vendors or factory workers.

In Charles's Cleveland circles, however, only the men worked.
The more elegant of these donned bowler or derby hats rather
than the stovepipe hats of earlier days. In cold weather they wore
straight coats with capes à la Sherlock Holmes. Their coachmen
took them to work in carriages drawn by high-stepping horses.

At home, their wives began the day by submitting to the tor-
tures of corsets designed to create tiny waists and dresses with such
slim skirts that they had to take tiny, mincing steps. To finish the
look, they swept up their hair, donned pillbox hats, and carried
parasols as they set out for tea parties or charity work. Those who
stayed home to oversee housekeeping affairs fought a dreary and
futile battle against the soot that belched out of Cleveland's industrial smokestacks and continually seeped into their houses, black-
ening their furniture and draperies.

Given its easy access to waterways and its role as a major rail
junction, the city was a natural crossroads for commercial traffic
and a magnet for industry. This was the main reason that George

Willis Pack had moved to Cleveland to expand his business: he could easily transport his Michigan lumber to Cleveland lumber-yards via Lake Huron and Lake Erie and then ship further orders out by rail.

Other entrepreneurs such as John D. Rockefeller also saw that Cleveland was a fine port of operation and set up businesses there. By 1882, Rockefeller's Standard Oil Company had hit its stride and created its famous trust agreement in which the stock of individual companies was held by nine trustees who directed the businesses, thus making Cleveland the cradle of the oil industry (at least until 1911, when the Supreme Court struck down the trust).[1]

Rockefeller was not the only successful Cleveland businessman. Rollin H. White, who created America's first steam automobiles in 1900, was producing the greatest number of cars in the world in 1906.[2] By 1900, as others prospered there the "hum of trade" had developed "into the roar of industry."

Over the flats, where cattle grazed and corn grew in the old days, there now hung a pall of coal smoke, beneath which great ships sounded their sullen signals, whistles screamed from locomotives and mills, riveters rat-tatted and presses pounded. Along the lake front east to Gordon Park, south of Newburg and west of the Cuyahoga River giant factories were making things with the iron ore which the ships brought them. The city had evolved from hunting settlement to trading post, to commercial cen-ter, and finally into a gateway for the "industrial Ruhr" extending south-easterly into Pennsylvania.[3]

Cleveland's importance was further enhanced when its own James A. Garfield was elected president of the United States in November 1880. His victory and the shared pride of his family and friends, who included the Packs, was short-lived; he was shot by a disgruntled office seeker, Charles J. Guiteau, on July 2, 1881, and died eighty days later.

The ever-observant Charles saw as early as 1882 and 1883 that Cleveland was growing quickly. Sensing that the business center of the city was shifting, he decided to survey business traffic. He hired men and women and stationed them on key street corners, where they counted how many passersby turned one way, how many another. By 1885 he had a set of statistics indicating that Euclid Avenue was destined to be the new business district.[4]

At this time, Euclid Avenue was an elegant showcase for Cleveland's wealthy citizens, who built their high, grand mansions high on a ridge overlooking Lake Erie. Set two to five acres back from the avenue, which was paved with Medina sandstone, the mansions seemed to float amid spacious, landscaped grounds. The area was a millionaire's dream. John D. Rockefeller lived in one of the Euclid Avenue mansions from 1868 until 1884, when he moved to New York. By 1870, no avenue in the world, it was said, could boast "such a continuous succession of charming residences and uniformly beautiful grounds." "Old families, very conservative, driving fat horses in fresh varnished carriages," daily paraded up and down the avenue on their way to teas, debuts, or grand openings, while the "British coachmen on the boxes dwelt in the lower stretches of the avenue in quiet magnificent and fancied security." The street was so elegant that it was a regular feature of sightseeing tours.[5]

In 1885, however, Charles was beguiled by neither the beauty nor the tradition of Euclid Avenue, despite the fact that he had lived on the avenue from 1875 to 1877 while attending Brooks School, and that his father was building a palatial mansion on Millionaire's Row. Rather, Charles, who was living at the Stillman Hotel with the rest of his family while the new mansion was under construction, was dazzled by his vision of Euclid Avenue turning into a thriving business district.

Charles contributed to this transformation by moving the Pack offices from Superior Street to 44 Euclid Avenue and by buying "mansions at the lower end of Euclid Ave . . . and putting up one-story buildings, which he [would rent] to small merchants, plumbers and other mechanics," in order to help transform Euclid Avenue into the commercial center he was certain it would become. He also took out options on other properties in the area. Predictably, the residents of Millionaire's Row were outraged by the actions of this young opportunist. "'You are surrounding us with yellow dogs,'—snarled a rich and outraged inhabitant who lived in the neighborhood."[6]

Charles stood his ground: "You are right," he retorted, "and the yellow dogs are calling to the bankers and the great merchants downtown to move up into what is going to be the permanent business heart of the city. Some day you will sell your ancient house for money enough to buy a better one, and the interest on the balance will be sufficient to support you the rest of your life."[7]

The trend that Charles had predicted and helped to launch grew stronger each year. By 1910, Samuel Mather was among the last people to build a mansion on Euclid Avenue. In 1913, an article about Charles reported that "inside of ten years . . . the yellow dogs have disappeared. In their stead are skyscrapers, great retail establishments, magnificent banks, and a hotel that cost $2,000,000. Much of the land is owned by Mr. Pack and is leased for long periods. He helped to organize the companies which erected the buildings. It is said that his rentals, out of which not a penny is subtracted for taxes or anything else, amount to $100,000 a year."[8]

By 1937, only seven of the forty great Euclid Avenue mansions were left, and by 1986, only one remained.[9] The loss of the great mansions was mourned as early as 1933: "One of the tragedies of progress is the obliteration of that beautiful ridge, the destruction of its noble and spacious homes and their replacement by business institutions,"[10] observed one of the authors of *This Cleveland of Ours.*

Charles lived on Millionaire's Row during the time that he was transforming the avenue into a business district. He moved there in 1887 or 1888—the date is in dispute—thanks to a gift from his father. George Willis had transformed two small houses on the estate of Peter M. Weddell, at 3333 Euclid Avenue, into a three-story, thirty-room mansion, intending to make it his new home. His plans changed, however, when a physician recommended that he and Frances move to a warmer climate for the sake of her health. Thus, George Willis and Frances moved to Asheville, North Carolina, where they built a showcase mansion that featured the city's first bathroom.

As for the newly remodeled house at 3333 Euclid, George Willis gave it to his daughter Mary and her husband, Amos McNairy, as a wedding present. He also gave an adjoining seventy-eight acres to Charles's new wife, Alice Gertrude Hatch Pack, whom Charles married in 1886. The couple built a small cottage called Norway Lodge, made of red, or Norway, pine on this land.[11]

Controversial though it was, Charles Pack's vision of a new

A self-made millionaire, George Willis Pack celebrated that fact by building one of the grandest mansions on Cleveland's famed Millionaire's Row, otherwise known as Euclid Avenue. This once elegant address, 3333 Euclid Avenue, now marks the site of a motel. (Courtesy of Elizabeth Boggs.)

business district on Euclid Avenue, coupled with his southern investments, got him off to a fine start in the world of business. In 1885, the same year he began investing in Euclid Avenue real estate, he was invited to become a director of the East Cleveland Railway Company. The next year, he became a director of the Detroit Street Railways, of which his Uncle Greene was president and cofounder.[12]

Sometime between 1881 and 1891, Charles also took over his father's business. Charles remembered the moment of the transfer like this: "[Father] sent for me one time. 'I want to turn the business over to you. I want you to manage it. Here's a memorandum

*Beulah Pack, Charles Pack's younger sister, grew up to
marry the lawyer and western historian Phillip A. Rollins.
(Courtesy of Virginia Lathrop [Pack] Townsend.)*

showing what Beulah, Mother, and so forth are to get. I want you
to get it into their hands as soon as you can, and what's left you
take and do anything you like with.' I said, 'O.K., I'll do the best I
can.' So all father's property was turned over to me."[13]

The exact year that this happened is unclear because the Packs'
business records have disappeared, and the accounts of when
Charles took over the family business contain some contradic-
tions. In one instance, Charles claimed his father "retired at fifty
and turned the business over to me in Asheville."[14] The problem is
that George Willis was fifty in 1881, did not begin visiting Asheville
until 1885, and did not move there until 1888.

Another account says, "When Charles Lathrop Pack took over his father's business, he was already richer than his father." If this account is true, then the transfer could not have happened when George Willis was fifty, since in 1881 Charles had not yet made his own fortune from his speculation in southern timber. Furthermore, Charles claimed that "by the time father was sixty years old I was richer than he was."[15] If these two statements are true, then Charles would have taken over the business in 1891, when his father was sixty, and by which time Charles was richer than his father, and not in 1881 when George Willis was fifty.

Although Charles's name does not appear in the Cleveland City Directory under the Pack, Woods & Company heading until 1887, he may have helped run the company as early as 1885, when his father began staying in Asheville. His association with Pack, Woods & Company continued until it closed in the mid-1890s.

When Charles took over the family timber business, in addition to running Pack, Woods, & Company, he was responsible for Woods, Perry & Company, which was established in Cleveland around 1883 and operated for some twenty-three years thereafter as "a dominant factor in the commercial life of Cleveland." In addition, Pack, Gray & Company, established in 1893, may have been founded by Charles, since its establishment postdates either of the years that he is said to have taken over his father's business. In any case, the Cleveland directory listed Charles as an officer of the company the year that it was founded. It operated until 1906. By 1904, Charles was head of a new company, Standing Pine Timber.[16]

"For a quarter of a century his father and himself were, perhaps, the principal manufacturers of lumber in the United States," a newspaper reported in 1913.[17]

By the early 1890s, between his southern timber holdings, his family businesses, and his various directorships, Charles was an important Cleveland businessman. As a director of the railroad companies, working elbow-to-elbow with the other directors, Charles sharpened his leadership skills. In 1893, "a group of local businessmen selected Mr. Pack to affect a merger of four street railway companies."

This merger, arranged by Charles as a director of the East Cleveland Railway Company with the help of other arbiters, enabled the East Cleveland Railway to acquire and merge with the Broadway & Newburgh, Brooklyn, and South Side companies. This created the Cleveland Electric Railway Company, also known as the Big Con(solidated).[18]

Charles was also operating as a "clever trader"[19] in banking. He had been on the boards of directors of the New National Bank and Euclid Avenue National Bank (headed by the Packs' old business partner, John L. Woods) for years and was also on the board of the Seaboard National Bank of New York. Although his fortune would have allowed him to be a passive director of these banks, Charles chose to be quite active.

"In the panic of '92," he recalled in an interview with Tom Gill, "I went to the Bank of the Republic and got a twenty-four[-hour] option on several shares. I made them take $10 down for the option. The next day it was all out that the First National was absorbed by the Republic, and I still have the First National Bank shares. It cost me all that I had in the world, and something over, but I've had my money back with six percent interest so many times that you can't count it."[20]

The next year, in the Panic of 1893, he was sent to New York to find a way of lending money: "I consolidated several banks," he told Gill, "and set up a plan of requiring thirty-three percent margin instead of twenty-five percent. At that time all money was between six percent and eight percent a year. I loaned the money out and made a killing for the Cleveland Bank. It made a reputation for me as a banker."[21]

His astute business insights, his wealth, his booming laugh, his open sense of humor, and his tremendous energy made Charles some strong business connections. In the 1880s, he had befriended his sister Mary's new husband, Amos McNairy, and advised him to invest in the paint industry, which he did, successfully. Amos and Charles also became friendly with Henry A. Everett, a wealthy young man who became head of the Cleveland Electric Railway Company; Harry A. Garfield, a Cleveland lawyer and future president of Williams College; and his younger brother, James Rudolph Garfield, who would become one of Cleveland's leading lawyers as well as secretary of the interior under President Theodore Roosevelt.

Charles first began associating with McNairy, Everett, and the Garfield brothers when the five young men were just starting out in their careers. Over the years they became such a dynamic group of business leaders and were so full of new ideas that, according to Charles, they were known as the "Pack Gang." As Gill described it, "This 'Pack Gang' . . . began making things hum in Cleveland. So newsworthy were they that reporters camped on the steps of Charles Pack's office, sure of stories of new developments in Cleveland."[22]

Key among these developments was the establishment of the Cleveland Trust Company, founded in 1894 against considerable odds.

Charles, McNairy, the Garfield boys, and an architect named Cobb had financed the building of a great steel skyscraper called the Garfield Building. They leased the basement of the building to the Boston firm, the Security Safe Deposit & Trust Company, which began building elaborate vaults and other deposit equipment in the space. At that time, all that the company could do legally was rent and maintain safety deposit boxes and "conduct a general business of holding property in trust."[23]

In May 1894, a new state law freed "safe deposit companies to do a trust business." "Immediately," recalled Harry Garfield, "some of those interested in the Garfield Building conceived the idea of buying out the Boston parties and building up a great financial institution, under the provisions of the new law."[24]

According to Amos McNairy, who became Cleveland Trust's vice president, "Credit is due Harry Garfield for thinking of it, and to C.L.P. [Charles's friends and family often called him by his initials] for putting up the money." This money must have been the one hundred thousand dollars needed to acquire the Security Safe Deposit & Trust Company's contract.[25]

Apparently the Pack family's wealth was one reason why Charles and Amos wanted to invest in the trust company: "George Willis Pack was busy handing around fairly generous portions of dollars to everybody," recalled a granddaughter of McNairy, Elizabeth

Monroe Boggs, "and it seemed desirable to have a trust company to handle" the money.[26]

That summer Charles became sick (with what illness is not known), and went to Karlsbad, Germany, for a cure. By the time he returned, Harry Garfield and Amos McNairy had rounded up twelve other men interested in forming a trust company. On September 19, 1894, a group of fifteen, including Charles, met at the Pack office, 44 Euclid Avenue, to confer for the entire morning about whether to go ahead with the plan for this "bank in the cellar." They decided to do it, and articles of incorporation were signed.[27]

Despite the enthusiasm of the group, the founding of the Cleveland Trust Company looked like a crazy move to some. Harry Garfield would later recall it in this way:

To carry out this plan involved certain departures from the preconceived notions of those familiar with the banking business in Cleveland. In the first place, to take over the vault and equipment . . . required approximately $100,000, an equipment charge thought by many to be unwarranted. To meet this outlay, it was proposed that in addition to the $500,000 capital, $100,000 be paid in as surplus. In other words, that subscribers pay [$]120 for the stock of the new company. This proposal was sufficiently novel in Cleveland at that time to meet with considerable opposition.[28]

Another drawback was that after spending so much for equipment, the company could not afford ground-floor offices. "The space rented by the Boston parties comprised about eight thousand square feet, but it was all in the basement of the building," an unheard-of location for a financial institution.[29]

Furthermore, a new bank seemed badly timed in terms of economics. Eighteen ninety-four was not a great year for banks in general, never mind starting a new one. America was still recovering from the Panic of 1893, which was brought on by a drop in the value of silver. Due to a silver surplus in the Treasury and a subsequent gold-buying craze in which Americans bought nearly sixty million dollars in gold options in the first five months of 1893, the silver market had bottomed out. As Harry Garfield explained it, when the group decided to start a savings and trust: "Times were threatening, business was slack, and money hard to procure. It was found necessary to call upon prospective stockholders and labor with them in behalf of the enterprise, for nearly everyone approached was wary of the 'bank in the cellar.'"[30]

Despite the obstacles, the group managed to subscribe two hundred thousand dollars of capital by November. Because the basement quarters were not yet ready, the company rented a tiny office on the ninth floor of the Garfield Building, from which it operated for nine months until the cellar was finished. By March of 1895, the first deposit had been received and the first issue of bonds certified, and on September 10, 1895, the Cleveland Trust Company opened its cellar doors.[31]

As chairman of the executive committee and one of the company's twelve trustees, Charles was critically involved with the company's development from the outset. His executive committee met twice a week and dealt with such issues as revisions in Ohio banking laws. As a trustee, Charles also made investment decisions such as whether to invest in foreign government bonds—which was done.[32] Reflecting on the importance of such decisions, Garfield observed,

Although comparatively insignificant in themselves, these items evidence the activity and resourcefulness of the officers and trustees of the institution. . . . No one desired, and all disapproved of the too frequent practice of one-man power. Loans to trustees or to institutions with which trustees were connected were scanned with a care amounting almost to suspicion. The inspection committee, elected annually by the stockholders, scrutinized the loans and investments, taking nothing for granted. At times a large excess of reserve was carried, in spite of the temptation to invest at low prices.[33]

Although people were at first skeptical of "the bank in the cellar," Cleveland's leading lights, including L. H. and S. L. Severance, soon began investing in the little bank. By December 31, 1896, deposits had passed one million dollars. Three years later, deposits had increased sixfold.[34]

Success continued to sweep over the bank; it merged with the Western Reserve Trust Company in 1903, and in 1905 ground was broken for a new building at Euclid Avenue and East Ninth Street. Charles is credited with having had the "wisdom and foresight" to have the company buy the land upon which the new building was built. Today, the company is known as AmeriTrust, with assets in the billions.[35]

The success of Charles's investment in the Cleveland Trust Company is best portrayed, perhaps, on a personal level: at least some of his descendants are receiving incomes on the order of twenty thousand to thirty thousand dollars a year from both stock in the bank and investments handled by the bank.[36]

As an officer and trustee of the Cleveland Trust and a director of the Seaboard National Bank in New York, Charles quickly established himself as a banker and economist. A staunch Republican as well, he came out against William Jennings Bryan's free silver campaign and, according to Gill, "fought vigorously for sound money."[37]

"Later," Gill wrote, "after the Republicans had succeeded in defeating the silver idea, a great Monetary Commission was called in Indianapolis in 1897 to work out methods for a sounder, more elastic monetary system for the country as a whole. To this meeting went the best banking and business minds in the nation, and at forty years old, Charles Lathrop Pack was not only Chairman of the Cleveland delegation, but the youngest delegate in the entire gathering."[38]

While developing as a financial leader, Charles also became a charismatic civic leader. Described in one newspaper article as being "among the more prominent" members of Cleveland society, Charles became a civic leader. He headed the ways and means committee that organized the Cleveland Chamber of Commerce. In 1899, as a member of the chamber of commerce building committee, he handed over the key to the chamber's new building. In 1901, he became its president.[39]

A look at his inaugural speech gives some insight into how Charles inspired others and achieved his own successes. In the speech he predicted that Cleveland's population would grow from 381,768 to 1 million in thirty years. The city, he said, should start preparing for this growth.[40]

The prediction captured the imagination of many. One Cleveland editor hailed the speech as a "sound statement" and urged Clevelanders to plan for this growth. Another said the prediction was too low—that Cleveland would reach the million mark in twenty, not thirty years. (Charles later revised his prediction, saying the moment would arrive in twenty-five years.) Cincinnatians were annoyed by Charles's vision, however, and responded with an article rebutting the idea under the headline "The Conceit of Some Clevelanders."[41]

Despite his pride in Cleveland, Charles did little during his year as chamber of commerce president. He was absent for 50 percent of the meetings, and aside from giving eloquent speeches when he was there, he accomplished little else but the formation of a music hall committee. The efforts of the committee proved fruitless, however. It would take John L. Severance to form the Cleveland Orchestra in 1912 and build Severance Hall in 1930–31.

Similarly, Charles's promise as chamber of commerce president to "secure a new uptown hotel for Cleveland" did not materialize until eight years later, when Elsworth M. Statler of Buffalo, New York, signed a lease agreeing to erect "an independent hotel building . . . of substantial character . . . the plans for which shall be prepared and approved by first class architects." Charles Pack, of course, owned the property that Statler leased.[42]

On opening night, October 19, 1912, Charles and Statler each held celebration dinners at the new hotel. Charles especially had a great deal to celebrate with the hundred businessmen who attended his dinner. He had bought the land in 1900 for $150,000. Now he was leasing it for ninety-nine years for $32,500 a year, not to exceed $34,000 a year.[43] Furthermore, the requirements of the lease—that a "substantial" hotel be built on Charles's land—had been more than fulfilled: "The Hotel Statler is an Aladdin grotto out of a page in 'Arabian Nights,'" wrote the author of *Cleveland Town Topics* on October 26, 1912. "It is entrancing, bewitching, wonderfully beautiful, yet withal idealistically homelike."

A writer for the *Cleveland Plain Dealer* reported on October 20, 1912, that the lobby alone measured 104 by 320 feet, boasting marble halls, an "exquisite aristocracy of blue and gold," walls and pillars of Botticini marble, and "one of the finest ceilings in the world" of plaster relief with panels of old ivory and blue. The furniture was of Italian walnut covered with blue silk brocade, and tables, desks, divans, and chairs were inlaid with beautiful blue medallions. The impression of luxury was completed by "decidedly Kauffmanesque" thick blue Chinese rugs, draperies of figured blue silk damask, and curtains of Arabian lace.

The numerous dining rooms were each done in an individual style, such as "the so-called lattice room . . . of [a] filigree and gold sort of daintiness . . . latticed with pretty little cameos interspersed on wall and ceiling and with the most novel and delicate Wedgwood cameo door knobs. The draperies are of soft green and yellow striped silk." The men's lounge was a study in perfection as well:

If the Statler had no other distinctive features, this lounge alone would suffice to spread its name and fame through the length and breadth of the country. Like the rooms adjoining it, it is severely Elizabethan in style. . . . The soft, luxurious carpet, the deep divans and easy chairs covered with old rose velvets invite a dreamful repose. The massive fireplace radiates hospitality and cheer, and the walls with built-in oak book cases contain hundreds of volumes of standard works as well as "best sellers," fiction, science, philosophy and poetry. . . . An expert librarian is in charge of the room. The elevated portion is equipped with desks and writing materials, and adjoining it is a small room for the public stenographer.

The seven hundred rooms each had private bathrooms with baths or showers, air and water filtering systems, and regulated thermostats, "giving the cold air or Turkish bath temperature enthusiasts exactly what pleases them most." And every room was color-coordinated:

There are four floors of blue, four of green, two of brown decorations, in which everything in the rooms is so arranged as regards color that no . . . jarring element is visible. . . . The innovations which make the Statler distinctive and apart from other places thusly named are numerous and each in its way helps to produce comfort. It may be the . . . arrangement of the wardrobe doors so that a triple mirror effect is secured, the air space between the solid mahogany doors of adjoining suites, the adjustable reading lamps, the glass topped writing tables . . . the lighting adjustment on the dressers, the emergency pin and needle cushions or the manner in which you are shown to your room, that makes a Statler enthusiast of each patron.[44]

While Statler received accolades for his creation, Charles also received a significant amount of credit for this magnificent hotel:

"It is now nearly ten years ago that Mr. Pack, as president of the Cleveland Chamber of Commerce, promised his best efforts to secure a new uptown hotel for Cleveland," reported the *Cleveland Town Topics* on October 12, 1912. "The opening of the Hotel Statler is the realization of his dream and he himself has made the realization possible."[45]

His energy, his enthusiasm, his vision for Cleveland, and his significant business successes made Charles a popular leader. At one point he was nominated the Republican party's mayoral candidate, but declined the nomination. His soirées were regularly reported in the society section of *Town Topics*. In 1901, for instance, it was reported that "one of the swellest stag dinners ever given in Cleveland was tendered last Monday evening by Charles L. Pack, to the officers and trustees of the Cleveland Trust Company, and including some other bank officials of Cleveland. After dinner the guests were most delightfully entertained by the Philharmonic String Quartette." The guests included the cofounder and president of the Cleveland Country Club, Samuel Mather, and James Parmelee, president of the Cleveland Stock Exchange. Another party made the news in 1912, when Charles held a banquet honoring one hundred men whom he felt "were helping the city and were not taking something out without putting something back."[46]

When Charles stepped down from the presidency of the chamber of commerce in 1902, he gave a farewell speech that reflected his own secret to success—pure vision and pure energy.

"How fortunate we are to be Clevelanders," he said. "Did you ever think of it? There is something inherent in our city that makes men energetic. There are men before me to-night who, before they came here, were willing to sell tape by the yard, but who are to-day selling goods by the car load. There are here men who were satisfied in other places to sell molasses in winter by measure, who to-day are sending car lots all over America and ship loads to foreign shores. There are men who, through our trade excursions, are carrying the gospel of Cleveland to towns and cities in many States. Why is it? It is because Cleveland makes its own type of man. The man that stands still is run over."[47]

Charles Pack was in no danger of being run over.

CHAPTER 5

Charles and Gertrude

S HINING IN THE CENTER of Cleveland society, Charles Lathrop Pack was one of the city's most eligible bachelors. When, at the age of twenty-nine, he married his distant cousin Alice Gertrude Hatch, he no doubt dashed the hopes of at least a few young ladies.

Charles and Gertrude, as she was known, were married on April 28, 1886, in her parents' home at 680 Prospect Street. The couple honeymooned for the summer in Europe. After returning home, the newlyweds spent the winter in Oscoda, where Charles oversaw the family mills, before settling in Cleveland.[1]

Charles married in part because he wanted heirs. As an only son, continuing the Pack line meant so much to him that he later offered a precious necklace as a reward to the first daughter-in-law to produce a male heir. The reward was never given, though, since the only grandson conceived in Charles's lifetime was born prematurely and died.[2] Charles Lathrop Pack II was born to Charles's youngest son, Arthur, one year after Charles had died.

The real question is not why Charles married but why, of all the eligible ladies in Cleveland, he married Alice Gertrude Hatch. The question intrigues her grandchildren and in-laws who, knowing Gertrude only as an older woman, saw marked contrasts between Gertrude and Charles.[3] By then, partially isolated from the world by near blindness and deafness, Gertrude seemed so reserved and stiff that one granddaughter described her as "iron-backed," "straight as a metal yardstick," "never relaxed," and with a barrier surrounding her that was "impossible to penetrate."[4]

Charles, on the other hand, was jovial and outgoing, and loved to laugh, drink, smoke cigars, tell jokes, and go dancing. How on earth, the relatives wondered, did Charles and Gertrude come to be married?[5]

Gertrude was a native Clevelander whose strict, old-school Presbyterian father, Henry Hatch, a leading Cleveland banker and businessman, raised her to be a stoic young lady. While Charles was running practically wild in the Michigan woods, Gertrude had a board strapped to her back to teach her good posture.[6]

But this strict upbringing did not break Gertrude's spirit. Although she always maintained formal, ladylike manners, inside she was an outgoing young woman. In fact, Gertrude's travel diaries from two European trips reveal a young lady who is open, sensitive, honest, humorous, fun-loving, deeply appreciative of beauty, and a keen observer of people.[7]

"Glorious moonlight nights and lots of fun," she wrote on June 3, 1879, while sailing to Europe on the steamship *Gallia*. She was twenty years old at the time.

Six years later, still single and in Europe once more, she wrote, "Had two or three good dances. A strange man asked me to dance, foolishly consenting, I was whirled once around the room and then sat down too dizzy too [*sic*] see."[8]

Far from being repressed, Gertrude was actually rather adventurous. While visiting Killarney in 1879 she wrote, "Papa and I . . . rode horseback through [Dunloe] gap. Our horses were led by guides all of whom were full of 'Blarney.' I enjoyed the ride very much as it was an entirely new experience."[9]

And in 1885, while touring Egypt, she "had the excitement" of falling off her donkey, and even drew a self-mocking, comic illustration of the event.[10] Two days later, with that incident behind her, Gertrude exulted in her beautiful surroundings: "Have had a lovely quiet day, the air is so soft and fresh from the sea it makes one feel happy in the extreme."[11]

These diary entries indicate that at least one year before she married Charles, Gertrude was a happy, outgoing young lady who was, in fact, not so different from her fiancé.

It is easy to imagine Charles being attracted to such a young woman, and there is evidence that he may have actually loved her. When Tom Gill interviewed him in the last year of his life, Gill asked Charles what his favorite tree was. Mishearing the question, Charles replied, "I have never been in love with any girl except my wife."[12]

No one knows when Charles and Gertrude first met, but since the two families were quite close, they probably met soon after Charles moved to Cleveland. Certainly they were close by 1884 or 1885. On January 1, 1885, while in Rome, Gertrude wrote that she had "received a pretty little New Year's souvenir from Charlie Pack." Upon her return home she wrote, "Frank [Elbert Frank Baldwin, her first cousin] was the only missing one of the family. . . . Charlie came last night, so little by little we are truly at home once more."[13]

A letter from Gertrude to her future mother-in-law, Frances, who now lived in North Carolina, indicates that Gertrude was engaged to Charles by February 1886. The letter describes a reception that was held for Charles's elder sister, Mary, and her new husband, Amos B. McNairy. In this letter, Gertrude let her mother-in-law know that she, Gertrude, had made quite a good catch in Charles: "Mrs. James Tracey came up to me in her usual gushing style saying, 'Allow me to offer my congratulations and let me tell you that you are going to marry one of the nicest young men in Cleveland. I am a great admirer of Mr. Pack, we used to be such good friends before I was married.'"[14]

Furthermore, Gertrude told Frances she was thrilled to be marrying into the family—"I am so glad I am going to belong to such a nice looking family"[15]—and that she also adored her future mother-in-law: "Ah! dear little woman if there is a particle of my heart that Charlie has not in his possession it must belong to you, we did have some happy times together did we not? Do you miss *Gertrude* just a little?"[16]

Thus, at the time of her engagement, Gertrude was not only in love with Charles but also extremely close to the family. This love for her husband seems to have lasted some time, if a letter written at least fifteen years later is any indication. It ends with Gertrude saying, "Lots of love and if that and good wishes could make you well, you would never be ill."[17]

But somewhere, somehow, the closeness between Charles and Gertrude began to fade. By the time Charles claimed that the only woman he had ever loved was Gertrude, he had been living a life apart from her for years.

Eventually, for the sake of the children's health, Charles moved his family from Cleveland to Lakewood, New Jersey. Charles, however, spent weekdays in New York, doing business from his Vanderbilt Hotel suite and going home only on weekends. Although Gertrude and the children visited Charles in New York for theater and dinner engagements, Charles had private parties on his own and was known to have mistresses, including a secretary for whom he created a lifetime trust fund.[18]

There is no documentation of how, when, or why Gertrude and Charles began to lead separate lives. By the time Gertrude was a grandmother, the split seemed extreme to some, and Gertrude especially seems to have suffered. As her granddaughter Eleanor Liddell put it in a poem:

> If you were touched
> I think you would have shattered
> into a thousand pieces.[19]

Charles, however, remained as genial as Santa Claus. Eleanor remembered her grandparents this way:

GRANDFATHER'S LAUGH

> As a child I had to lean way back to see
> his crinkled face. Blue eyes sparkled and
> a booming laugh came from his feet,
> ringing through the house. It shook the
> chandeliers! Ramrod straight my
> grandmother sat, tight lips pursed. . . .
> When he died, a plate was set at his empty
> chair, not to mark a loss, but balance to assign. . . .
> When he was gone, I tiptoed down
> thick carpeted halls, fearful lest my

grandmother appear and glare at me, her
owl-like spectacles glued firmly on her
nose. For years I crept down halls,
carpeted or bare, looking left to right
lest I see a stare of disapproval near,
until at last my silence-deafened ears
picked up the sound of laughter, a deep
rumble rising from my feet rushing through
my body, bursting freely forth, drowning
my grandmother in glee.[20]

By this time, Gertrude had endured numerous tragedies and losses—the loss of a stillborn child and another adored son, her father's death, and the deaths of her parents-in-law. In addition, she suffered from poor hearing and eyesight. Perhaps all of these circumstances combined to make her defensively more reserved, unfortunately giving the appearance of coldness.

Some relatives, however, saw past Gertrude's reserve and formality and caught a twinkle behind the thick glasses and an expression of amusement at the world. Even in her old age Gertrude was interested in world affairs and the new ideas of the young, but she never criticized others who were not as bright or well-informed as she. To one granddaughter, Virginia Lathrop (Pack) Townsend, Gertrude was "a very lovely and intelligent person—never a cuddly grandmother but warm-hearted, caring and dignified." Virginia and her sister Joan loved spending weekends with Gertrude, touring her beloved garden and going to the New York Philharmonic concerts on Friday afternoons.[21]

Nevertheless, given the differences in temperament between Gertrude and Charles in their later years, relatives could not help but wonder if the marriage had been arranged. Certainly such marriages were not at all unusual during this era.

Such an arrangement would have linked family fortunes. In addition to being a partner of E. I. Baldwin, Hatch & Company, Dry Goods, of Cleveland (which became Hatch & Company after the senior partner died), Henry Reynolds Hatch was a director of several banks, a Cleveland Chamber of Commerce member, and a Western Reserve University trustee. His fortune combined with that of the Packs would have made the families even wealthier and more influential than they already were.[22]

Relatives also remember hearing that the great love of Gertrude's life was not Charles, but her first cousin Frank Baldwin. Marriage to Frank was forbidden, of course, due to the close blood ties.

It is not known when Gertrude fell in love with Frank. Possibly the romance blossomed just one year before she married Charles, when the two met during their travels in Germany in 1884–85. But while Gertrude noted that they took tea and dinner together and went sightseeing, she said nothing of her feelings for Frank. If she did love him, she kept tight control of the emotion, for the two would be close throughout their lives. Frank also moved from Cleveland to Lakewood, New Jersey, and Charles and Gertrude's son Arthur wrote often in his diaries of visits with the Baldwin family.[23]

If Gertrude loved Frank, did she harbor disappointment over this thwarted love, and did her disappointment turn into resentment of Charles? Some descendents believe that the answer is yes to both questions. Yet at the time of her marriage to Charles, Gertrude seemed happy and well adjusted, indicating that she had not yet broken her heart over Frank.

In fact, if the evidence of the diaries and letters is to be trusted, Gertrude was very much in love with Charles when she married him. And as for Charles, when they honeymooned in Europe, he gave his bride a very loving gift—her first pair of glasses. "Oh, Charlie," Gertrude cried in delight, "I can see the leaves on the trees."[24]

CHAPTER 6

 The Family Man at
Home in Cleveland and
Lakewood

U
PON RETURNING to Cleveland from Oscoda,
Charles and Gertrude seemed to lead a fairy-tale existence. They moved in the center of Cleveland society,
were surrounded by close family and friends, and soon
were living in the most prestigious neighborhood. Their picturesque house, Norway Lodge, looked like an elegant variation on
the rose-covered cottages that one imagines newlywed couples living in, happily ever after.

Norway Lodge was built on the land Gertrude had received as a
wedding present, next door to Mary and Amos's new home, on the
old Weddell estate.

According to Charles, he and Gertrude moved into Norway
Lodge in 1887. A newspaper item dated December 24, 1887, however, states, "Mrs. Charles Pack of Huntington Street gave a reception on Tuesday." Unless the newspaper reporter was mistaken, it
appears that the couple stayed at Huntington Street while Norway
Lodge was being completed. Since it is unlikely that they would
have moved over the Christmas holidays, Charles and Gertrude
probably did not move into their new home until 1888.[1]

Their new address, 3307 Euclid Avenue, placed them in the center of Cleveland society. The importance of their new neighbor-

The home of Charles and Gertrude Pack presented a modest exterior, compared to those of its grand neighbors. (Courtesy of Elizabeth Boggs.)

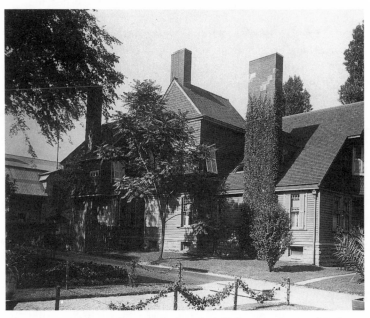

The unassuming front of Norway Lodge belied the fact that the rest of the house was copious enough for a family of five and the requisite servants. (Courtesy of Elizabeth Boggs.)

hood is made clear by a feature article that was published in 1888, describing a public celebration honoring President Benjamin Harrison, an Ohio native and a Republican. At the center of the celebration was Millionaires' Row, where Cleveland millionaires—staunch Republicans all—competed in decorating their mansions with banners and flags to honor Harrison: "Mr. Eells' house was ... distinguished by one of the largest and brightest flags on the avenue," the writer reported. "At each of the front windows the regular curtains had been replaced by the glorious colors of this country, and the porch was literally covered by handsome flag drapery."

The Packs, neighbors of Mr. Eells, were not to be outdone.

Mr. Charles L. Pack had the handsomest avenue of elm trees in Cleveland leading to his picturesque house. These elm trees were artistically decorated with fifty silk flags of various nations, and at the entrance to the grounds was a banner some twenty feet long with these words: "We Honor Garfield. Long Live Harrison." President Harrison left Mr. Eells' house a few minutes Thursday, and called at Mr. Pack's residence, wanting to see, he said, the people who had so kindly wished him great longevity. The residence of Mr. George W. Pack had as original and beautiful a design as any in the city. An enormous star was made by red, white, and blue streamers on the front of the large square house, and between the radiations a large number of small stars cut from tin added greatly to the effect.[2]

Despite his prestigious address, Charles lived in what, by Millionaires' Row standards, was a cottage-style home. In fact, tour-bus guides regularly pointed out that it was the smallest house on Millionaires' Row. With seventy-eight acres to build on, Charles and Gertrude could have designed a much larger house. Since they both had money, the decision had to do with personal taste, not finances.[3]

Although simple by Euclid Avenue standards, the two-story house was impressive. It featured three fireplaces, and what it lacked in sprawling width, it made up for in length. It was, in fact, large enough to accommodate Charles, Gertrude, a nanny, a maid and a cook, and four children who were all born in Norway Lodge: George Lathrop Pack, born in 1888, who was called Lathrop; Randolph Greene Pack, born in 1890; Arthur Newton Pack, born in

1893; and Beulah Frances Pack, born in 1896. Elegant in design, Norway Lodge was made inside and out of Norway pine from Michigan. Even the nursery was paneled in this beautiful, straight-grained, golden-red wood.[4]

Next door, Mary and Amos added Gladys and Elizabeth to the clan. Both girls were of an age to play with Lathrop, Randolph, and Arthur, but would have been too old to play well with Beulah.

When Charles Pack's son Arthur wrote his memoirs, it was not his own home, Norway Lodge, that he described in detail, but the McNairy's home, Ivywall. (The house had been named by George Willis, who had a penchant for naming things. He christened his Asheville home Manyoaks and called his horses Hector and Alcibiades, after the hero of the *Iliad* and a general who saved Socrates' life during the Peloponnesian War.)[5] The fact that Arthur focused on Ivywall, where he had played as a child, indicates that Norway Lodge paled in comparison.

Ivywall was a three-story mansion with massive front columns of stone. The bathroom, Arthur recalled, "offered gilded built-in fixtures concealed by hinged panels of solid mahogany, so that the actual plumbing became invisible and the whole room belied its intimate and practical purpose. Almost all of the ground-floor rooms had intricately paneled ceilings, cross-divided into squares of cabinet work. Hand-built of flawless lumber before the day of power tools, the painstaking mortise work had been done by a German cabinet maker."[6] On the third floor was Jubilee Hall, a great ballroom that "occupied the whole of the immense front gable above the multiple stone pillars."[7]

Spacious and elegant, Ivywall was a perfect homestead for the Pack clan. It was large enough to accommodate the McNairys and their children and servants, as well as George Willis and Frances and their entourage of live-in servants when they came for extended visits. Even the great, three-bay carriage house, situated behind the two houses, accommodated Hector and Alcibiades as well as the Pack and McNairy horses, buggies, and coaches.[8]

Ivywall was where the family gathered for Christmas. Soon a Christmas tradition, the Dolls' Ball, evolved; family members would arrange their dolls in attitudes of dance along the window

THE FAMILY MAN AT HOME

Randolph, Arthur, and George Lathrop Pack, playing with George Lathrop's wheel-chair in front of Norway Lodge. Randolph holds the chair with Arthur in it. George Lathrop is in back. *(Courtesy of Virginia Lathrop [Pack] Townsend.)*

OPPOSITE PAGE
Top, left: Alice Gertrude Hatch was known as Gertrude to her friends and family.
(Courtesy of Virginia Lathrop [Pack] Townsend.)
Top, right: Arthur Newton Pack at about the time he became his father's "partner."
(Courtesy of the Arizona Historical Society.)
Bottom, left: Randolph Greene Pack. (Courtesy of Virginia Lathrop [Pack] Townsend.)
Bottom, right: Beulah Frances Pack, Charles Lathrop Pack's daughter. (Courtesy of Virginia Lathrop [Pack] Townsend.)

seat of the great bay window of the library. While the library was also used as a living room and for Christmas celebrations, family dinners were held in the formal dining room. Grander parties were held in Jubilee Hall.[9]

The family appears to have been quite close. Every spring from 1890 to 1899 Charles took his family to Asheville, where they stayed near George and Frances.

Arthur's memoirs include notes about regular family visits among family members throughout his teen years. This was a continuation of a pattern set early in Charles and Gertrude's married life. Charles also provided business counsel for his family, advising his brother-in-law to invest in a paint business and including him in various of his own business deals. Given these connections and the fact that the senior Packs stayed with the McNairys for long visits, Charles and his extended family spent a great deal of time together.

Charles, Gertrude, and the children also spent time with Gertrude's father, Henry Reynolds Hatch, and his new family. Gertrude's mother, Eliza Newton Baldwin Hatch, died in 1886, the year that Gertrude and Charles were married. In 1887, Henry Hatch married a school chum of Gertrude's, Mary Cummings Browne. The two soon produced a new family. Gertrude graciously overcame the fact that her stepmother was a friend her own age, and that her half-brother and half-sister were her own children's age. The children from both families often played together.[10]

Between the Hatch and McNairy families, the Pack children had no shortage of playmates. Homemade programs for evening entertainment indicate that each year, from at least 1898 until 1909, the children put together regular and elaborate amusements for their parents. The groups they formed had various names—the Evening Amusement Club, the Three Cornered Orchestra, the Two Cornered Orchestra, the Three Cornered Dramatic Club, and the Sunny Side Club—and involved various combinations of members, ranging from all the Pack, Hatch, and McNairy children to just Lathrop, Randolph, and Arthur. Their programs included musical arrangements ranging from "Alpine Flowers" in 1905 to a nocturne and intermezzo by Mendelssohn in 1907, speeches such as "Foes of Little Boys" by Arthur, and plays ranging from the one-act comedy "Ou Est-Elle?" to "The Mad Tea Party (from *Alice in Wonderland*)."[11]

The programs themselves were often humorously written: one featured a list of "Masculine, Feminine & (Neuter)" patrons on its cover—Mr. Taft and Miss Maud Adams being of the first two genders, respectively, and a Mr. Bryan (possibly William Jennings Bryan, given Charles's well-known dislike of him) being neuter. This same program also included the notation that "not more than (5) consecutive encores will be played." Another program, with masculine and feminine patrons only, announced that its patrons —Theodore Roosevelt, the Mikado of Japan, Governor Hughes, Julius Caesar, and Mrs. Eddy—"are few but select."[12]

Given Charles's love of speech-making and humor, he must have enjoyed the performances greatly. Charles also loved to entertain the family himself, with stories and bad jokes, such as how Thanksgiving was like a world war because it involved the fall of turkey and the overthrow of grease.

He also engaged the children in his entertainment plans. The day after Admiral Dewey defeated the Spanish fleet in Manila Bay, Charles "was as excited as a small boy" and had Arthur memorize and recite to company a verse that had appeared in the paper:

Dewey was the morning of the second day of May
Dewey was the Admiral's name out on Manila Bay
Dewey were the Regent's eyes*
Those orbs of emerald blue.
Do we feel discouraged?
I do not think we do!
Do—we?[13]

When Uncle Arthur and his family came to visit, Charles and Gertrude entertained them with a grand family dinner and a "negro quartet" that sang a ditty reflecting Charles's feelings about that newfangled contraption, the gasoline car:

Gasoline, gasoline
First you put it in a tank
Then you turn a little crank.

*The Queen Regent of Spain.

Gasoline, gasoline
Put-put, put-put, put-put BANG
Gasoline. (The last word sung with all the heavy
implications of a funeral dirge.)[14]

Although the family roared with laughter, the cost of their laughter was sky-high. Charles's Uncle Arthur, like most of the Packs, respected Charles's financial genius and asked his advice, perhaps at this very dinner, about whether to back a certain automobile maker. At the time, Uncle Arthur was retired from the timber business and was living in Detroit, where he was a partner in the Welch car company. As Uncle Arthur explained it, a "more or less 'crazy' man" had asked if Arthur would rent him part of the Welch car plant where he would begin manufacturing cheap gasoline vehicles for the common man. Arthur would consider doing this, but all the man could offer in return was stock in his as-yet-unformed company. Charles told Uncle Arthur to "have nothing to do with such a ridiculous, fly-by-night scheme." Thus, as Charles's son Arthur observed, "Henry Ford had to look elsewhere for a partner."[15]

Charles was often engaged in serious business discussions such as these when he was at home. Yet he also made time for the children and for play—so much so that to the children, life with Father must have seemed rather like life with a large child. On Sundays, for instance, following services at the Second Presbyterian Church, Charles would have Frank, the coachman, harness Scrapper to a red and green painted wagon. With Charles driving, the family would set out for a picnic on their country property, which they called the Farm.

"If Scrappy was scrappy," Arthur recalled, "so was he—even on the day when the big red interurban trolley met us on the plank road and Scrapper ran away almost spilling us all." Soon after that incident, Charles invested in an electric car and stayed with this mode of transportation for years before switching to gasoline powered cars. Ultimately the family owned a midnight-blue twelve-cylinder Packard, with heather blue upholstery and a polished oak interior. Gertrude's lap robe featured the upholstery fabric on one side and brown curly fur on the other that matched the oak paneling.[16]

Charles loved to play. When the battleship *Maine* was sunk, supposedly by a mine, setting off the Spanish-American War, Charles brought home postcards that read, "Remember the Maine." According to his son Arthur, pasted onto each card "was a little channel of black powder that led to the vessel's bow. One could touch off the powder and blow up the *Maine* with a very satisfactory bang," much to Charles's delight.

Charles's boyish glee over blowing things up and making loud noises made the Fourth of July a brilliant holiday *chez* Pack. While the children set off their fireworks, Charles assembled his own collection of Roman candles, skyrockets, and pinwheels and set them off himself.

What he did not have time to do with the children, Charles hired someone else to do for him. For instance, he employed a Mr. Donkin to teach the children how to raise prize-winning pigeons, thinking this would teach them about business, just as his own tomato-growing project had once taught him.[17]

Charles clearly delighted in his children, but his enthusiastic method of fathering sometimes kept him from seeing what his children really needed or wanted, as opposed to what he felt they should need or want. As Arthur recalled, "Between the always dirty job of cleaning pigeon coops and perching shelves, the equally messy one of chopping off the heads of live squabs after first wringing their necks to make them hold still, and then plucking those seemingly endless pin feathers, my sister Beulah and I felt that we would have preferred tomatoes to pigeons."[18]

Although a perfectionist and driven super-achiever, Charles was not the sort of person who could not abide imperfection. Some men as ambitious and egoistic as he might have shunned an invalid son. Lathrop, Charles and Gertrude's firstborn, was a hemophiliac who also suffered from rheumatism or arthritis and alternated between bed, wheelchair, and crutches; Charles doted on the boy, as did Gertrude.[19]

Charles interested Lathrop in stamp collecting, a hobby that he could easily pursue from the confinement of bed or wheelchair. Lathrop avidly took up the hobby, writing letters to collectors around the world with his typewriter. He turned into an astute collector, acquiring at one time the only block of four of the Pan American Inverted Center Stamp.[20]

Although Lathrop was restricted to more intellectual pursuits than his siblings were, he was far from a stuffy child. He was always kind, especially to his little sister, Beulah, the youngest of the family. Whenever the others teased her, Lathrop would gather Beulah beside him in his wheelchair and, turning the wheels with his hands, chase the others until they gave up. As for Gertrude, she protected and cared for Lathrop by helping to nurse him and sleeping by his side every night.[21]

All the nursing and love in the world, however, could not change the raw climate of Cleveland; the winters were notoriously fierce, thanks to the effect of Lake Erie. The damp, cold air, heavily laced with coal soot from the factories, must have hurt everyone's health. When the children developed persistent throat and chest trouble, doctors advised Charles to move them to a drier climate. After researching various possibilities, Charles decided to have the family winter in Lakewood, New Jersey, which, studies showed, had as much sunshine as Florida.[22]

Lakewood was a winter resort for the wealthy. A major train depot allowed Charles to travel from Lakewood to Cleveland, to New York, and, later in his career, to Washington, D.C. He rarely, however, made daily commutes. Instead, he spent several days at a time away on business before returning to Lakewood.[23]

The neon and plastic signs that today crowd the main streets of Lakewood do nothing to distinguish it from any of its neighbors. But at the turn of the century when the Packs moved there, Lakewood offered great beauty and climatic relief from the cold, damp, dirt, and grime of Cleveland and other industrial cities. The key to this resort was its idyllic location in the famous pine belt of New Jersey. As one promotion piece of the time described the area,

In autumn, the brilliant sunlight, balmy air, sweet odor of pines, the exquisite tints of the foliage delight the senses. In winter, there is none of the penetrating dampness prevalent in our Northern States. These conditions in Lakewood are due to sand strata 600 feet in depth and the forests of pine trees which surround and protect the town. Through the sand, the water quickly percolates after a rainfall, leaving the ground dry and the atmosphere free of moisture. . . . The exhilarating atmosphere and dryness of the air incite the active to exercise . . . while those less vigorous find inspiration and renewed strength.[24]

The society people who flocked to this lovely resort supplemented its beauty by building elegant homes and hotels. They paraded up and down the boulevards and avenues in shiny horse-drawn coaches and open-air buggies; strolled along the walkways encircling Lakewood's Lake Carasaljo, wearing the lovely full dress of the day, complete with soft felt fedoras and walking sticks for the men and wide-brimmed hats for the ladies, extravagantly decorated with feathers and flowers; and took leisurely boat rides across the lake to have tea at the tea house.

The Packs belonged to a community made up of some of the most powerful and wealthy people in America's Gilded Age. Grover Cleveland had a cottage and John D. Rockefeller a mansion there, complete with a golf course and two lakes and streams. Rudyard Kipling, a Lakewood regular, often sat on the floor of a fashionable hotel, the Laurel House, near the fireplace, telling stories for children's ears only—no adults allowed. Elsewhere, the Lakewood Hotel, nestled on fourteen acres of grounds, became known as the winter headquarters of Tammany Hall. The Laurel-in-the-Pines Hotel was an opulent five-story hotel with two hundred rooms and spacious sun corridors. These and the other two hotels made Lakewood one of the gayest playgrounds of the Gay Nineties.[25]

In 1900, the Packs spent their first winter in Lakewood before eventually moving there permanently. That winter they moved into a great square white house. Unfortunately a fire soon forced them to move into a rental property on Forest Avenue, which they used until 1909 when they built their own three-story Georgian brick home at Forest Avenue and Third Street.[26]

The new home was named Lathrop Hall in honor, perhaps, of both their invalid son and Charles's grandmother, Maria Lathrop. Compared to some of its neighbors, the house was quite modest. Just down the road, for instance, lay Georgian Court, the great estate of George Jay Gould, son of the financier Jay Gould. In addition to featuring a palatial mansion, Georgian Court boasted sprawling and spacious grounds that included a Japanese tea garden, a grand fountain sculpture of Apollo that had been shipped from France, sunken gardens, and a stable and polo field for the best and fastest polo ponies in the country. Polo was George Gould's passion, and he provided regular weekend entertainment to the Packs and others by hosting games featuring the most famous international players. Afterward the local boys would mount their bicycles and play their own brand of polo, using "discarded balls and sawed-off mallets abandoned by the experts."[27]

Although a wealthy man, Charles did not favor the Goulds' flamboyant style. By contrast, Lathrop Hall was quietly elegant and of superior quality. Its rosy bricks were imported from England. The walls were two feet thick, built to last generations, and all the finishing details—the moldings, mantels, and floors—were the finest to be had. The architecture was of perfect Georgian design.

The grounds of Lathrop Hall, which included great pine trees, were no more than two acres but highly impressive, thanks to Charles's zeal for gardening. His azaleas, he once claimed, could have sold for fifty dollars each; some, seven and eight feet high, were irreplaceable, and his rhododendrons were even taller. By 1937, his garden boasted 4,500 gladioli and hundreds of picotee tulips, distinctive for their color banding, at one time cost Charles seven dollars per bulb. His passion for imported Holland tulips was unbridled. Each year his gardeners planted some seven thousand tulips. When they bloomed, he plucked and discarded imper-

This magnificent fountain of Apollo still graces the grounds of Georgian Court, now home to Georgian Court College. Its grandeur typifies the style of Charles Pack's Lakewood neighbor George Jay Gould, son of financier Jay Gould, and the opulence of the society people who graced Lakewood during the Gay Nineties. (Courtesy of Sister Mary Christina Geis.)

Charles Pack's garden at Lathrop Hall was so grand that it became a regular tourist attraction in Lakewood. (Photo by Frank P. Jewett. Courtesy of Virginia Lathrop [Pack] Townsend.)

fect specimens. People, he said, came from all over the country to see his garden. He loved to tell about how he invited a group of admiring onlookers to come in and look around. When one remarked that "Mr. Pack wouldn't like that," Charles, whose shirt-sleeves were rolled up, replied, "If anyone says anything, tell them the head gardener said it was O.K."[28]

Lathrop Hall's lush grounds, grand chimneys, elegant brick-work, and wrought-iron gate made it literally a picture-postcard house. For years, Lakewood tourists bought postcards with color pictures of Lathrop Hall as a memento of their visit.[29]

Charles was possessive and proud of his house. In the 1920s, he bought a neighboring estate next door in order to protect his wife from the tenants, who did not live up to his standards. He closed the house, and, it is rumored, used the ground floor of the mansion to store his fertilizer. He even bought Third Street from the town in order to stop the road from running through his property. Furthermore, he stipulated that should he outlive his wife, the house should be torn down after his death, for it was built for his family's use only, and none other. This sequence of events, however, did not occur. Gertrude outlived Charles, and after her death the house became a residence for the nuns of St. Mary's Academy. It was sold to developers in 1992 and torn down to make way for condominiums and townhouses.[30]

Compared to its neighbors like Georgian Court, the interior of Lathrop Hall was quite simple. While leaded-glass French doors connected the downstairs rooms, for instance, they were simply cut. Similarly, the columns on either side of the doorways were carved in relief from the walls in simple Doric lines; other houses of that period had elaborate, freestanding Corinthian columns.

The living room, decorated by the prestigious interior decorator Elsie De Wolfe, was done in tones of soft green, gold, and tan brocade. Chippendale mahogany curio cabinets displayed Sunday porcelain pieces and silver and ivory miniatures. A glass cabinet in one corner held elaborate gilt and enamel German wine glasses. The lampshades were fringed.

The dining room contrasted light walls with dark woodwork and heavy furniture, mostly mahogany, including high-backed chairs. Fine French meals were served on any of the various Bohemian china place settings that Charles collected, continuing a tradition set by his father. The meals were prepared by a Belgian chef from one of New York City's finest restaurants, Delmonico's, who came to the Packs after losing his leg in a tramway accident. Peas fresh from Charles's garden were served regularly, for Charles claimed he loved them so much that he could eat them for breakfast, lunch, and dinner.

On the second floor, Lathrop Hall offered beauty and convenience. The spacious bedrooms were done in soft colors, with walls of light cream or beigy pink. One bedroom featured furniture that had been painted white and decorated with dainty

Left: Charles Lathrop Pack hurrying up the walk to Lathrop Hall. (Courtesy of Virginia Lathrop [Pack] Townsend.)

Bottom: Charles was so possessive of Lathrop Hall that he wanted it used for no other purpose than to serve as the Pack family home. He stipulated that should he survive his wife, Lathrop Hall would be torn down upon the event of his death. (Photo by Frank P. Jewett. Courtesy of Virginia Lathrop [Pack] Townsend.)

flowers, while another featured light wood furniture, possibly fruitwood, with a delicate inlaid pattern. Three bedrooms had their own baths; two shared a bath. Each bathroom had marble sinks and monogrammed towels. Charles's and Gertrude's corner bedrooms, across the hall from one another, each had a fireplace.

On the third floor were servants' quarters and a large study for Charles, with a fireplace. Here Charles dictated his letters, sometimes keeping three to five secretaries busy all day.

Meetings, formal and informal, were most often held in Charles's den on the first floor, where Charles and cronies would retire behind closed doors to swap lies or plot new business coups over cigars and brandy; Gertrude could not abide cigar smoke in the rest of the house.[31]

Ensconced in the den, Charles conferred with fellow Lakewoodians like Dr. Charles J. Lindley, who had fought with the British in Africa and loved to tell war stories, or the war correspondent Stanley Washburn, who was deeply interested in politics. Washburn was one of Charles's best friends, as were John Hays Hammond, the famous mining engineer who worked with Cecil Rhodes in South Africa, and Lewis B. Stillwell, the electrical director of the Niagara Power Company, who designed the New York City subway system. With these men and others, including George Gould, Charles held forth on almost any subject, ranging from the state of the world economy to the country club's upcoming inaugural horse race (he, Gould, and Hammond were all on the board of directors).[32]

It is unclear whether Charles was actually on friendly terms with Gould. According to one account, Charles had not wanted to have the interview with George's father, Jay Gould, which had resulted in Jay's investing in southern pine. The reason Charles gave for his reluctance was that Jay Gould "had such a reputation for wickedness."[33] Yet Charles seems not to have extended this distaste for Jay Gould to George, since he served on the same social committees with George and apparently attended his polo matches.

What is clear is that Hammond and Stillwell became Charles's best friends. They served on conservation organizations he headed, as well as the National War Garden Committee. In fact, they seem to have allied with him in every activity he undertook from the early 1900s on.

While the move to Lakewood gave Charles a powerful group of new friends, this new life was not without hardship. On July 3, 1904, Lathrop died at the age of sixteen, just after the family returned to Cleveland for the summer, and five years before Lathrop Hall was built. Gertrude was so stricken by her son's death that for years she dreamed that he was still alive. She never forgot how once, after his death, she saw him coming down the sidewalk in his wheelchair.[34]

Gertrude's diaries and letters were destroyed in a move, so she cannot tell us how Lathrop's death affected her marriage. Years later, however, Arthur recorded in his diary that when Gertrude's father died in 1915, she grew withdrawn and depressed, so much so that he worried that she would become seriously ill. Charles, on the other hand, seems to have always been his cheerful and busy self. Given these differences in personality, it is possible that the death of Lathrop marked the beginning of a coolness between them. If Gertrude coped by withdrawing into herself while Charles continued to live an active business and social life, she might have resented Charles for not dealing with grief in the same way that she did.

Charles found a variety of ways to compensate for his loss, all expressed by outward activity rather than withdrawal. The unpublished biography by Gill states that he sought solace by throwing himself into stamp collecting and conservation work. Ultimately, with agents scouring the earth for rare and precious stamps, he acquired such outstanding collections that he became known as "the greatest philatelist of this country." According to one source, the entire collection was sold for $2.5 million after his death.[35]

"Mr. Pack's collection of early Victoria stamps," reported the *New York Times* on February 10, 1924, "is one of the finest in the world. . . . The only other collection that compares with Mr. Pack's is owned by King George. The King was so much interested in Mr. Pack's work that he sent him for study his entire collection of early

Victoria stamps—the first time that such an honor has ever been bestowed upon an American."[36]

Because Charles had introduced stamp collecting to Lathrop and Lathrop had thrived on it, it is possible that this activity helped Charles cope with the boy's death. The claim that Charles consoled himself over Lathrop's death by working for forest conservation, however, is less likely to be true, since all the evidence indicates that Charles did not truly immerse himself in conservation until four years after Lathrop died.

According to Arthur, however, Charles coped with his grief by spending more time with Arthur and Randolph. The first outing came a few weeks after the funeral, when the boys were eleven and fourteen. Charles took them to "look over" Williams College, with the idea that they might attend the college one day. As Arthur recalled:

Having gone by train from Albany to Bennington, Vermont, he hired an open carriage for the fifteen-mile drive across the state line to where the college campus nestled amid the northern Berkshire hills. I remember how the driver stopped his horses as soon as he saw the stone which marked the Massachusetts line. We all piled out and Father beat us in the ensuing foot race to cross the border.[37]

Two years later, Charles anointed Arthur as his favorite son. If age alone was the consideration Randolph should have received this honor, since he was now the eldest son. But while he was a handsome, charming, and confident child who made friends easily and excelled in sports, Randolph barely made it through school. To get him through the academic system, the family transferred him from one private school to another and hired tutors as well.[38] Perhaps Charles felt that Randolph's charm would carry him through life despite his academic difficulties, and thus decided that the boy did not need him. Possibly Charles dismissed him as a playboy, a son on whom he could not depend. Whatever the case, Arthur was another story; this insecure and awkward boy both needed his father and could be depended upon.

Arthur was small and frail, as Charles had been, and a redhead. He was serious and a diligent worker. Unlike Charles, however, he lacked charisma and confidence. A timid boy, he was saddled with the unfortunate nickname Artie the Shrimp. He adored girls from afar, and when one got wind of this, she wrote him a note that read, "The boys say that you are crazy about me. Please don't be because I never could be crazy about you." Sadly, it was a note that Arthur treasured.[39]

Arthur also adored his father. As a child, he was enthralled by Charles's stories of adventure, which ranged from how, caught in New York in the Blizzard of 1888, he had snowshoed down Fifth Avenue and saved at least one woman and her child, to how he had survived a wreck of the Twentieth Century Limited to make his way to the nearby station, rouse the dazed telegrapher, and instruct him to stop all trains. "Undoubtedly," Arthur wrote, "he did take charge of the rescue attempts and if there was a hero of that awful night, it was he."[40]

In selecting Arthur as his favorite, Charles did so in a firm and dramatic style. The event took place on the morning of the funeral of his own father. George Willis Pack had died on August 31, 1906, in his summer home at Southampton, Long Island. His body was brought to Ivywall for funeral services. Thirteen-year-old Arthur stood on the second-floor landing of Ivywall, looking down the grand staircase to his grandfather's coffin. Next to him was Charles. As the two stood together, Charles reached over to the boy and drew him into his arms.

"Your grandfather was my partner," Charles said to Arthur. "You will have to be my partner now."

Arthur gave his father his hand, in affirmation of what Charles had said. When he did this, he also silently made a pledge of loyalty to Charles that was as sacred to him as the pledges given to King Arthur by the knights of the Round Table. It was a pledge that he would never break. For the rest of his life, Arthur wanted nothing more than to please Charles, if not fill his shoes. For, as he would later recall, he always believed that there was a kind of magic about his father.[41]

CHAPTER 7

A Conservationist
Is Born

I N 1908, two years after his father died, Charles began to change: he launched a new career in conservation that ultimately would make him internationally famous.

One cannot help but wonder why he did this and, above all, why he did so at this time. For the twenty-two years before his father's death in 1906, Charles had immersed himself in business. Focusing his energies on one business venture after another, he had surpassed his father in wealth and established himself as a leading businessman in his community. Yet although Charles had distinguished himself from his father in business, he had not truly distinguished himself from his peers. It must be remembered that Cleveland was a thriving commercial industrial center, full of men as ingenious as Charlie Pack, if not more so. Rockefeller, for better or for worse, was making history with his growing oil monopoly. Furthermore, Charles's friends were making outstanding social contributions: Charles Franklin Thwing was president of Adelbert College and, later, Case Western Reserve University; George Washington Crile had performed the first successful human blood transfusion; and James R. Garfield had served a term in the Ohio Senate, in which he originated an election reforms bill. Even the Pack family's business partner, John Lund Woods, had paid for a new school of medicine at Western Reserve University.

And Thomas Edison, who as a small boy had sold chickens and eggs to George Willis and his family when they lived at Fort Gratiot, and who had dismantled a toy mechanical engine of Charlie's and been unable to put it back together,[1] was now catapulting the world into the modern age with his electrical inventions.

As for Charles, when his father died he was merely a capitalist's capitalist. Despite all he had achieved, his name would not go down in Cleveland history. He would not be singled out as a founder of the Cleveland Trust Company—too many others had been involved with that. Nor would he become known as the man who transformed Cleveland's business district—he had identified and encouraged the migration, yes, but others had followed. Besides, even if his name had been publicly associated with these developments, what of it? Banks were being founded all the time. And there were those who were appalled at the ongoing transformation of Millionaire's Row into a commercial district.

The fact was, despite all of his commercial successes, Charles Pack had done nothing exceptional for his community—nothing that would earn him the respect and adulation of all its citizens. He had founded no colleges or schools. He had made no great scientific or medical contributions. He had made no major charitable contributions. He had written no books. He was nothing more than a wealthy businessman and banker, and, in that abundant age, America had many of those.

By contrast, Charles's father had made himself indispensable to his new hometown of Asheville, North Carolina. After George Willis moved to that town, he practically acquired it as his own; he and his family, including Charles, owned thousands of acres of land in and around Asheville. But George Willis's influence went far beyond real estate ownership. He was perhaps the best-loved citizen of Asheville, and its biggest benefactor. When he died, flags were lowered to half-staff, and Asheville went into public mourning. On September 5, 1906, the secretary of the local newspaper, the *Asheville Citizen,* sent Charles Pack this letter:

Dear Sir:
    A mass meeting of the citizens of Buncombe County was held on the afternoon of September fourth to suitably honor the memory of Mr. George W. Pack.

The court room was crowded with people and the places of business were closed and the fire bell tolled from three to four o'clock.

Judge J. C. Pritchard presided at the meeting and addresses were made . . . when the chair extended an invitation to any citizen to speak.

I beg to enclose here with a copy of the resolutions presented by Hon. Locke Craig and of resolutions of the other organization which were approved by the mass meeting.[2]

Among these resolutions was one written by a committee of Asheville's leading citizens. It summarized George Willis Pack's contributions to the Asheville community.

He was the most generous citizen that Asheville ever had. . . . He gave us the library. . . . He gave parks to the city and to the county the site for the court house. He established and maintained the Kindergarten [the Free Kindergarten for poor children]. The Mission Hospital has been largely sustained by his bounty. The colored people too were the recipients of his unselfish beneficence. While in distant lands, never in the stress of winter did he forget the poor of Asheville. We will always feel grateful for his costly gifts, but the spirit in which he gave was priceless and infinitely beautiful. He belonged to the Mystic Order of that universal Brotherhood of Man founded by the Carpenter of Galilee. We mourn his loss. . . .

Through fretted vault the pealing anthem swells the note of praise. While wealth and culture pay to him just tribute in song and eulogy, the humble will know in sorrow that the heart that beat in sympathy with them is forever still.[3]

The Retail Merchants Association of Asheville said that to George Willis Pack "is due more than to any other one person the attractive beauty of our city, making it a better business center and a place of pleasure for thousands of visitors to spend their vacations."[4]

The Flower Mission board of managers stated that they had "sustained a great loss in the death of the noble benefactor and in this hour of sadness [we] recognize the many and generous gifts of Mr. Pack to a charity which his benefactions have so inestimably aided."[5]

The Asheville Free Kindergarten Association said,

While we bow in reverent submission before the decrees of the Almighty, [we] do deplore in unutterable sorrow the loss of one who has been our constant stay and counselor. . . . In his death the little children of the poor have lost a generous and unfailing benefactor, and the kindergarten association a far-seeing guide and friend; that even while our hearts are wrung in these first hours of loss we realize that in this noble life it has been vouchsafed in this community to see a daily example of how wealth may be so consecrated to the cause of patriotism, charity and truth as to render it an instrument for the uplifting betterment of all humanity.[6]

What must Charles have felt as he read these tributes to his father, or the huge feature article on George Willis Pack that ran in the *Asheville Citizen*? Surely he felt proud of his father. Yet if, as Charles told Tom Gill, he needed to be recognized as his own man and not just his father's son, did this posthumous praise of his father make Charles feel, at least subconsciously, once more over-shadowed by his father? Did he wonder whether he would receive such adulation should he drop dead that very day?

If Charles asked himself this question and was honest in his answer, the response would have had to be no. Charles had not contributed to Cleveland in the ways that his father had con-tributed to Asheville. His rich friends would mourn him, yes, but surely not the masses.

The next question would be, how could Charles surpass his father? Quite possibly, Charles saw the promise of fame and phil-anthropic opportunity in the growing forest conservation move-ment.

That Charles's new commitment to conservation was somehow connected to the death of his father is also suggested by the fact that the forest conservation movement had been well under way for decades and had gained momentum during the 1890s. Yet in this time, Charles had done nothing for the cause.

The first record of American forestry conservation goes back to the period just after the revolutionary war, when New England shipbuilders faced an alarming shortage of hull and mast timber. In response to the shortage, a fine was levied on anyone cutting pine trees two or more feet in diameter from state lands without a license. Following the War of 1812, Massachusetts authorized re-wards for growing trees necessary to shipbuilding. Then, in 1828, President John Quincy Adams ordered a survey of the southeast coast's oak forest and later established an oak reservation of thirty thousand acres on Santa Rosa Island in Pensacola Bay, Florida.[7]

Thus, in fits and starts, locally and nationally, the American forest conservation movement began to take shape. Between 1867 and 1887, studies were made of forests in seven timber states. In 1875, the American Forestry Association, a public organization, was formed. The next year, Congress appointed the first United States forest official, Franklin Hough, to conduct a study on forestry. By 1881, the Division of Forestry had been created within the Department of Agriculture, with Hough chief of the division. States lobbied for legislation to help prevent and control forest fires. In 1891, with the support of the American Forestry Association, Congress authorized the transformation of public lands into forest reserves. A year later, the Yellowstone National Park Timberland Reserve became the first reserve to be formed under this new law. Even the great timberman Frederick Weyerhauser got in on the act. He was one of the first to put patrolmen and post No Fires signs in his woods. In 1903, he asked the Bureau of Forestry to examine his lands and advise him on future management.[8]

Into this growing movement stepped a young zealot, born in Simsbury, Connecticut: Gifford Pinchot, a "young 'Lion of Judah,'" who gave to the forest conservation movement "a fervor of religious intensity and a magnetic personal leadership that have rarely been equaled in the American drama."[9] Among his many contributions to the field, Pinchot founded and became the first president of the Society of American Foresters in 1900 and headed the Bureau of Forestry.

Early in his career, Gifford Pinchot managed the Biltmore, North Carolina, estate of George W. Vanderbilt, located in the hills outside of Asheville. Pinchot first visited Biltmore in 1891 and began managing the forest in February 1892, two years after Charles started bringing his family to visit his parents in Asheville. In 1893, Pinchot set up an office as a consulting forester in New York City. For several years thereafter he split his time among Biltmore, New York, and the various places he worked as a consultant.[10]

Although Pinchot traveled a great deal, Charles and Pinchot

may well have been in North Carolina at the same time and have been introduced there. Thomas Gill's unpublished biography of Charles, which Charles most likely read, since corrections seem to have been made in his handwriting, states that Charles and Pinchot "probably" formed their friendship in Asheville. This statement was not corrected.[11]

The Biltmore estate forest that Pinchot managed was "to become a demonstration to all near and far that the harvesting of forest crops in this country could be conducted and controlled in such a way as to secure perpetuation of the forest, prevent unguided exploitation and devastation, and stave off the threatened timber famine."[12]

Given his avowed early interest in forest management, it is hard to believe that Charles did not hear about Pinchot's work at Biltmore. Since the two men were of the same social class, Charles would surely have been told of Pinchot and his work, if he did not already know Pinchot personally, when socializing in Asheville.

If, for some reason, Charles and Pinchot had not met during the early 1890s, then they probably met later through a common acquaintance, Carl Alwin Schenck.

Schenck was a German forester who founded, developed, and ran the Biltmore Forest School, the first of its kind in America, from 1898 to 1913. Schenck first came to Biltmore in 1895 to work, under Pinchot's direction, as forester at the Biltmore estate.[13]

A letter from Charles to Schenck, dated April 29, 1934, shows that Charles and Gertrude had known Schenck when he was at Biltmore and they were visiting Charles's parents in Asheville.

"I have given your regards to Mrs. Pack," Charles wrote to Schenck, "and she is delighted because she remembers you in connection with the good old Asheville days."[14]

If Charles knew Schenck, then he knew of the forest management work being done at Biltmore Forest. Yet the only mention Charles ever made of Vanderbilt and his Biltmore estate was in an interview with Tom Gill, in which he boasted of how he had sold a piece of property to Vanderbilt.

"I can still see him," Charles recalled. "I didn't state a price on it. I said to him, 'I would like to know what you will give me for this property that cuts your estate in two. How much will you pay me?' He didn't want to tell me, but I made him name a price, and then I said, 'It's yours.'"[15]

If Charles was at all interested in the work being done at Biltmore, beyond how he could profit from it, there is no record of this. Rather, the existing documentation indicates that Charles was concentrating not on forestry or forest conservation, but on his businesses in Cleveland and Louisiana and on acquiring property in and around Asheville.

The first documentation of Charles's active participation in conservation does not appear until 1905, when Charles attended the American Forest Congress in Washington, D.C. The purpose of the congress was to "foster public understanding of the economic importance of forests and advance the conservation of forest and related resources."[16]

The congress was sponsored by the American Forestry Association. Two thousand people attended the keynote address, given by President Theodore Roosevelt. Throwing down his prepared speech, the president "strode across the stage. With shaking fists and flashing teeth he thundered, 'I am against the man who skins the land.'"[17]

At the end of the conference, the American Forest Congress "urged enactment of long-sought reforms, including the unification within the Department of Agriculture of all federal forestry work, including the administration of forest reserves." The reserves (later called national forests) were transferred to the department's Bureau of Forestry the following month.[18]

Charles was merely one of 486 delegates and one of several other timber tycoons, such as Fred Weyerhauser, who attended the gathering. The five-day conference featured forty-three scheduled speakers and seventeen impromptu addresses. Charles was neither a scheduled speaker nor a member of the Committee of Arrangements. His only distinction was that he gave the seventeenth impromptu speech, the last speech to be given at the conference, in which he explained his stand on reforestation, forest management, and taxation.

There is little I can say to edify this Congress. I am simply a plain owner of trees, of forest lands in different parts of the country. I have taken great interest in this subject for many years, and I may say also that I have learned a great deal this week in Washington. I have studied the commercial side of forestry at home and abroad, and I have come to believe that the man who cuts down a tree should plant or cultivate or care for two new ones. Our economic laws do not make it an inducement for him to do so. We must do something to catch up, as we have been very tardy in applying what experience teaches on this subject. The problem of private forestry is a great one. I am caring for, at present, several thousand acres of small timber in different parts of the country, but I am faced with the taxation question; and I think one of the greatest questions of forestry within the States having to do with the private ownership of the forest and the promotion of forestry locally, is the taxation question. Much baby timber is cut because its owners can't pay exorbitant taxes. I will not detain you by giving my ideas at this time upon the subject, but I think an equitable State taxation scheme can be devised with the aid of those present. I believe that the time is long past when the Government should, through the operation of any law, sell or dispose of timber by the acre, but that every tree disposed of should be under the direction of the Forest Service, and be sold by the thousand feet. And, I believe, further that while in years past our forefathers cut the trees of the forest without leave or hindrance, that now we all readily see that no man has a private right to the timber on public lands without paying a full consideration. Under our present laws much timber is annually obtained, and at a fraction of its actual value. And, I believe that the same is true with regard to the use of the forest reserves by the stockman, by the sheep raiser and the cattle raiser. I think the time is at hand when they should pay a small, but equitable and just charge for the use of the ranges.[19]

This speech touches on the major topics of the time and, in some cases, echoes other voices. For instance, the term "forest service" refers to the Bureau of Forestry, which only later became known as the Forest Service. Charles's use of this term hints at the influence of Gifford Pinchot.[20]

The claim that Charles was "simply a plain owner of trees" who was "caring for" small timber is the only known record indicating that Charles was practicing forest management of any kind. Caring for small trees can include such management practices as fire and disease prevention and thinning out of poorly developed trees to give healthier trees more room to grow. Charles may have done these things. But he stops short of saying this care would end when he sold the trees to the highest bidder—unless the buyer also practiced reforestation. This happened in a few cases when Henry Hardtner bought land from Charles, but William Buchanan was Charles's principal buyer.[21]

Charles was not a major influence on the American Forest Congress, but it is likely that the conference influenced him. Many future associates of his were key players in it. Pinchot, for instance, planned the conference and wrote many of the speeches that were given. Hearing Pinchot passionately preaching forestry at this gathering, Charles might have begun to think of what he could do for the cause.

Nevertheless, three years passed before Charles began his own impassioned work for conservation, beginning with his attendance at the historic Conference of Governors in 1908.

Virtually every article ever written about Charles during his lifetime, including biographical articles approved by him, such as his entry in *Dictionary of American Biography,* cites his attendance as a forestry expert at this Conference of Governors as his first involvement with conservation. Clearly, Charles himself saw the Conference of Governors, rather than the American Forest Congress, as the birthdate of his twenty-nine-year campaign for forest conservation. From this point on, he would be as zealous an advocate of conservation as his friend Gifford Pinchot. Beginning at the age of fifty-one and continuing for nearly three decades, he would work ceaselessly for this cause and pour into it an estimated five-sixths of his fortune.[22]

CHAPTER 8

Charles and Gifford: Crusaders for Conservation

B ORN IN 1865, Gifford Pinchot was eight years younger, and probably a good foot taller, than Charles Pack. Although Charles was never fat, he was short, and he tended toward portliness as he grew older. He was always elegantly dressed and perfectly groomed, but he had the bad luck to be designed in such a way that he walked rather like a duck, with his feet splayed outward. This unfortunate trait, along with a somewhat pompous air for such "a short man," caused the girls attending his daughter's boarding school to twitter at him behind his back when he came to visit.[1] Pinchot, by contrast, was lean and handsome. He was elected best-looking by his Yale classmates and was quite a ladies' man.

Whenever the two men walked together in Lakewood, Cleveland, New York, or Washington, D.C., deep in conversation, they must have made an odd-looking pair, so different were they physically. Yet they had a great deal in common, including energy, intelligence, enthusiasm, charm, and wealth. Both men were so alive, so full of ideas and action, as to seem driven by some bottomless divine inner wellspring of pure energy. Both were quick studies of everything they took on, both had persuasive powers of oratory and great personal charm, both were members of America's wealthy elite, and both were highly influenced by their fathers. Small wonder then that they became friends, worked together for the conservation cause for five years, and remained friends afterward—until a scandal involving Charles severed the relationship.

Like Charles, Gifford Pinchot was the son of a wealthy businessman, a merchant who operated out of New York City. Pinchot, however, had more elite social training than Charles. He had attended private schools in Paris and New York City and Phillips Exeter Academy in New Hampshire. In 1885 he continued a family tradition on his mother's side by attending Yale University.

Before entering Yale, Pinchot had been torn between studying ministry and medicine. One summer day in 1885, however, James W. Pinchot asked his elder son if he wanted to become a forester.[2]

A forester? At the time, it was a strange question indeed for a man to ask his son. In 1885, there were no professional American foresters—only European. Nor did America have a forestry school. James W. Pinchot, however, had seen the well-managed forests of France and Germany. In looking at American forest consumption, he saw the forests were being depleted at an alarming rate. The timber industry had nearly exhausted great forests of the Northeast, first in Maine, and would soon do the same in the Lake States. There were growing fears that America's forests might turn into desert wasteland, as had happened in other countries. There seemed no reason why it should not happen here, unless forestry and foresters were to come of age in America and promote forest management.[3]

"Without being himself a forester," recalled Pinchot in his autobiography, *Breaking New Ground,* "my Father understood the relation between forests and national welfare, as another of his heroes, Colbert, minister of Louis XIV, had understood it three centuries before. He was sure that Forestry must come to America, he was convinced of the prodigious service it could render, he was confident that foresters would be needed, and he believed the time was ripe.

"He saw what nobody else had seen, that here was a career waiting for somebody's son."[4]

Although there were no American foresters or forest schools in

1885, when Pinchot decided to study forestry, there was the federal Department of Agriculture, which contained the Forestry Division. The Forestry Division head, Bernhard Fernow, was a trained German forester. He told Pinchot not to pursue forestry as a profession, but "only as a second fiddle to something else," because "under existing conditions Forestry was impracticable in the United States."[5]

Pinchot ignored this advice, which he had heard from others. At Yale he prepared for this almost unheard-of vocation by studying meteorology to learn about climate; botany to learn about the vegetable kingdom, in which he included trees; geology to learn about the earth from which trees grow; and astronomy, since the sun enables trees to grow.[6]

After graduation, he attended the French National Forest School in Nancy and studied model forests in France, Switzerland, and Germany. He returned to the United States in 1890 before becoming forester of Biltmore estate in 1892. From this point on, his career grew quickly. After opening his office in New York City as a consulting forester, in 1896 he was appointed to the National Forest Commission, created by the National Academy of Sciences for the purpose of recommending a national forest policy. The following year he worked for the Department of the Interior studying public forests. Then in 1898, he became chief of the Forestry Division, which became, successively, the Bureau of Forestry and the U.S. Forest Service.[7]

In his twelve years as head of the Forestry Division, Pinchot was a major force in forging the core of American forest policy. He created a program that showed private foresters how to manage their forests as crops; orchestrated the move of federal forest reserves from the Department of the Interior to his Forestry Bureau in the Department of Agriculture; created the foundation for a national forest system; and ran an extensive publicity program that brought the conservation cause to the general public. His regulation of the resources of national forests also influenced federal management of other natural resources.[8]

During Pinchot's era, the subject of conservation brewed distrust and division. While almost everybody agreed that natural resources should be conserved, different groups had different ideas of how this should be achieved. To begin with, America had long been the land of the free—at least so far as the colonists were concerned. But with the rise of men like Pinchot, as the forester William B. Greeley would later recall, "The conservation crusade ended a tradition of free land, free timber, and inexhaustible forests."[9]

In the course of this long crusade, battle lines were drawn over states' rights *vs.* federal rights, over waterpower monopolies and mineral leases, over timber industry taxes and regulations. How, then, did Pinchot do so much? His own personal vision and charm, combined with a healthy dash of perfect timing in working for a proconservation president, had much to do with his success. Two years after he became chief of the federal Forestry Division, Pinchot had a wonderful new boss, President Theodore Roosevelt. The two men saw eye-to-eye on conservation, and together they advanced the cause.

Pinchot's greatest victory came in 1907, when he persuaded Roosevelt to hold a national conference the next year for the purpose of studying the control and management of America's natural resources.

Roosevelt invited thirty-eight governors and their aides, territorial representatives, congressmen, leading scientists, engineers, labor leaders, cabinet members, industrialists, and spokesmen of seventy national organizations to attend the meeting, which he called the Conference of Governors, held from May 13 through 15, 1908. Pinchot was the conference chairman. Charles Pack attended the conference as a forestry expert, no doubt at the suggestion of Pinchot or James R. Garfield, who was a friend of Pinchot as well as of Charles.

The conference was an immediate success. As Paul Russell Cutright described in his book *Theodore Roosevelt: The Making of a Conservationist,*

The results of the conference were immediate and far reaching. The state governors drew up a unanimous declaration in support of conservation, thirty-six state conservation commissions at once sprang into being, scientific bodies appointed numerous conservation committees, and a

Charles Lathrop Pack on the steps of the White House, possibly in 1908, at the time of the Conference of Governors. (Courtesy of the State University of New York College of Environmental Science and Forestry.)

National Conservation Commission was organized. In short, the sum of these several events gave the conservation movement a prestige and momentum previously unknown and raised it to a plane that enabled it to survive the various reversals it later suffered as a consequence of periodic shifts in the political climate.[10]

Historians would praise the conference as "the single greatest stimulus to resource preservation and management" in U.S. history, and "one of the landmarks in conservation history."[11]

Indeed, as a result of this meeting, forty out of forty-six governors created state conservation commissions and organizations. The 1908 Conference of Governors has also been credited with enlightening governors to the point that by 1911, thirty-six states had forestry agencies or departments. Congress responded to the governors' support of conservation by passing the Weeks Act in 1911, authorizing federal matching funds to states for specified forestry purposes.[12]

Charles believed that he was at least partially responsible for the idea of the Conference of Governors. In at least two published articles and in the unpublished Gill biography, Charles Pack is credited, along with his friend Pinchot, with suggesting the idea of the first Conference of Governors to Teddy Roosevelt.[13] Yet, just like the story that Charles studied forest management in Germany, this "fact" seems to have had no substance; not a shred of documentation has surfaced to support it. In fact, the evidence contradicts this claim.

According to Pinchot, the idea was suggested by Frederick H. Newell, a member of the Inland Waterways Commission. After the commission members agreed to it, a letter, written by commission member W. J. McGee, was sent to Roosevelt, recommending that such a conference be held.[14]

Although Pinchot is known to have omitted key people from his biography or to have barely given them credit for their accomplishments, in this case his failure to mention Charles Pack is backed up by the fact that there is no mention of Charles in Pinchot's correspondence to the president concerning the development of the Conference of Governors, and that the letter written to Roosevelt was indeed from McGee.

Charles was not a member of the Inland Waterways Commission. If he had been, perhaps he could have claimed to have given Newell the idea and let him run with it. But that was not the case. Why then did he claim credit he did not deserve?

There are two possible answers: either that Charles and Pinchot or Charles and Newell discussed the possibility of doing such a thing before Newell suggested it to the Waterways Commission, or that Charles wanted to be thought of as powerful and would take credit wherever he could, right or wrong, in order to enhance his image. It is interesting to note that while Gill included this "fact" in his unpublished biography of Charles, written during the last year of Charles's life, he omitted it from his published biographical articles of Charles, which appeared after Charles died.

There is no question, however, that Charles was invited to attend the Conference of Governors. Afterward, he was made a member of the National Conservation Commission, which was formed on the recommendation of the Conference of Governors. Pinchot was chairman of this commission.

At first it appeared that the biggest victory for the Conference of Governors was the creation of this commission. The commission was charged with compiling the first comprehensive inventory of America's natural resources. Unbelievably, the commission completed this enormous task in just over five months. At the time, the study was "the most comprehensive inventory that had yet been made of the natural resources of the United States."

The commission conducted the study through four committees—on water, forests, land, and minerals in North America. Each committee consisted of twelve members, including senators, congressmen, industry heads, forestry professors, government officials, and private individuals. Charles Pack was on the forest committee. His friend John Hays Hammond was on the minerals committee, as was another friend, Andrew Carnegie.[15]

The commission drew up a three-volume report, based on the committees' studies, which was reviewed at a special Joint Conservation Conference (or Second Governors' Conference). This conference was attended by twenty governors, representatives of eleven others, members of twenty-six of the new state conservation commissions, and spokesmen for sixty national organizations.[16]

The Joint Conference unanimously approved the report, which urged, among other things, the disposal of public mineral rights by lease only, treatment of all watersheds as units, waterway development under an executive board or commission appointed by the president, the enactment of state laws regulating the cutting and removal of timber on private lands, and a plan for united action by all organizations concerned with conservation of natural resources. To this end, it urged the cooperation of federal and state governments in conserving natural resources, the creation and support of conservation commissions in every state, and the creation of a permanent national conservation commission.[17]

All of this was transmitted to Congress, via the commission's report, on January 22, 1909. Attached to the report was a message from Theodore Roosevelt:

[This] is one of the most fundamentally important documents ever laid before the American people. It contains the first inventory of its natural resources ever made by any nation. . . . The function of our government is to insure to all of its citizens, now and hereafter, their rights to life, liberty, and the pursuit of happiness. If we of this generation destroy the resources from which our children would otherwise derive their livelihood, we reduce the capacity of our land to support a population, and so either degrade the standard of living or deprive the coming generations of their right to life on this continent.[18]

Yet Congress was "becoming increasingly wary of the Roosevelt administration, which had appointed seven separate commissions to study national problems and provide expert information enabling the executive to act where the legislative branch would not."[19]

Thus, when Congress received a request to release funds to pay for the commission's expense, it lashed back by passing an amendment that forbade "the payment of salaries or expenses of any commission not authorized by law or the use of any employee of the government on work connected with the activities of any such commission."[20]

With no funds available, the National Conservation Commission's work came to an end. Furious at Congress's action, Roosevelt stated that if he did not believe the amendment to be unconstitutional he would have vetoed the bill which contained it, and that if he were to remain in office—which he was not; he was to be replaced by William Howard Taft—he would have refused to obey it. Taft, however, did obey it, and the National Conservation Commission became history.[21]

With Taft as president, Pinchot's power waned. Taft refused to indulge or follow him as Roosevelt had. Their conflict came to a head with the infamous Ballinger coal case, in which Secretary of Interior Richard Ballinger was charged with conflict of interest in approving coal claims in Alaska. When Taft dismissed the Interior Department field agent who made the charge against Ballinger, Pinchot continued to block the fraudulent coal claims. Taft, believing in Ballinger's innocence, fired Pinchot. Claiming victory nevertheless, "Pinchot flaunted his dismissal as evidence that his charges had been correct. Triumphantly he carried on the conservation crusade outside the government."[22]

What enabled Pinchot to carry on his crusade were his wealth, private conservation organizations he had already formed, and personal friends and associates in and out of government. Among Pinchot's supporters was Charles Lathrop Pack.

Charles and a number of Pinchot's other friends, including Overton Price, Pinchot's associate forester; R. S. Kellogg and William Cox, Pinchot's assistant foresters; and Charles Eliot, president of Harvard and a mutual friend of both Charles and Pinchot, became officers and members of Pinchot's National Conservation Association, which he had formed in 1909.

The NCA was a membership group open to the public. Membership fees ranged from one to three dollars. Eliot was its first president, Pinchot its second and last. Charles Pack was a director. The purpose of the NCA was to drum up public support of the Pinchot-Roosevelt conservation program. Pinchot envisioned a membership of fifty thousand to one hundred thousand; it is doubtful that the number ever passed twenty-five hundred. The association's budget came largely from substantial donations from Pinchot and the directors, including Charles.[23]

The conservation program that the NCA supported was opposed by industrialists and others, who believed it would keep America from using its abundant natural resources in accordance with its needs and the needs of each succeeding generation. The NCA countered that its proposed legislation would prevent the formation of self-serving monopolies by leasing rather than selling coal fields, oil fields, timber reserves, and waterpower sites to private individuals. It insisted that this leasing system would ensure resource development and a fair profit to developers while giving consumers reasonable rates. This policy was defined by Pinchot's friend W. J. McGee as "the use of the natural resources for the greatest good of the greatest number for the longest time."[24]

The NCA functioned as a congressional lobbying agency and fought primarily for waterpower and mineral lease policies.[25] Charles Pack was on the board of directors from 1909 until 1916.

From the moment the association was formed, it capitalized on the power of the press to aid its lobbying efforts. Weekly, monthly, daily, whenever the situation called for it, the association sent out press releases and editorials in support of or in opposition to various bills. For instance, when the waterpower monopolists landed a bill in Congress that would protect their interests at the cost of the public interest, Pinchot issued an acidic statement to the national press, asserting,

The bill as it stands is a thoroughly bad bill. It does not require the power companies to pay the public for the valuable privileges they receive . . . does not protect consumers within the states from extortion . . . makes substantially impossible the taking back of the public rights granted even when the . . . grant has expired . . . gives the waterpower people the right to saddle the Government with the unearned increment in land values . . . would apparently require the Government to take over the whole electric lighting plant of a city in order to get possession again of the waterpower owned by the people, if that power were the source from which the lighting plant was supplied. . . . The Adamson Bill in its present form is full of jokers, and is lacking in important safeguards to protect the public interest.[26]

While the association was often effective in manipulating the press to support its views, it did not totally control the newspapers' editorial stances on conservation. "Did you see the cunning editorial in the Washington Post of March 31st?" Charles wrote to Pinchot. "It entirely misrepresented our cause, and misquoted me. I suppose we cannot expect anything else from them as they are enemies of Conservation."[27]

The NCA did not limit itself to simply publicizing conservation. It also worked in the political trenches in Washington. For instance, to further derail the Adamson Bill, the association marshaled together an army of experts who presented important data that showed up the frailties of the bill. And when concerns arose over another bill, the Shields Bill, the NCA secretary, Harry A. Slattery, met privately with House and Senate members to call their attention to the bill and its problems. These politicians called the president's attention to the situation and pressed the secretary of the interior to make a tabulated comparison of the Adamson and Shields bills for use in the Senate, which he did.[28]

The NCA's efforts were applauded by many of the nation's leaders. "The Association has done magnificent work for conservation," wrote Henry T. Rainey of Illinois, who for several years led the fight in the House against waterpower monopolists. "Those of us who stand for conservation and against the program of the water power monopolists of the country, could not get along without the assistance of the National Conservation Association, and the information and data we receive from that organization."[29]

Victor Murdock of Kansas wrote, "I saw your association bring into legislation an understanding that was not only wholly illuminating to all of Congress but vitally effective in saving the measure under consideration from being evil. The many occasions when the Association isolated the vicious line or phrase in a bill and pilloried it before the public, are among the most vivid experiences of my terms in Congress."[30]

The association also managed to stay in the center of the conservation crusade by allying itself with an important annual congress, similar to the Conference of Governors. The National Conservation Congress, as it was called, was "an annual forum for the exchange of ideas, experiences, and problems among state, private, and federal conservation leaders, first called by the Washington [State] Conservation Association in Seattle in 1909." Thus it brought together all types of people who were key to the cause— timbermen, congressmen, senators, industrialists, and foresters. Its purpose was to "act as a clearing house for all allied social forces of our time, to seek to overcome waste in natural, human, or moral forces."[31]

Although all organizations and individuals interested in conservation were encouraged to participate in the congress, Pinchot's NCA had the greatest influence on choosing the issues it would address each year. At first, the NCA focused the National Conservation Congress on national legislation dealing with the controversy over fees charged to utilities operating hydroelectric power sites.[32]

Furthermore, the NCA used the press to publicize the congress and its pet issues. The public-relations skills that Charles learned from Pinchot and the association's secretary, Slattery, would serve Charles well in later years, when he set out on his own as a conservation crusader.

In the meantime, Charles was growing closer to Pinchot. The two corresponded regularly and met whenever possible for "conferences" or luncheons, usually in New York, where Pinchot attended to family matters, and Charles handled his family's vast finances from his office on Wall Street.

As their friendship grew, so may have Pinchot's faith in Charles's organizational and publicity skills. Possibly it was Pinchot's trust in Charles that played an important part in Charles being named president of the Fifth National Conservation Congress, which was held November 18–20, 1913. By this time, the congress had become one of the biggest annual events in conservation, and being its leader was a heavy responsibility.

CHAPTER 9

The Pack-Pinchot
Friendship Nearly
Drowns in a Water Fight

C HARLES LATHROP PACK was elected president of the 1913 National Conservation Congress in part because he was a strong advocate of the party line Gifford Pinchot wanted the congress to promote—the use of natural resources "for the greatest good of the greatest number for the longest time." In addition, Charles was emerging as a consummate leader. As Arthur W. Greeley, retired associate chief of the U.S. Forest Service, noted, he was "a commanding person, and although he was not a large person when he walked into a room you knew that somebody had come in."[1]

The abundance of energy that fueled Charles during his twenties had hardly slackened. At fifty-six he fairly vibrated with vitality. He knew how to concentrate his attention, thus accomplishing a great deal in a short amount of time. Furthermore, he had a marked talent for homing in on others who also possessed great energy and talent and for tapping their skills to the full. These qualities combined to make him the obvious leader of the 1913 National Conservation Congress, which by then was highly visible at the national level and one of the most powerful lobbying vehicles for what Charles termed the "friends of conservation."[2]

When Charles agreed to run the 1913 congress, the organization was under heavy political fire. It had adopted "perhaps the broadest statement of purpose of any conservation organization: 'to act as a clearing house for all allied social forces of our time, to seek to overcome waste in natural, human, or moral forces.'" But how these goals were to be achieved was a subject of vast dispute.

Pinchot wanted to achieve these goals while adhering to the Roosevelt-Pinchot policy of the use of natural resources for the greatest good of the greatest number for the longest time. He also envisioned a unified conservation program and tried to impose this vision on the congresses. But some participants resented this, at one point claiming the congresses were simply vehicles to "support both the Republican insurgency against Taft and Theodore Roosevelt's aspirations for reelection" in 1912.[3]

Nevertheless, from 1909 to 1913, the congresses put legislative conservation issues in the national spotlight and molded national policy. Senators, governors, and secretaries of war participated in each congress. Returning to Capitol Hill with the Roosevelt-Pinchot viewpoint in their minds, they were more likely to vote against bills that the National Conservation Congress viewed as detrimental to the cause or to draft legislation that followed the Roosevelt-Pinchot party line. In addition to influence at this level, the National Conservation Congress always sent its recommendations to the U.S. Congress as a whole, hoping to influence its conservation votes.

This is not to say that the congresses were always influential, that they always ran smoothly, or that they were attended exclusively by people who all agreed with each other. To the contrary, conservationists of all persuasions, including preservationists, states' righters, and those who, like Pinchot, were in favor of federal controls, flocked to the congresses, each ready to fight for his own viewpoint.

In 1913, the Fifth National Conservation Congress, headed by Charles Lathrop Pack, reached a fever pitch of fighting over the regulation of hydroelectric waterpower.

Originally the 1913 congress was to address two issues: "fair play for the forests"[4] and how to regulate hydroelectric power development.

Working closely with Pinchot, Charles appointed two committees, one on forestry conservation and one on waterpower, to conduct national studies of these issues. The committees were made up of influential senators, governors, statesmen, and businessmen. The members of the forestry committee conducted the most intensive study of national forest resources that had ever been made. The waterpower committee gathered equally detailed data concerning the practices of public waterpower utilities. Their results would be presented to the National Conservation Congress and, using these reports, a resolutions committee was to make recommendations that would be presented to the U.S. Congress.[5]

Charles and Pinchot decided that if these recommendations were to have any punch, the Fifth National Conservation Congress should be held in Washington while the U.S. Congress was in session so that congressmen and other policymakers would be around to sit up and take notice.[6] The meeting was set for November 18, 19, and 20 on the tenth floor of the new Willard Hotel.

Fourteen hundred delegates flocked to the congress. Among these were industrialists—timbermen, waterpower men—as well as more foresters than "had ever heretofore attended any similar meeting in the country."[7]

Under Charles's direction, there had been an onslaught of advance publicity promoting the wonders of the upcoming congress. "Fierce fighting promises to confront conservation interests in the near future," declared one of his press releases, "and official Washington is taking deep interest in the plans for the contest. There have been intimations of trouble for several months. The warfare has been expected to crop out at any moment. . . . The protection of the country's forests and waterways will command the Conservation Congress."[8]

A couple of weeks later, however, Charles issued a press release downplaying the waterpower issue and stating that the congress was "to be devoted largely to forest conservation, because of the national importance of the subject in its many phases."[9] As it turned out, though, fair play for the forests got little attention. The congress focused instead on hydroelectric power regulation.

The issues at stake were whether states or the federal government should regulate waterpower and whether hydroelectric power company monopolies were the evil that Pinchot, Charles, and their friends claimed they were. The conflict received national attention.

Neither Charles nor Pinchot could have been surprised that the water fight broke out. On August 26, 1913, Charles had issued a press release that described the goals of the Conservation Congress as

bringing to a head the contest between the advocates of Federal [waterpower] Control and those who demand control by the individual states or the distribution of resources owned by the public among private individuals. In certain parts of the West an active sentiment is said to exist in favor of abolishing the system of national forestry. It is understood that at the session of the [National Conservation] Congress the conservationists will concentrate the fire of some of their heaviest batteries on the enemies of Federal Control of the people's resources.[10]

The "enemies" attending the Congress were westerners who were loath to give up their freedoms, industrialists with strong interests in existing hydroelectric power monopolies, and senators with states' rights and hydroelectric power constituents to protect.

In accordance with the standard program for the national congresses, at the end of the congress all delegates were to vote on "unanimous recommendations" for waterpower development drawn up by the resolutions committee. Signed by the committee on waterpower, the resolutions would be routinely passed by the delegates and submitted to the U.S. Congress. As far as Charles and Pinchot were concerned, in the best possible case, Congress would follow the recommendations and create antimonopoly regulations—including federal controls—for the development of waterpower.

Charles and Pinchot planned that the recommendations would push their vision of federal control of hydroelectric power development. But to have the unanimous recommendations passed, they would have to convince the states' rights delegates that federal control was necessary. Thus, the water committee's report and subsequent recommendations would have to be highly persuasive.

To ensure that the waterpower committee would come up with

a report in favor of federal controls of hydroelectric power to prevent private industry monopolies, Charles and Pinchot tried to rig the committee so that it was made up entirely of people who were sympathetic to their viewpoint. They appointed ten committee members who seemed to be on their side. Then, with Pinchot's consent, Charles made George F. Swain, president of the American Society of Civil Engineers, chairman of the committee.

Shortly afterward, Charles assured Pinchot that they had made the right choice. "I have just had a talk with Professor George F. Swain at the Manhattan Hotel in New York, and I think he will be alright. If we can bring much of the influence of the engineers with us this time, it will be a big step forward."[11]

The two obviously considered Swain little more than a puppet. In fact, Charles believed Pinchot to be the actual leader of the committee on waterpower. "We want you to do a lot of work in regard to the water-power matters as soon as we get this committee organized," Charles wrote Pinchot in May. "I want to put some men on the committee that will need some starting by an experienced water power man, and you are just the man to do it. If we can get a report from the committee that is rather wide in its influence it will help a big lot. I want, as soon as I can, to have a talk with you about this."[12]

Throughout the summer the two believed the committee they had appointed would unanimously lobby against monopolies and for federal waterpower controls. Then, on October 13, just one month before the Conservation Congress was to begin, Charles sounded the first warning bell that all was not under their control: "I am not certain that Dr. Swain realizes what is really expected from the Water Power Committee," he wrote to Pinchot.[13]

Swain, who had supported their point of view, had reversed himself. According to Pinchot, Swain's report proposed that "the only question concerning waterpower was that of immediate development; that monopoly was not dangerous; and that the question of who gets the benefit from such development does not come within the consideration of the Committee."[14]

To put the conflict in context, it is important to note that at this time public utilities already existed, as did monopolies. As both

Pinchot *and* Swain would note, ten groups of interests controlled 65 percent of all the developed waterpower in the United States, and "some of these groups [were] closely related through inter-locking directors."[15] Pinchot felt such monopolistic control was a public threat; Swain did not.

Pinchot responded to Swain's treasonous majority report by writing a minority report with the support of two fellow water-power committee members, Henry Stimson and Governor Joseph N. Teal of Oregon.

Pinchot then decided that when the Conservation Congress's agenda turned to waterpower, he was not simply going to read his minority report to the assemblage after the majority report had been read and then quietly sit down. No, he was ready for a fight. And, according to one news article in the *Boston Evening Transcript* headlined "The Mad Hatters of Conservation," a "white hot fight" was what he got.[16]

The battle lines were clearly drawn. Swain was so confident of victory that his committee issued a press release that claimed victory over Pinchot in advance:

The overthrow of Gifford Pinchot as the dominating figure in the National Conservation Congress will be attempted tomorrow when that body takes up for approval the [majority] report of the committee on waterpower. Adoption of that report will signify that the congress has passed from the control of the former forester. Mr. Pinchot suffered his first defeat when the waterpower committee decisively voted to condemn the existing Government policy, which he himself had dictated, and rec-ommended the adoption of a new or amended policy intended, while safeguarding public interests, to yet invite investment of capital in water-power projects coming under Federal control. Encouraged by their first victory, the revolutionists will press hard to unhorse Mr. Pinchot, and wrest the Conservation Congress from his control.[17]

The *Transcript* described the "great battle" that broke out the next day, Wednesday, October 19:

The waterpower report was to be "discussed," Mr. Pinchot was to talk on waterpower; "letters relating to the waterpower situation from the stand-point of the investor" were to be read; Senator Burton of Ohio was to speak; Senator Newlands of Nevada was to make an address; and eight important papers on forestry were to be read. . . . This carefully arranged schedule, however, was almost wholly upset.[18]

To begin with, Pinchot arranged for a move that guaranteed victory over Swain and his majority report. Pinchot had his friends Stimson and James R. Garfield suspend the rules so the congress could take up the unanimous recommendations, dispose of them, and then take up the majority and minority reports.[19] This disposition consisted of the two committees signing the unanimous recommendations before discussing the reports. Thus, Pinchot and his cronies laid "a clever trap into which the enemy walked."

Swain and his committee signed the unanimous recommendations without carefully reading them because they believed they had "fixed" the resolutions committee which had written them and the recommendations would reflect the views of the majority report. But as the *Transcript* explained, "Those who knew . . . realized that the 'unanimous recommendations' contained exactly what the minority report contained, namely, an indorsement [*sic*] of strong Federal control, fixed terms for franchises, and the Government compensation scheme."[20]

The fact that the waterpower committee had tried to fix the resolutions committee, and thus the "unanimous recommendations," was exposed later. The moment arrived at the peak of the debate over the issue of state control against federal control in waterpower development, a debate in which "at half-hour intervals a wild man in the audience let out an Indian yell for States' rights."[21]

As the day drew near its close the convention drew nearer and nearer to pandemonium. The dramatic climax broke when C. L. Watts of Huntsville, Ala., one of the delegates, rose and gave away the game of the packed [resolutions] committee. . . .

"I came here," he told a congress now white hot, "supposing that there would be fair treatment. But I found in five minutes that the waterpower interests dominated the Alabama delegation. J. W. Worthington, vice president of the Alabama Water Company, and chairman of the committee, told me that the plan was to refer all resolutions to the resolutions committee, 'and when we get it there we will fix it.'"

At this disclosure, the Congress howled with delighted rage—the kind of delighted rage which virtuous people have when the cold evidence is handed down to prove what they know is the truth, though direct evidence be lacking. The righteous howling lasted some time.[22]

But somehow, Pinchot had managed to keep his opponents from fixing the resolutions committee. Having signed the "unanimous recommendations" drawn up by the resolutions committee, thinking they supported their own majority report, Swain's committee was forced to either vote for its endorsement or contradict it.

"'Do you mean to say,' Pinchot shouted to one of the opposition leaders, 'that you do not believe in the principles to which your name is signed?' Again the Congress howled with righteous delighted rage, and the opposition was forced to admit 'Certainly we do. . . .' The vote was taken, and by a score of 434 to 154 the 'unanimous recommendations' were adopted. That was all. The conservationists had won their victory."[23]

And where was Charles Lathrop Pack, president of the congress, during this brouhaha? At first Charles appeared to be in Pinchot's antimonopolist camp. He had, after all, conferred closely with him in appointing the waterpower committee in the first place. He had told Pinchot that he expected him to indoctrinate some members of the committee who would "need some starting by an experienced water power man." Yet as the fight grew, his stance became questionable. On November 25, James Garfield wrote to Pinchot, "Write me about the result of the fight the day after I left. I see that some of the papers announce that Pack was unhorsed. Where did he finally stand in the water power question?"[24]

Garfield's confusion arose from the fact that Charles decided his stance should be viewed as neutral. When the committee split over the waterpower issue, Charles wrote Pinchot that he was not reading either report, as he did not "want to be put in a position were [sic] it may be thought I am trying to influence individual members in any committee."[25]

This desire to appear neutral may account for the fact that the *Transcript* gives no hint that Charles tried to quell the fight, which reportedly broke out on the afternoon of Tuesday, November 18, the first day of the congress,[26] resumed Wednesday morning, and raged on throughout the day until the congress voted on and passed the signed "unanimous recommendations."

By Thursday morning all was quiet. A number of delegates had gone home, assuming that, right or wrong, Wednesday's battle had been resolved. But trouble broke out again Thursday afternoon when Pinchot proposed that an antimonopoly amendment be tacked onto the resolution committee's report, which was based on his "unanimous recommendations."

The *Transcript* viewed the amendment as one with "full-grown teeth in it" that strengthened the otherwise "lifeless resolutions." Pinchot's move proved inflammatory, however. "We had the same old fight over again led by the same people," he wrote to Garfield.[27]

As the brawl overflowed once more, Charles panicked, possibly fearing, among other things, that the entire convention would be remembered only as an endless free-for-all, a travesty of political lobbying. He moved to adjourn the entire convention. Pinchot described Charles's actions in this way: "Charles Lathrop Pack . . . got the most aggravated case of cold feet I have ever happened to meet, during which he vainly attempted to get the convention adjourned without action either on my amendment or on the report of the Committee on Resolutions."[28]

The press gave a much more melodramatic account of this event. Charles is said to have exclaimed to Pinchot, "Oh, Gifford, Gifford! We have been friends for years. For ten years I have stood by you in everything that you have urged. But we have reached the parting of the ways. I cannot follow you in a course that seems to me destined to disrupt and nullify every bit of good the Conservation Association has done. I am through."[29]

Charles failed to adjourn the meeting, and Pinchot's amendment passed by a majority vote of three to one.[30] The press, however, did not let the matter drop. Two days after Charles's melodramatic outburst was reported, this item appeared in the *Sun:*

Oh Gifford, Gifford, I am through—*President Pack of the conservationists to Amadis of Gall.*

Comrades, round me strew rosemary and rue, lay a cypress tree over dolent me; love has turned to tiff, with a breaking heart I am forced to part with my hero GIFF! To the pines and firs where the wildcat purrs, lead me, O, bohoo! GIFFORD, I am through!

Snivel, sob and sniff, woe is me, alack; cruel, lovely GIFF, you've gone back on PACK! Oh dear conservation you have brought damnation; given a fatal gliff to the virtuous, GIFF!

Wield the saw and wield the axe, let the forest's pride be bust; wood-men, mighty be your whacks, serve the victory lumber trust! What care I what woe ye do? All my hopes are turned to dust. Hew and hack, you lumber jack, whom so often I have cussed. Hew and hack, for Pack's a wrack. In the forest solitude like another Bab i' the Wood, bury me 'neath yellowest leaves; bury me as one who grieves till his heartstrings snap and crack; vain, treeless world, adjoo, adjoo! alas, for PACK! Oh, GIFFORD, GIFFORD, I am through!—From "Sylvan Songs and Lamentations."[31]

The satire failed to mention that Charles had retracted his out-burst almost immediately and replaced it with one that was less inflammatory. On November 21, the *New York Press* reported,

Charles Lathrop Pack . . . denied to-day having said that he had come to the parting of the ways with Gifford Pinchot on the water power question as was said by some newspapers this morning.

"What I did say to Pinchot," said Pack, "was this: 'Gifford, I have worked with you for ten years and have been your friend. You can't drive me away from you now, even though I think it is a grave mistake of judg-ment for you to bring this question up at this time. The congress already has acted favorably upon the unanimous recommendations of the water power committee, and most of the members of the committees and a majority of the delegates interested in water power have gone home believing the water power subject finally disposed of. To force a vote by a minority of the delegates would be unfair to these people, and might alienate many men who have shown themselves true friends of the cause of conservation.'

"I have been interested in conservation all my life, and I am not through as my friends know. I am a friend of Gifford's and I differ with him only as to the manner of treating the subject and the absent dele-gates."[32]

Pinchot responded to the retraction the next day:

The calm and balanced little speech which Mr. Pack quotes himself as having delivered to me in the turmoil of the Conservation Congress sounds like the happy thought that came too late. The fact is that when I told Mr. Pack of my intention to introduce the resolution against water-power monopoly shortly before I did so, he gave it his cordial assent. His subsequent weakening under pressure is cause for regret. Efforts to encourage him failed. He declared that the resolution would be lost, and attempted to have the Congress adjourned rather than face a possible defeat for principle.

The contention that it was unfair to bring up the resolution against waterpower monopoly when the other resolutions were presented cannot be taken seriously. As it happens, that was the only time during the Congress when it could have been brought up, and it was as much and as fairly in order than as any other subject considered in the resolutions. Mr. Pack is in error when he intimates that only a minority of the delegates were present on the third day of the Congress. The largest vote on November twentieth was only one-sixth less than on the nineteenth. On both days the proportion of the votes was substantially three to one. . . .

Mr. Pack says he is the friend of Conservation. In a historical sense that is true. But the fight for Conservation calls for men who will fight.[33]

Charles seemed to ignore his friend's rebuttal. A few days later he wrote to Pinchot, expanding on his own retraction:

Personally, I believe the [amendment] of which you secured the adoption on the last day of the Congress is in the right direction, and I believe it was the sentiment of most of our mutual friends. We simply differed on the way of doing it. I find that a good many good Conservationists were somewhat sore, but I think that part will pass off as it is unimportant. It still remains that the Fifth Conservation Congress made a good step forward in both forestry and waterpower matters.[34]

In reviewing how Charles dealt with this affair, it is important to note that his handling of this conflict had in it a single element that would show up again and again in his life: a powerful need to manipulate reality—through denial and through manipulation of the press. Charles denied that he ever told Gifford he was through with him. Yet the two eyewitness press accounts of his outburst and Pinchot's account of the incident indicate that Charles had told Pinchot he was through. Later, an embarrassed Charles tried to erase his words by re-creating reality.

This element of denial emerges again upon examination of Charles's press releases summing up the whole waterpower affair. After the congress ended, Charles made no mention of the fighting that had fractured it—despite the fact that he himself had predicted such fighting would occur. Instead, he produced gushy press releases that not only ignored the fighting entirely, but painted, instead, a picture of wholesome accord:

The adoption by the conservation congress of the recommendations unanimously presented by its committee on water power [note that there is no mention of the minority report] was a long step forward in the development of a definite governmental policy recognizing clearly the principle of federal control. . . . The committee on water power was made up of ten men, exceptionally qualified by knowledge of this subject in all its aspects. Under the able chairmanship [blatantly denying that Swain had, much to Charles's dismay, changed sides] of Dr. George F. Swain, president of the American Society of Engineers, it worked out and presented not a mere declaration of principles but, concrete and specific recommendations which should be of great value to the government in framing the legislation that is needed.

And then the clincher:

The fact that a committee made up not only of professional experts of the highest distinction . . . *were able to agree upon a definite and constructive program and that this program received the emphatic endorsement of the conservation congress,* [italics added] is demonstration of the public spirit of the committee and the ability of the congress to accomplish effective and constructive work.[35]

Given the national press coverage of the congress's infighting, it is incredible that Charles could issue a statement that makes no mention of the division within the water power committee and the congress itself. Even a positive acknowledgment of the row, such as a reference that it had been overcome, would have been a huge improvement over this saccharin statement.

Nevertheless, Pinchot agreed with how Charles handled the affair. On December 1, after receiving a copy of the statement quoted above, he told Charles, "I am much pleased to get your letter . . . and the statement which accompanied it. Your view that the Congress has achieved important results is exactly my own."[36]

Furthermore, Pinchot forgave Charles his transgression at the congress. On December 4, he wrote to James Garfield that he and Charles were "now thicker than any thieves you ever saw."[37] They continued to stay friends and confer on conservation matters for the next three years.

Charles's outburst at the end of the congress was further forgiven when the congressional members "insisted on" reelecting him as their president for the Sixth National Conservation Congress. A press release stated, "The Convention insisted on the [re]election of Charles Lathrop Pack as a recognition and approval of the fair, able and impartial manner in which he has conducted its affairs."[38] Given his commitment and dedication to the congress, this is not surprising.

As president of the Fifth National Conservation Congress, Charles had devoted more than half of his time to handling all of its details, including planning the entertainment, arranging for forestry displays at the conference, appointing members of the committees, arranging for and participating in precongressional conferences and meetings among the delegates, overseeing the national surveys conducted by the forestry and waterpower committees, raising and contributing money to support the congress and publish its reports, and directing the congress's public-relations campaign. Furthermore, he had accomplished much of this while battling various minor illnesses during the summer and fall, including ptomaine poisoning.[39]

Charles had led the congress with great skill. Above all, his public-relations campaign had succeeded quite well. He had hired a publicist to write and distribute press releases, dictated largely by him. The press ate them up. In the month before the congress was held, newspapers across the country published *daily* "not less than" five hundred articles about the upcoming congress.[40]

Despite the literal vote of confidence from the delegates in reelecting him, once was enough for Charles. He declined the nomination, claiming that "others" in his life had allowed him to devote most of his time to the Fifth National Conservation Congress, but that now he had a duty to attend to them and other "sacred trusts."[41]

Apparently no one else was ready to take on the job. There was no congress in either 1914 or 1915. The congress was resurrected in 1916 by Charles and Pinchot's enemies, the waterpower monopolists and states' rights men. Among the resolutions adopted by this congress was the endorsement of the Shields Bill, which would allow for state control over waterpower development. This time, there was no question that Pinchot and Charles were united in their stand against the monopolists.

"I am delighted that the change in the date of the meeting of the Conservation Congress makes it possible for you to be in Washington on the day when both the Association and Congress hold their meetings," Pinchot wrote to Charles. "I very much hope you can attend the meeting on the 18th, for with your help this big plan can be put through."[42]

Ultimately, Pinchot's plan was to keep the Sixth National Conservation Congress from endorsing the Shields Bill and sending this endorsement to the U.S. Congress. He failed. Furious, Pinchot claimed that in endorsing the Shields Bill, the congress "destroyed itself" and now "ceased to be."[43] He was right. There were no other congresses after 1916.

But the Shields Bill was only a temporary victory for the congress. Thanks to the continued lobbying efforts of Pinchot, Charles, and others through Pinchot's National Conservation Association, the Senate did not ratify the bill. Rather, in 1920 Congress passed the Water Power Act, which provided for federal control of waterpower on the public domain generally and along navigable streams elsewhere in the nation.

The battle for control of the Shields endorsement in the spring of 1916 was the last time that Charles and Pinchot worked together closely. By then, Charles had resigned his directorship with the National Conservation Association, claiming he did not have enough time to devote to it.[44]

Charles submitted his resignation to the association's secretary, Harry A. Slattery, since Pinchot was in the hospital, recovering from "an operation for rupture."[45] In his response to Charles, Slattery urged him to reconsider: "Your help and support to the Association from the beginning has been so large a factor in its work and success that I, personally, really hope you will not decide to terminate your connection with this organization of over seven years."[46]

Although there is no record of Pinchot's feelings about Charles's resignation, it is likely he regretted it as well. In a letter written just two months earlier, he had told Charles, "In the event that it is impossible for you to be at the [National Conservation Association directors'] meeting, I would like sometime to talk over the conservation situation with you."[47]

In resigning from Pinchot's National Conservation Association, Charles did not renounce his interest in conservation. Rather, he left in order to develop a career as a national conservation leader in his own right: in January 1916, at a meeting in Boston, Massachusetts, he was elected president of the American Forestry Association. He was also about to extend his conservation activities by forming the National War Garden Commission. And, unbeknownst to his "friends of conservation," he was about to expand his timber empire by selling off his southern lands and investing in Canadian forests.

CHAPTER 10

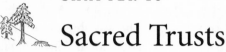 Sacred Trusts

W HEN CHARLES DECLINED his reelection as
president of the National Conservation Congress,
he cited some "sacred trusts" as needing him
more. Although the trusts were not specified, they
probably included his Cleveland and southern business interests.
One of his most sacred trusts was that of shepherding his sons into
the family business. By now both boys were grown, and Charles
was hoping to rely on them more and more—even on Randolph,
who, until he was sent to work in the lumber business, had given
Charles and Gertrude no end of headaches.

Over the years, Randolph had been transferred "from one private school to another, with tutors on the side." After loafing
through classes in a private school in Tarrytown, New York, he had
been sent to join his younger brother, Arthur, at Ransom School
on the misguided theory that since Ransom had begun to increase
Arthur's self-esteem it might help Randolph mature in other
ways—for instance, by teaching him to study.[1]

Ransom School catered to a small group of eighteen to twenty
boys and offered a college preparatory curriculum that included
studies in mathematics, English, Latin, and Greek. What distinguished it from any other prep school, however, was its outdoor
curriculum, which included forestry, trailblazing, bridge building,
boating, swimming, and sailing.[2]

The school had two campuses—one in the Adirondacks for the

fall, and one in Coconut Grove, Florida, for the winter and spring. The boys lived in log-cabin dorms, worked by kerosene lamps, kept warm by coal and wood, and used either chamber pots stored under their beds or the outhouse.[3]

The smallness of the school gave Arthur a sense of belonging, and the outdoor work bolstered his self-confidence, although he was still slight of build, very self-conscious, and far from the most popular boy. Seeing that Arthur was blossoming there, Charles and Gertrude sent Randolph to this school as well.[4] But unfortunately this well-intentioned move dealt "a shattering blow" to Arthur's "struggling ego" and did nothing to improve Randolph.

Arthur had never measured up to his older brother, who had the incredibly dark, romantic Byronesque good looks of his grandfather, George Willis. In addition, Randolph had equally generous doses of charm and sophistication, all of which made him a leader with the boys and a sought-after beau by the girls. Now, after settling in on Arthur's turf at Ransom, Randolph once again outshone poor "Artie the shrimp" and walked away with the one award that Arthur coveted, the school medal as the best-liked and most useful boy in school.[5]

Randolph won no scholastic medals at Ransom, however. He passed his entrance examinations to Williams College conditionally—with the agreement that he take extra tutoring in some subjects—and entered Williams with the class of 1913.[6] If the president of Williams had not been Harry Augustus Garfield, an old family friend, a member of the Pack Gang, and a cofounder of the Cleveland Trust Company, this condition would probably not have been extended to Randolph.

Once at Williams, Randolph followed his lifelong pattern. "With the students," Arthur recalled, "he rated as a Sophomore, but the Dean's Office had different ideas, and it had been his failure to pass Freshman requirements [that] had prevented his joining one of the 'houses' with top social prestige." In 1910, during what should have been his sophomore year, Randolph and Williams "parted permanently by mutual consent."[7] The handsome, racy Ran, as he was called, then transferred to Penn State's forestry school.

Given the fact that Randolph had shown little interest in anything beyond girls and parties, it is likely that this transfer had been Charles's idea, that Charles had pulled strings to have Randolph admitted, and that Randolph had had no choice but to follow his father's wishes. He was admitted as a special student studying forestry with the junior and senior classes, but earned no degree.

Randolph may have shirked his studies because he knew he had little need of them. After all, as the son of a multimillionaire, his future was assured. Indeed, in 1912, when Randolph was a mere twenty-two years old, he became vice president of a new Buchanan mill, the Tall Timber Lumber Company, which was established that year. Degree or no degree, Randolph had it made.

Given Charles's efforts to educate his son, it is probable that he wanted Randolph to be a working man rather than a spoiled rich boy. Thus one can assume that when Randolph did a stint as a Montana logger, sometime after entering Penn State, it was Charles's idea. Apparently this work was to give Randolph at least some slight preparation for the timber company he was to help manage as its vice president. Randolph headed south to begin working for the Tall Timber Company in 1913, by which time he had acquired 279 shares of its stock.[8]

Randolph did manage to get out from under his father's thumb long enough to have one significant success of his own. Somehow, in between stints in Pennsylvania, Montana, and Louisiana, he managed to make it back to Cleveland often enough to court and win "one of the loveliest girls of the younger set," Miss Georgia Fuller.[9]

Randolph and Georgia's wedding was the toast of Cleveland. On April 18, 1914, the *Cleveland Town Topics* reported that during the week prior to the wedding Miss Dorothy Stephens and Mr. Park Wilson gave the couple a dinner of twelve "covers" (or place settings) at the country club on Wednesday. On Thursday the couple was fêted with a dinner of sixteen covers, given by the Kenneth Allens at the prestigious Union Club, and this was followed by a theater party thrown by W. H. Cottingham, president of the Sherwin-Williams Company, and his wife. On Friday, Mrs. J. A. Stephens and her daughter Oriana threw a buffet luncheon for the bridal party. That night Georgia gave her spinster dinner and Randolph gave his bachelor dinner.

"Miss Fuller's home on Shaker Heights," reported *Town Topics,* "was the scene of a dinner of eighteen covers. The young women in spinster costumes were really very attractive in their quaint attire. . . . Mr. Pack's dinner was given at Norway Lodge, the home of the family on Euclid Avenue. The table was decorated to represent a lumber camp in every detail and gave the guests some idea of Mr. Pack's life in Louisiana."[10]

The couple was married the next day, Saturday, April 18, at four o'clock at Trinity Cathedral. The wedding was described as being of "unusual beauty." The wedding cake was decorated in roses and forget-me-nots, the bridal table seated eighteen, and the large centerpiece was of Killarney roses, white lilacs, and blue forget-me-nots ornamented with stunning bows of pink and blue ribbon. Pink and blue bows were tied on the handles of silver baskets of bonbons.[11]

Leaving this picturesque setting, the young socialites moved to the much less sophisticated town of Good Pine, Louisiana, just across the border from Randolph's place of business, the Tall Timber Lumber Company, which was situated in Arkansas. They set up housekeeping in what was described by the Cleveland paper as a "charming bungalow." Their stay there was short-lived, however. Ran contracted malaria, could no longer live and work in the hot, humid climate, and returned to Cleveland with his bride. In 1916 he joined the American Multigraph Company. He would stay there until 1923 as its vice president in charge of engineering. His father's friendship with Harry C. Osborn, president of the company, may have helped get him this job.[12]

In the meantime, Arthur was coming into his own. After graduating from Williams in 1914 he entered Harvard Business School. The story behind Arthur's entry into Harvard is typical of how subtly Charles could manipulate people to get what he wanted. Arthur had long dreamed of studying engineering at the Massachusetts Institute of Technology. Years later, he would record in his memoirs how his plans were changed:

It appeared that my father had accepted my choice of electrical engineering rather than entering his business and I suspected nothing in the urgent plea by one of his associates that on my arrival in Boston [to enter MIT], I call on some particular friends of his who might be useful to me. These friends turned out to be the charming Edwin F. Gay family, and Professor Gay was no less than the Dean of the Harvard Graduate School of Business Administration. I came to tea at this house and a few days later telegraphed my father that I had changed my mind and was registering not at MIT after all, but in Harvard Business School. This was my first exposure to subtle salesmanship, but I realized also that my none-too-successful struggles in college with higher math had already weakened my belief in myself as a potential engineer and there was no doubt about my welcome of a dignified way out.[13]

There is also no doubt that Charles had decided Arthur could become a real partner to him. After sending him to Harvard Business School for one year, Charles informed Arthur that "the plans of the family" did not include his return to Harvard for another year. "Father wants me to help him," Arthur wrote in his diary that day, "& as for myself, I shall be glad enough to get to work for a definite aim."[14]

Arthur had spent summers working half-days for his father for a mere three dollars a week, doing such menial tasks as coloring in land maps of their timber holdings. Now he was to be a real businessman, working for "various timber and mineral lands owned in the name of family corporations."

Charles had moved the Pack offices into the prestigious new Citizens Building at 850 Euclid Avenue. Here he ran not only his Cleveland-based business, Pack & Company, but also the River Land and Lumber Company, a New Jersey–based organization that Charles had taken over sometime between 1907 and 1910, which held most of his southern land; the George Willis Pack Land and Lumber Company, which Charles had inherited from his father and which he also headed; Jena Company, another southern timber company; and the Tioga Company, also operating in the South, which appears to have been involved in iron-ore strip mining, if not other operations. This involvement in mining is indicated by the fact that in October 1915 Arthur was sent to Birmingham, Alabama, to buy Birmingham acreage for Tioga Company, which land shows up in various geological surveys as having been mined for its iron ore.[15]

By now, Charles's Cleveland and New York financial interests had also expanded. In addition to his involvements with the Cleveland Trust Company and the Seaboard National Bank in New York, he was also a special partner with a New York investment firm, Bayne, Hine & Company.[16]

As his father's helper, Arthur set up shop in the Citizens Building, working at his father's desk and learning the ropes from R. K. Gowanlock, a dour and serious man who nevertheless enjoyed poems and stories about wood fairies and who had for years served Charles as office and business manager. Arthur took over some of Gowanlock's duties and was soon given a great deal of responsibility.[17]

With one year of business law and accounting behind him, Arthur took over the River Land and Lumber Company books, did his family's taxes, and helped manage the Tioga Company beginning with the Birmingham land deal. This job taught Arthur two valuable lessons: not to take people at their word—the land seller tried to sell Arthur more acreage than actually existed—and that even the poor can have dignity. During the trip to Birmingham, he wrote that he "saw and met some of the Tioga tenants, who were not at all 'poor white trash' but a clean industrious lot, marveled how they could live in such shacks & asked many questions."[18]

In addition to handling the Tioga deal, Arthur also managed most of the Packs' Cleveland real estate. The family was starting to develop some fifty acres, divided into two sections—one of forty-six acres bordered by Mayfield and Yellowstone roads, and one of just over four acres running between Taylor and Yellowstone roads. Known to the Packs as the Farm, for it was made up of farmland acquired since 1898, it was now part of Cleveland Heights village and would soon become a housing development. Arthur had been in charge of laying out its streets and housing plots but turned this work over to someone else when he was conscripted into the military.[19]

Arthur was extremely high strung, and suffered from a digestive and nervous condition. He took his responsibilities, as he did everything, far too seriously. After returning home to Lakewood from a business trip to Birmingham in the fall of 1915, for instance, he wrote in his diary that he almost had "another nervous breakdown."[20]

Arthur's nervousness would be treated both at a sanitarium in May 1916, and then by the local doctor with "strychnine tonic" and "special bathing." Not surprisingly, these treatments afforded little help.[21] A notation in Arthur's diary on December 4, 1915, however, indicates that no medicine could have solved the problem, for the real cause of his nervousness was not physical, but emotional. Ironically, the cause seems to have been Charles Lathrop Pack himself: "Father arrived this morning. Worse luck, just when I wanted to feel my most efficient best, my head clouded up again & along in the afternoon I was no good. It is too bad that he seems to work on me nervously that way. I couldn't stay down in the evening and listen to him talk, that is always the worst nervous strain of all so I went up to my room."[22]

On his own, though, Arthur managed quite well. Living in an apartment in Cleveland with a housekeeper and three roommates, Arthur attended dinners and dances at the country club; had business lunches at the Stillwell; entertained his mother when she came for visits; and visited all his Cleveland relatives, including Georgia and Randolph, with whom he still had a sibling rivalry, who were living in their new home at 2224 Tudor Drive in Cleveland.[23]

Although Arthur worshiped his father, he was closer to his mother. His diaries are full of Gertrude—talks he had with her about girlfriends, her visits to his apartment in Cleveland, their outings to visit relatives. Two weeks after Gertrude's father died on May 20, 1915, Arthur noted that Gertrude looked "very weary & worn & sad," and that he was glad to be with her that day. The two spent the entire day together in Lakewood, talking, and Arthur read aloud to her, for she was too shortsighted to read for herself.[24]

Whether Charles was able to console Gertrude over her father's death is unknown. It is possible that by then the two of them were estranged. The numerous family outings to catch a musical or dramatic play at the elegant Hippodrome Theater in Cleveland, recorded in earlier years of Arthur's diaries, seem to have dwindled. More and more the family seems to have been operating singly or in pairs. If Charles and Gertrude spent time alone together, there is no indication of it in the diaries. Nevertheless in 1916, in accordance with the social custom of the day, which demanded recognition of major anniversaries, Arthur and Beulah threw a surprise party to celebrate Charles and Gertrude's thirtieth wedding anniversary.[25]

Arthur's diaries from this period clearly indicate that one member of the Pack family, his sister Beulah, was not doing well. Arthur seems to have been Beulah's closest friend. His observations of his younger sister, recorded in 1915 when she was nineteen years old, evoke a picture of a lonely girl, wandering unnoticed in the background.

"B & I had a talk," Arthur noted on July 2, 1915. "Although the boys seem to fall for her even less in a way than the girls do, for me she certainly is a wonderful sister. She is very pretty at times especially & the boys do like her a lot in a more quiet way."[26]

One month later, Arthur observed: "I like to go around with B she is such a good companion, but I'd like to see her take an interest in people and be popular, she doesn't seem to care for that sort of thing."[27]

By this time Beulah had graduated from her private boarding school, Bennett School in Millbrook, New York, and was living at home in Lakewood. As foreshadowed by Arthur's observations, her life was to be rather lonely. According to surviving family members who knew Beulah, she was engaged twice, and both times her parents ended the engagement. Apparently they were afraid that Beulah, like her mother, would produce a hemophiliac child.[28]

How such interference may have affected Beulah's relationship with her parents is unknown, but there is no evidence that Beulah was close to Charles. In fact, according to Arthur's second wife, Phoebe Finley Pack, Beulah was estranged from her father for many years as a result of some action on her mother's part. It is not known whether this break occurred before or after Charles provided Beulah with an independent income. Eventually Beulah joined the Christian Science church. She lived at various times in California and Union, Maine, where she had "a charming white home . . . complete with lake to swim [in] and canoe on." From there she also ran a summer camp for girls. In her later years, she lived with a succession of paid companions from the her church. True to her religious beliefs, she did not treat the cancer that eventually caused her death. She is remembered by her niece Virginia Lathrop (Pack) Townsend as being a warm person, with pretty blue eyes and a lovely smile. She willed her entire fortune to the Church of Christ, Scientist.[29]

Yet in 1916, all this was far in the future. As families go, the Packs seemed relatively happy. If Charles was focusing on Arthur to the exclusion of Beulah, this was typical behavior of the times; daughters were not expected to run family businesses. With Randolph now working for the American Multigraph Company, Arthur became Charles's business heir apparent.

In 1916, Charles brought Arthur with him to St. Louis for a big meeting involving the sale of the bulk of Charles's southern pinelands to the Buchanans.[30] It was not Arthur's first exposure to his father's southern business interests. He had gone to Texarkana with his father in 1911, at the age of eighteen, for a tour of the mills. On that trip, they had traveled on the Louisiana and Arkansas Railway, which Charles had started with William Buchanan. As the train moved through and around the vast pine forests owned by the Packs and Buchanans, Arthur sat in on numerous business meetings held in Will Buchanan's luxurious private car, "a dandy car," as Arthur noted then, "with observation room, estate [*sic*] rooms with bath room, 2 ordinary Pullman sections, kitchen etc. & dining room."[31]

Arthur had noted even then that the grown-ups had plans for him: "Mr. William Buchanan is an awfully nice, big hearted man," he wrote in his diary, "& he talks to me & gives me advice about honesty etc. once in a while in a way that I rather like. I would have left the car this evening only he came out with a 'Stay right here son, some day you will have to help us out of difficulties. . . . There is plenty of room at the top, Son.'"[32]

Now, at the age of twenty-three, that time had come. Arthur

was going to St. Louis to help his father conduct a business deal with Will Buchanan, and to begin working with attorneys to see that squatters "were promptly ejected from our properties lest they established squatters' rights."[33]

During this trip, Arthur watched his father closely to see how he operated. He was especially taken with his father's understanding of the moody Will Buchanan and his ability to handle him. For instance, Charles, who wanted to sell the bulk of his lands to Buchanan, should have been worried about the fact that Buchanan was "about as blue as could be in his general outlook," including the future of the timber industry. Yet Arthur noted that his father, "having often seen [Buchanan] that way before, knew that he would soon rally, & was not concerned at all."[34]

The next day, Arthur watched Charles charm Will out of his slump. Later, he also observed his father in behind-the-scenes negotiations that would assure him of getting the price he wanted from Buchanan. Charles accomplished this by taking Will's right-hand man and adviser, a conservative Texarkana banker named William Rhoads (W. R.) Grim, to lunch, and persuading him that the timber Charles wanted to sell was worth what Charles wanted to ask for it. The subsequent sale went exactly as Charles had planned: "Mr. Grim [was] won over to our side by Father's clever arranging of the conference with him & our side privately," Arthur recorded, "& thanks to this, [the price was] agreed upon and [the] sale passed on." The sale in question consisted of 14,757.73 acres in La Salle Parish, Lousiana, selling for $1,180,000, or $79.96 an acre. Not a bad profit on land that had cost no more than $2.50 an acre.[35]

Although Arthur would later become a devoted conservationist, he recorded almost no observations on this topic in his 1916 diary, except to mention that he had run into a conservation friend of his father's on the train, the timberman John Barber White, who was also a National Conservation Association director. Later that year, Arthur referred briefly to his father's election to the presidency of the American Forestry Association but did not expand upon it. Instead of conservation, what seemed to have been most promi-nent in the minds of both father and son at this time was the need to run a profitable business. Watching his father manipulate Buchanan and Grim gave Arthur a valuable lesson in salesmanship. Soon he and his father would make a formidably effective good guy–bad guy team as they negotiated the expansion of another timber empire, this time in the Canadian Pacific Northwest.

CHAPTER 11

Staking Out British Columbian Green Gold

A L M O S T   A L L of the papers relating to Charles Lathrop Pack's business interests have disappeared over the years, and those documenting his Canadian timber investments are rare. Thanks to a flood, the industriousness of clerks determined to clean out files, and filing systems containing only vague descriptions of some timber locations, no full record of Charles Pack's Canadian timber investments exists.

Nevertheless, information in Arthur's diaries and memoirs, coupled with the diligent research of Dorothea Hammond, a Canadian Ministry of Forestry employee, reveals that Charles and his sons held, over a thirty-seven-year period, at least 22,670 acres of timber on the British Columbian mainland and Vancouver Island. The words to note here are "at least." The records pertaining to these holdings were unearthed "through sheer luck," according to Hammond, so there is no way of knowing if other records exist or where they are. It is clear, though, from Arthur's unfinished memoirs and the testimony of his first wife, Eleanor Brown Pack Hibben, that his Canadian holdings were limited exclusively to British Columbian coastal lands and islands.[1]

British Columbian timber was outstanding. Nowhere else in the country were forests so massive and varied, or the geography so diverse. The province of British Columbia lies on the west coast of Canada and consists of two distinct parts: To the east of the Cascade Mountains lies the drier interior region. Here trees are small, or normal size. To the west of the Cascades, however, lie miraculous stretches of forest, growing up from a wet and wild landscape along the coast, as well as the offshore islands. Both the coastal land and the islands have been shaped by the deep, pervasive, and penetrating presence of the Pacific Ocean, whose unceasing rhythms have carved out of this land staggeringly steep cliffs and mountains. Warm, damp westerly winds blowing from Japan across the colder Arctic current to the British Columbian coast bring enough moisture and rainfall to produce what may well be "the greatest coniferous forest in the world."[2]

Bathed in this mild, damp climate along the rain coast, British Columbia's dizzying, precipitous cliffs gave birth to ancient and dense forests of mammoth cedar, spruce, and Douglas fir that grew nearly as large as the great redwoods along the coast of California. All of these species are used around the world for construction, Douglas fir being in greatest demand. Farther inland, but still bordered by the Cascades to the east, the forest seems to cover the land, mountains, and valleys of British Columbia as densely as the thickest coat of a great black bear. Once, untouched by humanity, this sea of forests was spellbinding. Even today, these forests are magnificent and are known for their powerful capacity for natural regeneration.[3]

The very geography that nurtured these amazing trees also protected them for centuries. Although Britain settled the area in the late 1770s, it took almost one hundred years for the new inhabitants to recognize the great industrial potential of the massive forest surrounding them. Decades passed before settlers and hand loggers cleared the vast timber lining the coast of British Columbia. Once they cleared the coastal forests, they then faced ocean-carved cliffs that rose sickeningly high above them, covered with unreachable forests. To harvest these steep forests was to court disaster. Only much later would machinery be invented that could cut and transport these trees from their great steep perches.[4]

Still, with or without such machinery, utilizing this great natural resource was never a priority for the colonists. Instead fur, a much easier commodity to obtain and transport, became a primary staple of the economy. Then, from 1858 to 1862, a gold rush swarmed over the province.[5]

Furthermore, when Britain began settling the area, it viewed the vast forests not as a potentially lucrative industry, but as an impediment to farming. The British government wanted its settlers to invest in agriculture, so it urged them to "improve" the land, meaning clear the land for farming. Thus trees acquired a low value. Nevertheless, the farmers needed wood for houses and barns. By the time British Columbia joined Canada in 1871, it had established a solid logging and timber mill industry. The bulk of the orders came not from Canada, however, but from overseas—Hawaii, Australia, and, later, Chile and China. With portages to the Pacific, international trade would flourish. In 1891, Vancouver's future as a trading port and exporter of lumber was assured with the establishment of a steamship line connecting it with the Orient.[6]

Significant timber consumption did not begin in British Columbia until the construction of the great railway system, the Canadian Pacific Railway. Completed in 1885, it traversed the whole of Canada. The railway was extended into Vancouver in 1886, connecting this former gold rush town and now growing lumber town with the interior.

Before the railway line arrived, it had been nearly impossible to move major amounts of timber eastward into Canada's interior. In fact, without rail transportation, large quantities of timber that could have been sold in the interior had been burned instead. Now, with the advent of the railway, mills began to multiply along the railway district. The coastal mills of British Columbia produced no more than 75 million board feet in 1885, but were producing 535 million board feet by 1906.[7]

Despite this tremendous growth of the industry along the railway district, the industry as a whole was plagued by the depression of the 1890s. The industry revived in 1898, however, thanks to an influx of settlers to the Canadian interior who required vast quantities of lumber for barns, fences, and wagons—but rarely for their houses, which were usually made of sod. The industry boomed from 1901 until 1913, when migration tapered off and orders to the coastal timber mills dwindled. Then in 1914 rumors of impending war in Europe began to spread; service industries and transportation companies canceled timber orders by the thousands. Mills closed, and unemployment lines grew as timbermen swelled their ranks. When war was declared and ships for transporting lumber overseas were taken for war use, Canada's international timber connections dwindled as well. And since Canada had focused its timber trade on international markets rather than its American neighbor, which had an abundance of timber itself, the Canadian timber industries "could do nothing but close down and await better times."[8]

With an eye to the future, Charles seems to have first invested in British Columbian timber in 1914, when the industry hit perhaps its lowest ebb. And it was against the backdrop of World War I that Canadian timber broker Judson F. Clark and Charles Lathrop Pack met in New York City in 1916 to discuss the possibility of Charles investing further in the dormant British Columbian timber industry.

It is important to note that what Charles had bought, and was considering buying more of, was not a forest and its land, but a license that gave him the right to cut timber. Since 1861, the British Columbian and Canadian governments had leased and licensed the rights to cut timber. Leases were let to mill owners, and licenses granted to people who did not own mills. Annual fees were paid on these leases and licenses, which were renewable. The fees and terms of renewal changed over the years, but the fees were always well below two hundred dollars a year. The advantage to this system was twofold: the government filled its coffers with rents, fire protection fees, and royalties on cut timber; and the lessees benefited by being able to invest in timber at minimal cost.[9]

By the time Charles met with Clark, licenses, which previously could only be renewed for up to twenty-one years, were now renewable indefinitely. The government had stopped issuing new licenses, but existing licenses were still valid and could be transferred from one party to another.[10] Thus, timber brokers such as Clark were selling their licenses.

Arthur's diaries indicate that when Clark and Charles met in 1916 to discuss the sale of thirteen timber limits in British Columbia, they probably had known each other or at least known of each other since 1908, through other leading timber brokers, like Frank H. Goodyear, who had interests in British Columbia.[11]

Like Charles, Clark was a timberman and forest conservationist. His recommendations had shaped Canada's first major piece of forest conservation legislation, the Forest Act of 1912, which gave the government more control over and support of the timber industry, with an eye to conservation. The act also led to the formation, under the Ministry of Lands, of the British Columbia Forestry Branch, which was modeled after the U.S. Forest Service.

When Charles and Clark did business in 1916, the Canadian timber industry was still foundering badly. In this case, the buyer—Charles—held all the cards. Charles skillfully played Clark out and got a bargain price for thirteen of Clark's coastal timber licenses near two connected lakes, then called Gordon Pasha and now known as Lois Lake and Khartoum Lake. Although Charles quickly took control of the negotiations, he accomplished this largely through his son Arthur, who recorded in his diary a day-by-day account of the scenario:

October 13 [1916]
New York

—Met Father at Manhattan. During the day we had several conferences with Dr. Clark—later final conference with Dr. Clark, Mr. E. A. Sterling [a director of the American Forestry Association and forest and timber engineer operating out of Philadelphia], & Father. Dr. Clark still wants to sell Father the Gordon Pasha Tract. Father expressed no eagerness as he is uncertain about the future in an economic & business way. I know Clark thinks Father goes the limit in pessimism.[12]

October 19
New York

Dr. Clark is still here. He appears to show a willingness to try & meet Fathers [*sic*] ideas of what he would be willing to give for the Gordon-Pasha limits. I had a long conference with him of a most interesting nature.[13]

October 20
New York

Dr. Clark has sold some of the timber since our former negotiations. First in the roll [*sic*] of scout I found out his ideas of the value of the timber sold. Then after a consultation with Father I lunched with Dr. Clark & got his ideas about proper adjustment on the basis of $200,000 being the price at which Father said he might become interested. After that I searched out Father again from his refuge over at the Biltmore. He & Mr. G[owanlock] had talked it over & agreed that $175,000 was enough to pay for 13 limits under the circumstances. I was elected to continue the negotiations alone. After more interviews before which I carefully planned just what I was going to say the question still hangs in the balance. I am playing the part of the enthusiastic son who is enthusiastic over B.C. timber & these limits in particular. Clark's best price is down to $181,000, but tomorrow I am going to him & report with apparently some regret that Father is busy with other matters & doesn't seem to take much interest in this affair. I am very sorry to say that $175,000 is the very best he can do—[14]

October 21
New York

I closed with Dr. Clark & diligent use of the method aforesaid & giving the matter much thought got off at least $1,000 besides in the method of adjusting the license dues. We drew up a temporary contract memorandum & signed it—[15]

In addition to these limits, the Packs held licenses to limits further north along the British Columbia coast: on the southeast side of Toba Inlet, in the eastern and northeastern section of Kingcome Inlet, on Broughton Island, and in sections south of Seymour Inlet. They also held timber on Vancouver Island, west of Cowichan Lake and southwest of Discovery Passage.

According to the Ministry of Forestry, the Packs did not cut their timber themselves but contracted it to be cut by other mill owners. They dealt almost exclusively with Clark's firm, Clark & Lyford. Survey maps from 1917 indicate that most of their land held the best timber available in terms of board feet per acre; it was also the most varied, with western hemlock, Sitka spruce, western red cedar, some Douglas fir, and possibly western white pine.[16] Arthur's diaries indicate that the Packs may also have invested in timber along the northern section of Washington State, in the vicinity of Clallam Bay.[17]

Although the Packs were not known for owning and operating mills outright, it appears that they were involved with at least one firm in British Columbia, the Philadelphia-Vancouver Timber Company. The firm had gone idle after using up its timber in the Gordon Pasha area, but Arthur later revived it with the acquisition of more timber and renamed it the Sutlej Timber Company. This revival began in the summer of 1919, when Arthur toured British Columbia to inspect Pack timber holdings. During this time he became involved in a "full discussion and executive session regarding the proposed re-organization of the Phila-Vancouver Timber Co." By October, the company, which had been incorporated in the state of Delaware in 1913, was revived with E. A. Sterling, who had served as the Packs' timber consultant during their first investigations of Canadian timber, as its president.[18]

Charles and Arthur do not appear to have been officers in the company. In 1920, when the company became the Sutlej Timber Company, its directors did not include the Packs. From Arthur's comments in 1919, it seems that he and his father preferred the role of silent investors: on August 25, he noted that "S[terling] and I discussed further the 'Sutlej Timber Co.' & I brought up the matter of an underwriter's percentage for myself."[19]

Arthur was also linked with the Deserted Bay Logging Company for a time. "Unfortunately," he wrote in an unpublished memoir, "the Deserted Bay Logging Company, with which I became associated, soon closed down its operations because of a great post war [sic] depression that struck the West Coast lumber industry." We may never know what other timber companies the Packs invested in, but Arthur's diaries suggest that the Packs may also have been involved with the Lappan Logging Company Ltd.[20]

What is known is that Charles took advantage of the depression that crippled the Canadian timber markets, bought low, and held onto his limits for many years.

In 1920, Arthur again played agent for his father. By this time Arthur had married his first wife, Eleanor Brown "Brownie" Pack, and the two spent six months based in Vancouver, from whence they traveled to inspect the Packs' British Columbian timber limits, both current and prospective, on behalf of Charles.[21]

"[My father] never saw his British Columbia investments," Arthur wrote. "In fact, he had ceased to travel even to Louisiana. He left field contacts largely to me while he sat in the rooms he kept at the Vanderbilt Hotel in New York or his Georgian brick home in Lakewood, New Jersey, puffing at his ubiquitous cigar and dreaming up new ways to publicize forestry."[22]

One day, while working in Vancouver, Arthur received a telegram from his father: "Understand British Columbia timber limits being offered at very low prices. Suggest you investigate and perhaps we will make some offers. We are having beautiful weather here. Affectionately, Partner."[23]

As a result, Arthur recalled in his memoirs,

I found a number of timber bargains available. . . . Good western hemlock, Sitka spruce and western red cedar with a sprinkling of Douglas fir "limits" were being offered as low as twenty-five cents per thousand board feet. I transmitted to my father what I thought were terrific bargains only to have him counter with offers of half of the lowest price. In my inexperience I was almost ashamed to pass on his proposals, but I learned something about business negotiation. The sellers almost wept with frustration on finding that their supposed wealthy easterner was no sucker but a hard bargainer. We acquired more and more limits. . . . My father was once more buying not "hog pastures," but trees frequently clinging to slopes so steeply inclined above tidewater that it was a standard joke to say that a man could fall right out of his "limit."[24]

The Packs held on to their licenses for years, with the last one expiring in 1951.

Charles kept few of the licenses in his name. Of the 22,670 acres of timber he acquired between 1914 and 1922, only 5,055 acres were ever in his name, and all but 613 of these were later reassigned to Arthur. The majority of the timber—17,126 acres—was, in fact, in Arthur's name, with the remaining 5,544 acres in Randolph's name.[25]

While Charles probably had his sons' financial welfare in mind when he put most of the British Columbian timber in their names, it was also in his own best interest to do so. In 1916, shortly after acquiring the Gordon Pasha timber, he became president of the American Forestry Association. It would not have boded well for the president of the largest public forestry conservation association in America to also be known as an active timberman. In fact, this would be perceived as a blatant conflict of interest.

CHAPTER 12

President Pack

W HEN CHARLES BECAME president of the
American Forestry Association, he took control of
the most influential conservation organization in
the country. He ran the AFA for seven years, from
1916 until 1922.

The AFA was and is a public organization to which anyone willing to pay the dues may belong. In this respect, it is distinctly different from the Society of American Foresters, which is open only
to forestry professionals. Nevertheless, AFA members, directors,
and officers have always included the leading foresters of America,
who have regarded membership in this association as an obvious
duty. The purpose of the association is "to promote public understanding and support of sound national, state, and private forest
policies."[1]

The AFA was established in 1875 by a group of horticultur-
ists and nurserymen during an annual meeting of the American
Pomological Society in Chicago. By the time Charles became AFA
president in 1916, the membership had grown from 25 members in
the year of its founding to 8,039.[2]

By that time, the AFA was known as a significant lobbying force
for forest conservation legislation. In 1885, together with the First
American Forestry Congress, it had lobbied for a comprehensive
and healthy national forest policy. In 1905 it sponsored the American Forest Congress, which adopted some critically important resolutions, including one to unify government forestry work under

one roof, which resulted in the national forest reserves being transferred to the Bureau of Forestry (renamed the Forest Service in the
same year). The AFA also helped create the national forests of the
southern Appalachians and the White Mountains in New Hampshire by successfully lobbying for the passage of the Weeks Act of
1911. The act authorized the federal government, for the first time,
to purchase forests for watershed protection and provided for federal-state cooperation against forest fires. To this end, the Weeks
Act provided an annual budget of first one million, and then two
million dollars.[3]

By 1924, 2.5 million acres of national forest had been purchased
at a total cost of $12.5 million. In 1928 the AFA sponsored the
McNary-Woodruff Act, which expanded the budget set aside for
forest acquisition for eastern national forests. Since the legislative
goals and lobbying efforts of the AFA were nearly identical with
those of Pinchot's National Conservation Association, the National Conservation Association merged with the AFA in 1923, when
Pinchot began his first term as governor of Pennsylvania.[4]

Since the AFA had a history of getting things done, Charles no
doubt believed that he was elected to the presidency of this organization because of his leadership skills. He had ably demonstrated
his organizational skills during his tenure with the National Conservation Association and the National Conservation Congress,
with which the AFA was involved, and there he had also demonstrated his talent for garnering publicity. Furthermore, he was
known to hold sound conservation views. Certainly all of these
attributes were familiar to AFA members, since Charles had been
an AFA director since 1910.[5]

Of course, there was also his personal style. By now, Charles was
fifty-nine years old. As he had grown older, he had become more
and more benign in appearance. Small, thin, and pale during his
teens and early twenties, Charles was now the picture of a short,
slightly portly, prosperous gentleman. His glistening bald dome
was encircled by neatly cut white hair. Small, sparkling blue eyes
shone above a generous white mustache and a tidy white beard.
This diminutive man's public persona was friendly, warm, open,
humorous, and highly energetic. To a startling degree, he resem-
bled no one more than Santa Claus.

This resemblance was not lost on the members of the AFA, who elected Charles as their president not only for his leadership skills, but also for his great personal fortune—"He is very energetic and generous; his helpfulness to our association in time of need should not be forgotten," one director pointed out when Charles was being considered as a candidate. Nor was his ability to manage money lost on AFA officers. As another director remarked to a colleague, "You know that a strong reason for making Mr. Pack president was that he would bring a good financial mind" to the organization.[6] There was little doubt that Charles would pump enough of his personal fortune into the organization to expand its membership, improve its magazine, and continue its lobbying efforts.

The AFA had started to crumble under its previous president, Henry S. Drinker, who was also president of Lehigh University, a member of the Pennsylvania State Forest Commission, and active in the Pennsylvania Forestry Association.[7]

Drinker headed the AFA from 1913 to 1915. His downfall came when some states began questioning the wisdom of the national forest policy and Drinker refused to take a public stand in favor of it, claiming, "It is not—decidedly not—the function of the American Forestry Association to take sides in this matter." Yet despite this stance, in 1915 Drinker wrote an article that supported the waterpower lobbyists who wanted state control over hydroelectric power development. In the eyes of the AFA, this was a stand in favor of waterpower monopolists and against the Roosevelt-Pinchot ideologies of federal controls, which the association had so long supported. Drinker defended his article by insisting that it represented his personal views, not the AFA's.[8]

By this time, Drinker was on shaky ground with the AFA directors. His controversial personal stand on waterpower and his refusal to have the association take a public stand on national issues weakened his prestige.

So did his handling of AFA finances. In 1914, he supported a movement by one of his fifteen directors to have members subscribe to bonds bought by the AFA, which would pay 6 percent interest and be redeemable within twenty years, in the total amount of fifty thousand dollars.[9]

The idea was that these investments would provide the association with working capital, of which it had little, although it also had no debts. The bond sale proceeds would improve the AFA magazine, *American Forestry*, increase membership, and extend the association's educational work. But with Europe at war, the American economy was in poor shape, and few AFA members invested in the bonds. According to one AFA officer, "Eventually, the bond issue was retired, largely by purchasers donating to the Association. President Charles Lathrop Pack made a donation of $11,500."[10]

In 1915, twelve of Drinker's directors rose up against him. Key among these insurgents was H. H. Chapman, a young Yale forestry professor who would one day become a leading figure in conservation.

A colleague of Chapman's once said that there was no truth to the rumor that Chapman's initials stood for "Hell and Highwater." They really stood for Herman Haupt, but the nickname could not have been more apt. It is hard to find in the annals of conservation history a more zealous and self-righteous figure than H. H. Chapman. Tall, serious, and born of stern New England stock, Chapman defended his convictions with such tenacity that he was viewed as a troublemaker almost as often as he was seen as an effective watchdog and guardian angel of the movement.

It was Chapman who led the move to oust Drinker from the AFA. In doing so, he worked closely with three other directors, Charles F. Quincy, E. A. Sterling, and Alfred Gaskill.

In Chapman's eyes, Charles Lathrop Pack was a leading candidate to replace Drinker. Quincy, however, told Chapman that he "would not stand for the election of Charles Lathrop Pack." To pacify Quincy, Chapman in 1915 "endeavored to discover any thing de-finite against Mr. Pack," but "developed nothing."[11]

Sterling suggested another possible candidate, the timberman John Barber White, who was also an AFA director. Chapman killed the idea when he wrote to Sterling, "I have always desired [that] representative lumbermen be members of the Board and I shall hold to this policy but the president occupies a peculiarly public position and I hope you can realize that it would be as great a mistake to elect a lumberman to this position as to elect a member of the Forest Service."[12]

Clearly Chapman—and probably Sterling—had no idea that Charles was still an active timberman. Yet during Charles's AFA presidency, Sterling would work for Charles as a timber consultant and as his agent in his Canadian investments. Furthermore, both Sterling and Quincy would become directors of one of Charles's Canadian timber companies, the Sutlej Timber Company. But in 1915, Sterling apparently had no inkling of Pack's active interests in the lumber industry, nor did Chapman. The strange thing, however, is that Quincy wrote Chapman, "My objection to Mr. Pack is that he is a lumberman; on the other hand he is very energetic and generous; his helpfulness to our association in time of need should not be forgotten."[13]

Chapman ignored Quincy. Writing to another director, he said that Quincy "made that statement to me after I had told him that I objected to having a lumberman as president. This is not his reason. I really believe that he dislikes Pack excessively and has no other good grounds for his stand." Chapman, it seems, had so set his heart on making Charles AFA president that he simply refused to heed Quincy's warning. As far as Chapman was concerned, Charles was "not actively connected with the industry," and that was that.[14]

Although Chapman had to persuade Quincy to back Charles, he had no problem with Gaskill. On December 15, 1915, Chapman wrote him, "I fully agree with you in the opinion that Mr. Pack is the best man for president of the American Forestry Association who has yet been suggested." Chapman also considered Liberty Hyde Bailey, the first dean of Cornell's college of agriculture. Yet Chapman felt "Bailey would not take as much interest as Pack [although] he is equally well known. . . . Frankly I am perfectly willing to have Mr. Pack elected over Mr. Quincy's head. . . . Pack, I believe, has sounder ideas of finance."[15]

In the end, Chapman and Gaskill's first choice prevailed, and in January 1916 Charles Lathrop Pack became president of the American Forestry Association.[16]

Charles inherited a staff that included the executive secretary and editor of *American Forestry* magazine, who had served under Drinker—Percival Sheldon (P. S.) Ridsdale. Little is known about Ridsdale except that he was a newspaperman, that he was originally from Wilkes-Barre, Pennsylvania, and that he went to work for the AFA in 1911.[17] Given what can be deduced from photographs, he was probably much younger than Charles. Charles and Ridsdale were to become lifelong partners.

Ridsdale has been described as dynamic, and an excellent writer of popular conservation articles. As one forester observed: "[He] could write entertainingly about the less technical aspects of conservation, for example, bird life and protection, urban tree planting. . . . He had a flair for the news value of current public interests."[18]

As a talented writer and publicist, Ridsdale brought forestry and forest conservation to the attention of the general public. Previously, this issue had been of interest primarily to professional foresters, timbermen, and cattle and sheep ranchers who fought with timbermen over land-use rights.

Ridsdale's articles made Americans of all walks of life care, for instance, that the government could save a part of their heritage through the national forest program and that this heritage could one day be lost if they, the people, did not support conservation legislation. Through Ridsdale, the AFA made Americans see that their very livelihood could be threatened if timbermen cut too many trees without planting new ones. In essence, Ridsdale and the AFA functioned much as private interest groups do today, when they ask the public to pressure legislators to support their private interests. Likewise, Ridsdale's articles influenced Americans to pressure their representatives to enact conservation legislation. By writing popular articles in *American Forestry* magazine, he attracted a larger AFA membership, which, in turn, meant both larger AFA and grass-roots support of or opposition to upcoming conservation legislation. By 1920, thanks largely to the magazine, membership had doubled to 16,402 people. According to Ridsdale, fewer than 500 of these were foresters.[19]

By the time Charles became president, Ridsdale was established as the AFA's leading publicist, had expanded the format of *American Forestry,* and was changing its editorial policy to include mostly nontechnical articles that were connected, at that time, to current social issues.

While the First World War raged, Ridsdale focused on the connection between forests and war. Topics included Germany's voracious exploitation of occupied Belgium's scientifically managed forests; the destruction of French forests by enemy shells and the French army's use of wood for roads, shelter, and trenches; foresters in the German army; and the wartime condition of German forests. Ridsdale assigned and wrote many of these articles, but Charles jumped on the war conservation bandwagon with him at least once while still only an AFA director. In 1915, Charles invited his friend and Lakewood neighbor Stanley Washburn, a well-known war correspondent, then covering the Russian front for the *London Times*, to send the magazine his firsthand observations of forests in the Russian war zone.

When Charles became AFA president, he and Ridsdale kept the war and forestry topics going. In 1918, Charles sent Ridsdale to Europe to research articles on war conditions there. There were also articles on the planting of memorial trees and groves honoring war heroes, a hall of fame for trees, and a national honor roll of memorial trees. After the war, the focus shifted to American nature issues such as the wonders of national parks, the uses of the pine tree, and the teaching of forestry in schools.

"Imperceptibly," observed one of the AFA's leading members, Henry Clepper, under Charles and Ridsdale's leadership, *"American Forestry* became a magazine of conservation education and nature lore, avoiding policy controversies and ceasing to take sides on national and state issues affecting forestry. Having formerly been the defender of forestry at all times and everywhere, the Association had become an interested observer and detached reporter, as it were."[20] This did not bother Charles. He and Ridsdale saw eye-to-eye on how to run the magazine—and the AFA.

Thus, in replacing Drinker with Charles and keeping Ridsdale, Chapman soon found that he had failed to solve the AFA leadership problems he was fighting. Trouble first arose in February 1916, when Chapman alerted Charles to some questionable activity on the part of Ridsdale and Quincy:

I wish to call your attention to a tendency in the management of the association which, I think, must be overcome. Mr. Quincy and Mr. Ridsdale believe that the affairs of the association should be placed in an executive committee of about three men, with a dummy board of directors. I think they conscientiously believe that in this way the business of the association will be performed with neatness and dispatch. . . . I am sorry to take issue with this point of view but experience has lead me to believe that "in a multitude of counsellors there is wisdom."[21]

Chapman also complained to Charles that Quincy pushed Ridsdale's new contract through without anyone but Quincy seeing it; that a project for enlarging the magazine was "shoved through the board by letter ballot"; that the auditors' report and details of financial operations for 1915 were not presented at the annual meeting; and that quarterly board meetings were being held in distant places, rather than in the more central location of New York City, thus preventing "the attendance of certain directors."[22]

Chapman took it upon himself to go over the AFA's financial report for 1915 with an auditor, and circulated a memo on this report to his fellow directors. He also told Charles that "the Association must adopt a standard form of cost analysis supplementary to and in addition to the present form of accounting" and that he disagreed "with the policy of executive secrecy apparently favored by Mr. Quincy [and Ridsdale]."[23]

Alfred Gaskill also told Charles of "several things that did not look right" to him. Charles convinced Gaskill that he, Charles, would set things right. As a result, Gaskill told Chapman:

Mr. Pack will have told the Board, and I hope satisfied you, that the faults in the administration of the Association's affairs can be corrected. In fact, you know that a strong reason for making Mr. Pack president was that he would bring a good financial mind to this question. . . . He is determined, I think, to increase the efficiency of the organization and there again was shown the wisdom of his choice [as president].[24]

Gaskill's faith seemed well placed. On March 2 a meeting was held of the executive committee, at which Chapman explained a "cost accounting system" for the association. Charles then moved that Chapman, Quincy, and Ridsdale recast the 1914 and 1915 accounts in accordance with the new system and submit them to the board.[25]

By the summer of 1916, all was beginning to seem right in the world of the AFA. In July Charles assured Chapman that the association's finances were sound and told him: "With the plans I have in mind, I feel confident that the Association will be greatly expanded in numbers and financial strength. This will do away with any anxiety you may have had on this score." Having tidied up these difficulties, in a warm, confiding tone he urged Chapman "to be very careful not to talk among the members of the Association, or among the Foresters, about some of the little difficulties we have in the Association."[26]

Chapman was reassured, both by Charles's action on the matter of recasting the AFA's accounts and his attitude toward the association's stance on a federal forestry policy.

As AFA president, Charles made it clear, in the June issue of *American Forestry,* that the association supported national forest policy legislation. He rebutted his predecessor's stance on behalf of the AFA in the July and August issues. The June statement elicited a great deal of support from AFA members: "Mr. Pack has been in receipt of numerous telegrams and letters," Chapman wrote, "and is as pleased as a child with a new toy concerning the effect of his pronunciamiento."[27]

Chapman, too, was elated by this and other of Charles's actions. On July 7, 1916, he told Charles, "I wish to say most emphatically that I am in sympathy with your desire for harmony and loyalty in the Association. I am absolutely confident of your ability to swing the Association affairs and to secure a tremendous advance in membership and enthusiasm during the present year. I am not only confident of your absolute loyalty to the best tradition and policy of the Association but am more grateful than I can express at the tremendous boost which you personally gave to this policy by being willing to take the action which you did lately in the matter of publication."[28]

The Pack-Chapman honeymoon did not last long, however. Although Chapman had written anonymous editorials for the AFA magazine during 1916 and part of 1917, from 1917 to 1919 he worked for the U.S. Forest Service in New Mexico, as chief of forest management in the Southwest. He did not involve himself with AFA affairs until his return in 1919. During his absence, the magazine ceased publishing editorials altogether and, as far as many foresters were concerned, avoided taking "sides on national and state issues affecting forestry."[29] In fact, by 1918, *American Forestry* was almost fully devoted to features on war and conservation. This was due not only to Ridsdale's vision, but also to Charles's own patriotic fervor.

The war had occupied Charles since 1915, when he and a group of influential Clevelanders organized the World Court Congress, which led to the formation of the World Court League. The efforts of the World Court League ultimately helped form an international court known as the Permanent Court of International Justice. Charles's good friend John Hays Hammond headed the league from 1915 until 1917, when Charles succeeded him. Charles resigned the position on February 8, 1919, stating as his reason that he "had too many other commitments" and could not give his full attention to league affairs.

Key among these commitments was the National War Garden Commission, which Charles organized in March 1917 and which he headed until it was terminated on June 1, 1919. The commission's purpose was to promote, through articles, poster art, editorials, and brochures, the planting of war gardens. (These gardens were popular in World War II as well, but were then called victory gardens.) The idea behind the movement was that by planting and preserving their own food, Americans could free much-needed commercially grown food to be sent to the Allied soldiers and citizens overseas and also free such scarce and expensive commodities as gasoline, labor, and transportation that would otherwise distribute commercially grown food to markets across the country. Charles personally contributed $375,739 to the commission and raised other donations for it.[30]

The National War Garden Commission was hugely successful, producing $1.2 billion in foodstuffs. The commission was highly visible and, as its president, so was Charles. His name was prominently displayed on the commission's posters, and he was quoted regularly in articles—issued by the commission—that were published by magazines and newspapers, ranging from the *Ladies Home Journal* to local dailies.

Charles operated the commission out of the AFA offices and

often displayed the AFA name, along with his own, on publicity sheets and posters put out by the commission. He made Ridsdale, the AFA's executive secretary, secretary of the commission. Under Ridsdale's direction, Charles's personal publicity agent, Russell T. Edwards, conducted the War Garden Commission's public-relations campaign. When the commission folded in June 1919, Charles donated its publicity department to the AFA and maintained it with personal donations of eight hundred dollars a month.[31]

Not all of the directors were pleased with the AFA's connection with the commission. Chapman complained to Gaskill in 1919 that the AFA had not profited by the commission's publicity propaganda. Gaskill, however, disagreed:

I take distinct issue with your contention that the Food Garden Commission, and not the Forestry Association, gained by the propaganda carried on during the war. It was the money spent on behalf of the Food Garden Commission which brought the Forestry Association into prominence, which gave the magazine a hearing, which provided a mailing list that is now being used for the benefit of the magazine and the Association, which more specifically helped to prevent the reduction in the Association's membership that must have occurred, as it did in other Associations, without the stimulus of the War Garden effort.

My feeling distinctly is that while the War Garden work was extraneous, and had no relation to forestry, it was distinctly worthwhile, and did us upon the whole credit rather than discredit in the emergency.[32]

Chapman, however, contended that Charles Pack's greatest love was to promote his own name, and that he had used the commission for this purpose: "After the war," Chapman stated, "Mr. Pack retained this organization for publicity which he had built up, under Mr. Edwards . . . and turned its energies to securing publicity for forestry, his own name continuing to appear frequently."[33]

Chapman may have been right. Charles seems to have been driven by a need to be well known and admired, and he could well have been using the war, war gardens, and forestry to achieve this end. Following the war, his picture appeared in magazines and newspapers as he sent millions of tree seeds, collected by the AFA, and also donated by him, to the Allies—France, Belgium, and England—to reforest those war-torn countries. He continued to send tree seeds overseas for several years.[34]

By the spring of 1919, even Gaskill conceded that Charles might be overly fond of obtaining personal publicity at the cost of forestry. After a directors' meeting in April 1919, Gaskill wrote to a fellow forester that Charles and Ridsdale were "so full of the publicity that has been secured through the Memorial Tree effort, the Tree Seed program, and the War Gardens campaign, that they were unable to see that the advancement of forestry, which is the real object of the Association, had had little consideration; or that in that success lay the opportunity to carry out important measures. They did indeed promise to devote more space to forestry, but the program was very nebulous and every suggestion that a forester editor or assistant be provided [to the magazine] was rejected."[35]

Gaskill claimed that previous to this meeting, Charles had told him "that if [his] program was not approved, [he] could easily withdraw and find something else to do."[36] The threat hit home with Gaskill. "Now we cannot afford to antagonize Mr. Pack," he cautioned. "He has found the means to give the magazine a circulation and the association a reputation that are not to be despised. We must use that strength to the profit of forestry."[37]

Charles tried to pacify the directors by publishing a separate foresters' edition of the magazine, to be circulated for free to foresters at home and abroad. The directors rejected this solution, claiming that a foresters' edition would compete with the professional publication, *Journal of Forestry*, put out by the Society of American Foresters. Furthermore, this solution failed to address the issue, which was that the AFA magazine should provide leadership by taking a stand on serious legislative issues.

Charles produced two foresters' editions, in November and December 1919, before responding to member protests and laying it to rest. As for *American Forestry*, the foresters did not consider it satisfactory until, under threat of a total revolt, Ridsdale and Charles hired a forester, Ovid Butler, to act as adviser to the magazine, and began publishing a few more technical and policy-oriented articles.[38]

Yet the magazine's policy was the least of the directors' worries. By 1920 they believed Charles was bent on turning the AFA, a public organization, into a private dictatorship under his full control. Chapman charged that Charles, Ridsdale, and Charles F. Quincy, a director and chairman of the finance committee, were trying to set up "a centralized oligarchic autocracy of what was previously a democratic and representative form of government."[39]

Chapman based this charge in part on the fact that Charles wanted to keep the AFA's financial affairs private. In 1917, Charles and Quincy decided to stop giving the directors copies of auditors' reports—a practice that until then had been commonplace.

"We are conducting a *business*," Charles told Quincy, "and we should not let the secrets of that business become known to everybody. I happen to know that there are certain people that are very curious at this time."[40]

Thus, between 1917 and 1921, Quincy and Charles only *read* the reports to the directors, but never gave them copies. Finally, in January 1920, the directors passed a bylaw requiring that *American Forestry* publish an abstract of the previous year's financial report. This was done.

There is no evidence that in trying to keep the AFA's finances secret Charles was hiding any serious wrongdoing on his part, such as siphoning funds from the AFA. In fact, the evidence points to his generosity. He donated $12,656.60 to the AFA in 1915 and $19,689 in 1920. Although he only gave $500 directly to the AFA in 1919, in that same year he personally spent $10,595 for "publicity and forest propaganda," including the printing and distribution of 25,000 copies of *The Forest Poetic,* a hardback book featuring a compilation of tree and forest verses and poems; 65,000 bulletins on the selection, planting, and care of shade trees; 20,000 copies of an eight-page brochure titled "Memorial Trees"; and the printing of the foresters' edition of *American Forestry.* All of these contributions, however, were handled as a separate account and were not counted as donations to the AFA.[41]

Charles claimed he did not want to become the sole support of the AFA. He may have chosen not to contribute directly to it in order to push others to make contributions.[42]

But if Charles was even partially supporting the AFA, why did he want to keep the AFA finances secret? Aside from the power this gave him, it also kept secret the remarkable salary and commission that were being received by Ridsdale, Charles's right-hand man.

From 1912 to 1914, Ridsdale had worked for the AFA under a contract in which he was to receive a percentage of the AFA's *net income*. This was a successful arrangement: by 1915, Ridsdale had helped bring the association out of debt and also accumulate a profit of $14,000. As the *Journal of Forestry* reported, "The Association, through its Secretary, had raised itself by its own boot straps from insolvency to the position of a solvent concern."[43]

Then in 1915, Quincy, "in whose hands the general guidance of finances had come to center," was empowered by the board to draw up a new contract. When Quincy brought the contract before the board for its approval, he failed to give the directors copies of the contract or read aloud its terms. Instead, he requested a blanket approval of Ridsdale's employment contract, which was granted. What the board did not know was that in addition to a salary of five thousand dollars a year, this contract gave Ridsdale "20 per cent of the gross income of the Association for five years" rather than of its net.[44]

"The nature of this contract," Chapman observed, "is such that by increasing the gross expenditures of the Association, and by that means increasing the gross income, the Secretary's compensation is increased, regardless of whether a profit or loss is shown by such expenditure." The financial difficulties that could arise from such a contract are obvious. Yet Charles, though he had not originated this contract, allowed for its renewal.[45]

As a result, the AFA operated at a loss four out of the six years Ridsdale held this contract, from 1915 through 1920. The worst year was 1920, when the AFA recorded a deficit of $11,922.72, despite Charles's donation of nearly $20,000. Ridsdale, however, made $13,177.17 in salary and commissions.[46]

Charles's only sin regarding Ridsdale was a sin of omission— his failure to change Ridsdale's contract to comply with more economical management. Why did Charles not have it changed? After all, Ridsdale's $13,177.17 salary for 1920 was far in excess of the normal rate of pay for the times: the dean of the Yale School of Forestry had a salary of $7,000, the chief of the U.S. Forest Service earned $5,000, and a cabinet secretary made $12,000.[47] How could Charles justify Ridsdale's earnings?

The answer might be found in a story about Governor Nelson Rockefeller, a multimillionaire himself, who once responded indignantly to the pressings of reporters by saying: "Don't tell *me* about the common working man! I have lots of friends who make $100,000 a year!"[48] Since Charles was himself a wealthy man, he probably did not find Ridsdale's salary excessive. And, as a man who valued publicity, he may have felt that Ridsdale's contract was worth every penny.

But what of the argument that this was simply bad business? As Chapman pointed out, "This contract did not hold any inducement to economy or efficiency in business management, but stimulated effort to bring in additional gross income regardless of expense."[49]

Surely, as a sound businessman and banker, Charles saw that the AFA would never be solvent under such a system. Why, then, did he not modify Ridsdale's contract to a saner system of financial reward? Chapman put his finger on the answer; this "financial parasitism ... made the basis for [Charles Pack's] arguments for abandoning the old democratic by-laws in favor of ... autocratic control."[50] In other words, the AFA's financial mess gave Charles the perfect opportunity to present himself as the AFA's savior by taking it over and ensuring, through his wealth, that it need never again worry about money.

By the time this drama would play itself out, Charles would have changed the bylaws to much less democratic ones and have tried, in essence, to buy the AFA. No one knows whether Charles planned all along to do this. As for Chapman's motivations, his articles and correspondence indicate that behind his seemingly heroic efforts to keep the association on its original path was an egocentric need to have things his own way and an extreme intolerance to anyone else's opinion. In some ways he was as much an autocrat as Charles—if not more. Given their strong personalities, it was inevitable that the two men would clash.

On January 13, 1920, Chapman, Charles's former champion, rose up against him. The occasion was the AFA's annual meeting, at which both the board of directors and the presidency were up for election. Charles had his slate of directors and was running for president. Chapman had his own slate of directors, which he had drawn up with the assistance of the Northeastern Forestry Association. This slate included a new presidential candidate, George D. Pratt, conservation commissioner of New York State.[51]

Chapman tried to keep his slate and the existence of a presidential candidate secret in order to take Charles by surprise. As he said in a letter to one of Pratt's staffers:

Mr. Pack has tremendous facilities for collecting information, and . . . people are prone to talk. Personally, I have felt from the first that if Mr. Pack got wise to this situation in time, he would probably resort to such means as he possesses, which is [sic] considerable, in securing an attendance at the meeting which would make it very difficult for us to throw him out of office. On the other hand, Pack might of course surrender without a fight. I do not for one moment think he will do this. His conceit is too colossal and his desire to run that association is firmly imbedded, being the result of many years of waiting.[52]

Despite his self-righteousness, Chapman used tactics that were less than democratic. He promised Pratt to provide him with a loaded board of directors who would be "in absolute sympathy" with their program.[53] It was on these terms that Pratt agreed to run.

Chapman's efforts to maintain secrecy were in vain; Charles learned in advance of the attempted coup. In response, he did exactly what Chapman feared: he had the "nerve to bring a large number of people to the meeting for the purpose of voting for him." The election was held on January 13, 1920, and Pack won, 75 to 53. The new directors included men from both Chapman's and Charles's slates.[54]

Charles did not take the coup attempt well, and so his victory was bitter. According to Chapman, during the meeting Charles expressed the opinion "that the foresters did not count and were a bunch of cranks and impractical knockers to be laughed at up one's sleeve for their impudency and to be generally ignored." Later Chapman told another forester, "The feeling of bitterness and hostility displayed by Mr. Pack was very marked."[55]

Anyone might make nasty asides during the course of a meeting when faced with an uprising of this sort. Yet Charles also railroaded the meeting through, ignoring both AFA procedure and bylaws. Six weeks later Gaskill, who had repeatedly defended Charles to Chapman, sent Charles his letter of resignation. Key among his reasons was Charles's behavior at this meeting:

It surely was not courteous, or regular, to submit an official slate that had not been represented to the old Board of Directors. Furthermore, ground for just complaint was given everyone by your failure to present to the meeting any statement of the affairs of the Association, any Treasurer's report, or to provide for an audit. . . . I cannot but feel that the failure to make public what the membership has a right to know about the Association's affairs was a serious mistake.[56]

But later, despite misgivings, Gaskill continued to defend Charles. On March 22, he urged a fellow forester to work with Charles as long as possible: "He has kept the Association going, and is willing to keep it going. For my part, I am ready to take that as a counter to the many things that he does which I do not like."[57]

It looked as though Chapman, too, finally decided to accept defeat and go along with Charles. "It is settled now, and I have very little expectancy of the Association accomplishing the things which for years I had planned and hoped it would achieve."[58] Yet just two weeks later, Chapman rose against Charles once again.

It happened on February 4, 1920, when Charles pointed out that the treasurer, J. E. Jenks, was ineligible to hold that position, since a bylaw amendment, which Chapman had promoted, required the treasurer to also be a director. Jenks, who had annoyed Charles and Quincy by repeatedly asking for financial statements and records, was replaced by fellow director Quincy,[59] who, as Chapman well knew, went along with Charles's code of financial secrecy.

Chapman was infuriated by this move. More important, he was also angered by Charles's attitude toward him at this meeting, the first since Chapman's attempted coup in January. Although Charles often appeared to be the epitome of a kindly soul, he was not a gentleman who took well to being challenged. According to Chapman, Charles did not hide his feelings when the two met again on February 4.

"Mr. Pack ... bitterly attacked me personally," recalled Chapman, "for having pulled the rawest deal and rottenest move that had ever been perpetrated in forestry." Although Chapman said nothing at the time, he confided to his correspondent that he was now "going to make [Charles] sweat for it, if I can only get the goods."[60] First, however, he was going to put Ridsdale in his sights as well. He wrote:

I have made up my mind finally, definitely and conclusively regarding Percival Sheldon Ridsdale. I am slow to wrath as the saying is and it has taken me several years to thoroughly get to the bottom of that gentleman. I have now arrived. Mr. Ridsdale is directly responsible for every crooked piece of work and every diversion from the straight and narrow path which the American Forestry Association has suffered since Ridsdale's incumbency. It was Ridsdale who induced Mr. Quincy to advocate the bond issue. It was Ridsdale who got Quincy to sign that iniquitous contract which gave him 20 percent of the gross revenue. It was Ridsdale who, in six months after Pack became president, had him switched over from opposition of Drinker to support of Drinker [who was now a board member] and it was Ridsdale who convinced Pack that I was a dangerous character. It was Ridsdale who persuaded Pack to take the course that he has taken with regard to the last election. . . .

I shall not reveal my hand in this matter until the proper time but some day there is going to be a show down. Meanwhile Ridsdale is at present having things his own way, bleeding Pack for thousands of dollars and will no doubt continue to pull ten to fifteen thousand out of the Association annually even if the Association goes bankrupt in the process.[61]

Chapman had been thinking along these lines for some time. He told a friend that when he had nominated Pratt for president, he had refrained from open criticism of Charles "out of courtesy to Mr. Pack, who in a way is the victim of his own vanity and of Mr. Ridsdale's deceit."[62]

In April, Chapman wrote to Charles asking if he wanted Chapman to resign. "Yes," Charles responded, "I naturally expected your resignation after the position you took." Chapman, however, refused to step down from the board:

This would be an admission that I concur in the view that the association is a private business to be conducted largely for the purpose of publishing an attractive magazine on subjects of popular nature, and that as I am not in sympathy I should cease to embarrass those financially responsible for its success. Since I believe instead that the Association is supposed to be the mouthpiece of public sentiment on forestry and the defender of public interests in forestry as against private interest . . . I shall consider it my duty to remain on the Board until the expiration of my term and aid in every way I can to enable the association to do what it claims to be doing and should be doing.[63]

At last, Charles realized just how serious Chapman was. He began to ready himself for battle.

CHAPTER 13

 Charles Lathrop Pack *vs.*
the American Forestry
Association

I N D E C E M B E R 1920, Charles began fighting Chapman in
earnest. The fight would be long and bitter. In the end, it
would cost Charles not only the leadership of the AFA, but
his friendship with Gifford Pinchot as well. Charles began
the fight by creating a self-perpetuating board of directors, by
making himself and current directors life members of the board.[1]

Other directors were sounded out for their opinions of this idea
before it was proposed at the December 16, 1920, directors' meeting. W. B. Greeley, then chief of the U.S. Forest Service and an AFA
board member, responded with "a violent protest" against the
idea. The proposal was nevertheless made at the December meeting. When Chapman also protested, an alternate plan was suggested: half the board members would be permanent, half elected.
Although Charles was absent from the December 16 meeting, his
presence was felt. He had promised to buy the AFA a new headquarters. Minutes for the meeting indicate that this gift and the
promise of additional gifts were used to pressure the board into
voting for this change. "It was stated," the minutes read, "that as
the Association has an opportunity to become the recipient of a
building in Washington for a permanent home and also for receiving endowments for carrying on its work, *it is essential that provi-*

sions be made to prevent any radical changes in the present public policy of the Association [italics added]."[2]

Certainly, the association needed a new building; fire had destroyed its previous headquarters, and it was now renting office space. And there was no question that it was in need of money.[3] But if Charles gave them a new building and the promise of funding them forever, the cost would be the members' freedom to shape the association's policy.

Chapman opposed the motion. To appease him, he was named to a committee that would review the motion, and final action was postponed until February 1921. On January 13, 1921, Chapman submitted a minority report "in favor of a board, none of whom should be life members but all elected, as before." The directors then, "again emphasizing the financial condition of the Association . . . expressed themselves in favor" of Charles's plan. Chapman was one of the seven men nominated to be life directors. The nominations would be voted on at the February 25 meeting.[4]

Shortly before this meeting, Chapman discovered that Charles and his directors had modified a draft of the bylaws, which were to be voted on as well. As amended, the bylaws would allow the executive committee of seven to "control the Association and the financial reports would not be published." The directors would also have the power to elect vice presidents and the treasurer, thus ensuring that the AFA officers would be men who were in agreement with the directors and their—and Charles's—administrative methods. The directors could also amend the bylaws as they wished, thus assuring that their power would remain intact.[5]

Charles did not want anyone to know the details of these amendments, but hoped to railroad them through the February 25 meeting. He planned his strategy carefully. To begin with, he advertised the February 25 meeting in an inconspicuous place in *American Forestry* magazine, where few of the AFA's sixteen thousand members would see it, thus ensuring that few would attend the meeting. Second, he packed the meeting. The majority of the AFA members were not foresters, but citizens from all walks of life, including schoolchildren. Rounding up enough high-school girls to load the meeting in Charles's favor, Ridsdale apparently told them to vote for whatever Charles Pack wanted. A reporter would later ask if the association was not made up largely of high-school children.[6]

Realizing he probably could not stop the amendment allowing for seven life directors, Chapman put together, along with twenty-four other outraged and concerned foresters, an opposition slate for the role of lifetime directors. Ralph S. Hosmer, head of the Cornell University forestry department at Cornell, was chosen to present this slate.[7]

Chapman and his supporters and Charles and his supporters—and schoolgirls—met in Washington, D.C., at the Willard Hotel, on February 25, 1921, at 10:00 A.M. to vote on the new directors and the amended bylaws. Both men distributed leaflets before the meeting that listed the candidates for directors and officers. Charles was on both slates as the AFA's presidential candidate, so he faced no opposition on this count. But what happened at this meeting made AFA history.[8]

Charles opened the meeting and delivered a brief address, which he concluded by calling attention to an AFA deficit of about nine thousand dollars. He then got down to the election of officers, presenting what Chapman and company called his "steam-roller slate" of directors. Hosmer then moved to submit the opposition slate. His motion was seconded by Philip P. Wells, vice president of the Connecticut Forestry Association, who then began to speak for this slate of directors, beginning with an explanation of the bylaws and the proposed amendments. Presumably Wells planned to explain how the amendments would give the lifetime directors total power and why his opposition slate would better serve the AFA.[9]

But just as Wells began speaking, Charles declared him out of order. Charles's action was sustained by a 95 to 15 voice vote, amid considerable hand clapping. The forester J. G. Peters noted that while Charles was within the rules, his discourteous action showed poor spirit and lack of consideration. According to Peters, "The hand clapping was rather significant and carried with it the suspicion that somebody was there to put something over." A vote was taken on the two slates, with Hosmer's permission. Charles's slate passed, 157 to 15.[10]

Next came the proposed bylaw amendments. Charles asked Ridsdale to read them; instead he only summarized them. In speaking for their adoption, Charles covered only the first—an amendment to increase subscribing membership dues from three dollars to four dollars a year.[11]

Charles also explained that the bylaws were necessary to protect the AFA from outside attempts to control it. As Peters recounted, Charles said,

Two men, whom he chose to call stool pigeons, had approached the American Forestry Association with a suggestion that it be combined with two other associations, the three to issue jointly a magazine dealing with the out-doors. He stated that this was an attempt on the part of the "Lumber Trust" to get hold of the magazine. I was rather surprised that he used the expression "Lumber Trust," because I am not aware there is such a trust and, if there were, I thought he would be among the last to use the ugly term. This was sheer demagoguery on Pack's part.[12]

After Charles concluded his remarks, Wells managed to take the floor to speak against the proposed amendments. After making "a brief introductory statement opposing the amendments," he read aloud a letter from Harris A. Reynolds, secretary of the Massachusetts Forestry Association, opposing the amendments. Charles tried to discredit Reynolds and his association. Reynolds defended himself, and a lively argument ensued for several minutes. At one point the schoolgirls started to leave, but Charles called out to them, "Please don't go, please stay!" and assured them that the meeting would only last a few minutes longer. This last comment, one observer noted, was "another significant statement and quite in line with [his] steam roller tactics." At last a vote was taken, and the amendments passed.[13]

Chapman claimed there were not as many members present as there were votes counted. Ridsdale and Charles objected; Charles then hastily called for an adjournment, which was seconded and carried "while several persons were on their feet desiring to be recognized and heard."[14]

"It was evident from the beginning," Reynolds recalled, "that the opposition was not intended to be given a fair chance to present its side of the controversy. Some idea of how it was conducted might be gathered from the remark of an aged reporter to one of the minority after the meeting, in which he said, 'I have been reporting for thirty years, but I have never seen a minority get so raw a deal.'"¹⁵

But the minority did score two points in the meeting. Chapman carried a motion that the AFA publish its financial report in the magazine following each annual meeting. He also stated that the AFA "had lost the confidence of foresters," and a motion was passed to have Chapman and Ridsdale survey the foresters on their feelings toward the association. The results of the survey would be submitted to the board.¹⁶

These victories were insignificant, though, compared to what Charles had just accomplished. As Reynolds put it, under the new conditions, AFA members now had "little or no part in the affairs of the Association, (except to supply the money,) which is practically in the control of this little group of seven directors who are elected for life. Four of these seven directors are lumbermen or closely associated with the lumber industry."¹⁷

The victory captured the attention of outsiders as well. When the U.S. vice president Calvin Coolidge got wind of it, he wrote to Charles in protest. Charles responded by giving two reasons for his action:

To prevent control of the Association by groups of lumbermen, commercial interests, or other interests, which would not have been truly representative of the public. Such control was attempted at our Annual Meeting in New York in 1920 by a group of foresters. Efforts have also been made by a group of lumbermen and recently certain commercial interests were making inquiries as to how they could get control of the Association and our magazine.

To protect properly the sixteen thousand members, and to represent properly the sentiment of the American public in forestry, the Board of Directors, after careful consideration of the situation, decided the danger of such control as I referred to, would be best overcome by making seven of our fifteen directors permanent directors.

This action was also necessary in order to secure money for the development of the Association, and the improvement of the magazine, and for the gift of a building on Sixteenth Street, Washington, D.C., as a permanent home, and also for the purpose of acquiring an endowment for forestry work, which it is hoped will reach a large sum and enable more effective work.

This money and this property could not be secured by the Association unless the Association could show the donors that the property and funds could not possibly come under the control of any one particular group or interest not truly representative of the public or of the democratic membership of the Association.

The seven men selected for permanent members of the Board of Directors are men who have served as directors of the Association for more than the past ten years, and who have been instrumental in building up the Association from a bankrupt uninfluential organization with a small membership to one which has over sixteen thousand members, has tremendous influence and prestige, and is financially sound [a strange statement to make considering he had just announced a $9,000 deficit], and very actively engaged in the promotion of forestry in the best interests of the United States.

I am glad to say that the amendment was adopted ... and that as a result of its adoption, I am sure that the influence and the service of the Association in the cause of forestry will be greatly increased and the Association will be enabled to do more effective work for forestry than it has ever done before.[18]

But Charles could not savor his victory for long. He soon faced a massive attack, led by Chapman and backed by leading foresters.

First, Chapman had the National Information Bureau, whose function was to publicly endorse or discredit organizations, investigate the AFA. After completing its investigation, it refused to endorse the organization as "a body worthy of public support."

Second, Chapman completed the survey he had been invited to take on in January. Of the AFA's 500 professional foresters, 322 responded. Of these, 152 felt the AFA had unqualifiedly failed to "fulfill its function." Only 92 said it had unqualifiedly succeeded, and 78 felt the AFA had partially succeeded.[19]

Chapman next launched an unprecedented public attack on Charles in the form of editorals—four written by Chapman's supporters—and an eight-part article written by Chapman himself, detailing all the charges Chapman had ever made against Charles. The editorials and article ran in the Society of American Foresters' prestigious professional magazine, the *Journal of Forestry*, from March through May and again in October 1921, since the *Journal* was not published during the summer. The series was launched by an editorial by Henry S. Graves, who had recently left his post as chief of the U.S. Forest Service to become a forestry consultant. Graves stated,

If the function of the Association were only to publish a popular magazine, and carry on general publicity in forestry, but little harm would result. But great issues are ahead of us. The Association should be the instrument through which all friends of forestry could speak. But now that is impossible. The Association should be the strong right arm of the forests and friends of forestry to fight for right principles. But it is ruled by a group of men entrenched permanently in full control, and these same men have already repeatedly failed to make it an aggressive force in critical issues, and have refused to take any part at all in various of the most important situations.[20]

Another editorial invited Charles and his board to "justify" the charges against them, "if they can."[21]

This piece was followed by an article that included the following observations regarding the February 25 debacle:

What a spectacle to see men with a quarter century of public service outvoted by mere slips of girls impatient to be gone to their work or pleasure. How many of them knew the meaning of American forestry? Had they ever seen a commercial forest? They had been asked to vote and they voted—perhaps a little wearied of hearing discussions of life directorships—but committed to the faithful support of that great patron of generosity and of publicity—CHARLES LATHROP PACK! whose name is certain to go down in forest history. "What do foresters know of the art of publicity," he said after sternly shouting a tribute to his Secretary paid at the rate of a cabinet minister from the coffers of the American Forestry Association. What would the sixteen thousand members have decided had they not been denied a referendum vote? We shall never know.

In the American Forestry Association the spirit of Fernow and Pinchot has died. From now on it will be like a battery firing blank charges. Noise to be sure, but never the telling effect of honest shell.[22]

These editorials alone would have been damaging to Charles's reputation, but they were nothing compared to what came next—Chapman's eight-part article, "Has he American Forestry Association Lost Its Former Usefulness? Reflections of a Life Director."

Beneath this benign title lurked a battery of cannons aimed squarely at Charles Lathrop Pack, and fully charged with a complete history of every misdeed, real or imagined, that Charles had committed, in the opinion of H. H. Chapman. Charles had heard most of it before. But this time the charges were being aired publicly in the most respected professional forestry journal in the country. Furthermore, there was one additional charge.

In looking at the backgrounds of the seven life directors, of whom Charles was one, Chapman blasted Charles clean away. In describing Charles's Louisiana lumbering connections, he stated,

The cutting methods employed in stripping . . . long-leaf timber from Mr. Pack's lands as witnessed in the vicinity of Jena, Winn Parish,* Louisiana, and photographed by me, constitute the worst examples of complete forest denudation in the South and cannot be exceeded in complete destructiveness anywhere in the United States. So bad has this condition become in the South that the State of Louisiana in the Spring of 1920 passed a law, the first of its kind in America, compelling such operators to leave seed trees, at the time of logging, in order to provide for reforestation. This practical and simple measure Mr. Pack had no hand in advocating, nor did the American Forestry Association lend any support in the passage of this bill. . . . Mr. Pack has stated in a Board meeting that if there were even a possibility of getting back the principle [sic] of any money invested in forestry, there would be some excuse for lumbermen to practice it, but that up to that time such was not the case.[23]

Chapman concluded his series with the statement, "'Something is rotten in the state of Denmark,' and it is time to do some housecleaning. Mr. Charles F. Quincy himself remarked some five years ago, 'A Forestry Association which cannot retain the support of foresters will fail in its mission.'"[24]

Charles did not challenge the claim that William Buchanan's lands had suffered the worst of clear-cutting practices. Rather, he privately told one of his opponents, William B. Greeley, that he had disposed of all his holdings in the South.

Chapman decided to investigate this claim. As a result, he found that Charles was a stockholder in the very companies to whom he had sold his land. On May 27, 1921, Chapman boasted to Gifford Pinchot that "I now have in my possession, proof of Pack's ownership of stock in the Buchanan interests, which is the firm that is denuding the Longleaf lands in this vicinity. I have wanted this for some time."[25]

*Chapman was mistaken. Jena was part of La Salle Parish, never Winn Parish.

Chapman wrote up this and other findings in a manuscript titled "The American Forestry Association versus Charles Lathrop Pack." In this article, Chapman wrote that Charles had washed his hands of the property he sold to the Buchanans, "with the statement that to hold him responsible for its present condition is a calumny. It is not surprising that a 'forester' should wish to disclaim all connection with these lands in their present condition, for they are one of the worst examples of forest destruction to be found anywhere in the United States."[26]

He went on to describe these conditions and Charles's involvement:

The policy pursued on these lands has been to "cut clean" removing every stick that has a sale value, even for small ties or posts. Fires are then allowed to sweep over the area, consuming the slash and with it all seedlings or unmerchantable saplings that have escaped the logger. These fires continue year after year, destroying the grasses and reducing soil fertility. The lands so devastated cannot be successfully used for agriculture, and the forest is forever destroyed. . . . For these conditions the purchasors of the Pack timber are responsible. This timber was purchased by incorporated companies [Tall Timber Lumber Company, Good Pine Lumber Company, and Trout Creek Lumber Company]. . . . The stockholders of these companies are the owners and are therefore the purchasors and are responsible.

A large number of shares of stock in all three of these companies was owned on April 14, 1917, by Pack and Company, of 901 Citizens Building, Cleveland, Ohio, namely in the Tall Timber Lumber Company, 960 shares, in the Good Pine Lumber Company, 353 shares, in the Trout Creek Lumber Company, 583 shares.

The office at 901 Citizens Building is occupied now and has been for years by Charles Lathrop Pack. . . .

In the period following the organization of the Tall Timber Lumber Company, previous to 1917, Randolph G. Pack, son of Charles Lathrop Pack, was made Vice-President of this company, which erected a home for him. He had active charge of operations during his incumbency. But photographs taken of the lands cut over by this company during this period tell the same tale of desolation.

The inhabitants of La Salle Parish La. have never questioned Mr. Pack's responsibility for these conditions: For many years the denuded areas surrounding Jena, Eden, and White Sulphur Springs, in La Salle Parish have been known as PACK'S DESERT.

The worst feature of this situation is that it is entirely unnecessary.

Even a rudimentary knowledge of forestry . . . would have indicated what steps to take to prevent this ruin of a property which had immense potential value if rightly used.[27]

Chapman also charged that Charles had invested heavily in Louisiana and Arkansas Railway stock (which railroad had been built by William Buchanan with Charles's financial backing). The railroad carried the Buchanan mill timber between Alexandria and Shreveport, Louisiana. This railroad was "known as a profitable investment," Chapman wrote, yet had "the reputation of being the worst fire trap in Louisiana. Fires originating along its right of way have annually burned almost the entire area of Longleaf pine lands through which it passes."[28]

He continued,

It happens that the State of Louisiana possesses an active and increasingly efficient forestry department . . . which is attempting to put a stop to these fires; and state laws exist requiring railroads to prevent the occurrence of such fires by using suitable devices on their locomotives. In spite of these facts, the local inhabitants of La Salle Parish openly state that it is useless for them to attempt to keep fires out of lands in the vicinity of this railroad because the railroad is certain to set these fires.

In view of the fact of Mr. Pack's ownership in the stock of this railroad and of his position in forestry, the state forester more than a year ago appealed to him by letter to exert his influence to secure compliance with the laws of the state on behalf of this railroad. To this letter Mr. Pack made no reply nor was there any indication that he had undertaken this responsibility. Conditions continued as bad as before.[29]

In the end, Chapman did not publish these revelations because he felt that while he had "perfect moral proof" that Charles owned stock, he did not have "one single document of direct evidence" that Charles owned stock privately; he only had evidence of Pack & Company owning stock.[30]

Had Chapman seen the 1917 minute books of the Grant Timber & Manufacturing Company of Louisiana, Inc., he would have found that Charles, Arthur, Randolph and his wife Georgia, Charles's sister Beulah Pack Rollins and her husband Phillip A. Rollins, and Charles's office manager, R. K. Gowanlock, all owned stock in this Buchanan company and that Randolph and Georgia held stock in others as well. If he had dug farther back, he would have found that Charles had also held stock in the Buchanan mills in his own name from 1907 until 1912, at which time his stock was transferred to Pack & Company.[31]

Although Chapman did not publish his article, he did send copies of the manuscript to J. E. Jenks, Charles's former AFA treasurer, who was no longer in Charles's corner, and Gifford Pinchot, who was backing Chapman's efforts to oust Charles.[32] While these findings went unpublished, word no doubt spread through the grapevine that Charles was not only a didactic autocrat eager to take full control of the AFA but also a hypocrite, since his company, and probably he, owned stock in mills allegedly practicing the worst of forestry and fire safety.

In October, the *Journal of Forestry* printed a petition titled "Demand for a Change in Policy of the American Forestry Association," signed by seventy-seven of the country's leading foresters, including the former U.S. Forest Service chief and Charles's former friend, Gifford Pinchot; the current U.S. Forest Service chief, W. B. Greeley; the former chief of the U.S. Division of Forestry, B. E. Fernow; the dean of the Yale School of Forestry, James W. Toumey; the Louisiana forester and lumberman Henry Hardtner, who was practicing natural regeneration and forest management right next door to the Buchanan mills; the chief forester and commissioner of conservation in Ottawa, Canada, Clyde Leavitt; and numerous for-estry professors from across the county.[33]

The petition was sent to Charles in May. It stated that before the AFA could become "worthy of the confidence of the public and capable of performing the functions for which it was organized," the recently passed bylaws must be rescinded; the management of the AFA must be "brought into complete conformity with the standards" of the National Information Bureau; and the AFA must "take a real and vigorous leadership in initiating and advancing measures to bring about the practice of forestry, even when this involves public controversy."[34]

Charles responded with a letter that he had had printed in magazine-article style, which he sent to the signers of the petition: "We do not think that the management of this Association has been taken out of the hands of its members. . . . It is modeled on the similar provision of the National Geographic Society providing for an entire permanent Board of Directors. When an Association advances from an inchoate groping for existence into a broad, national, representative organization . . . some measure of stability and steadiness becomes necessary in its government."[35]

He denied that the amended bylaws had been briefly and incompletely summarized at the meeting or that the financial management of the AFA was unsound, stating that the finances "have always been open to inspection and study" by the members. As for complying with National Information Bureau standards, the AFA was under no obligation to this association. Regarding Ridsdale's contract, Charles claimed that the "management have had under consideration the discontinuance of the payment of such commissions, and they will be glad to receive suggestions and practical aid in the matter of raising money to carry on the work of the Association without this aid in the acquisition of members and of advertising."[36]

In response to the charge that the AFA had failed to take leadership in important conservation issues, "especially where controversies are involved,"[37] Charles made the cunning observation,

To what extent the Association shall engage in controversies must, of course, depend on the circumstances and merits of each case, not on the views or desires of members of the Association who may be interested on the one side or the other of such controversies. No better illustration of this can be cited than that, at this very time . . . Greeley and the National Forest Service are on one side, and Mr. Gifford Pinchot, one of the fathers and leading exponents of forestry in this country, is on the other side, and they are decidedly and diametrically in opposition [regarding] the matter of National or joint National and State control over forest devastation.[38]

He also declared that he had "actively led" the AFA "in many issues vital to forestry."[39] An accompanying list of such activities stated that the AFA had been "assigned the task of public education regarding" the Snell Bill to authorize the federal government to lay down essential requirements for the control of forest fires and timber cutting and removal by states and regions. Although the bill never passed, it ultimately led to the passage of the Clarke-McNary Act in 1924, making possible federal-state cooperation in forest fire control and authorizing further acquisitions of timberland to be placed under federal protection. Charles and Ridsdale gave testimony supporting the Snell Bill and also urged editors throughout the country to appeal to the Senate to increase fire protection appropriations, which resulted in an increase.[40]

In addition, Charles stated, the AFA raised money for new forest experiment stations for the U.S. Forest Service; helped pass a bill in Tennessee "for the purpose of teaching forestry in the public school"; advocated the passage of a Wisconsin forestry bill; assisted Texas forestry lobbyists; provided information on the organization of forestry associations to two states planning on forming such organizations; launched a publicity campaign in Minnesota "when the stability of the state forestry department was threatened"; helped pass a save-the-redwoods bill in California; and helped increase a congressional appropriation to the Forest Products Laboratory in Wisconsin.[41]

Charles also denied that his management of the AFA was undemocratic, asserting instead that it was "eminently democratic" and that the AFA would consider revoking Ridsdale's commissions.[42] Then, as he had in his tiff with Pinchot during the Fifth National Conservation Congress, he ended on a highly conciliatory note:

Far from desiring to exercise any autocratic or personal control over the Association's policy, its management is animated only by a patriotic desire to further the best interests of our country by the promotion of forestry and we believe that we are all seeking to attain the same end for the common good and greatly hope and desire that differences may be reconciled and the cause may be aided and supported by your co-operation and kindly feeling. We will gladly confer with you in the matter.

We earnestly request individual answers and suggestions from those of you who may feel interested to respond.[43]

The man who wrote this sounds as much like a demagogue as Thomas Jefferson did. But at the same time that this statement was being prepared, Charles was battling Gifford Pinchot over a little matter—the AFA membership list.

Pinchot wanted a copy of the list and Charles refused to send it.

As a vice president of the AFA, Pinchot claimed he had every right to see it. Ultimately, Charles pointed out that the board of directors had passed a bylaw amendment forbidding the list to be sent to anyone, on the grounds that it "is a valuable asset of the Association and that it is not in the interest of the association to furnish this list to any person or organization." In fact, this bylaw had only recently been passed, in response to Pinchot's request for the list. So much for cooperation.[44]

The battle dragged on until August 25, when several directors, excluding Charles, met by appointment at the University Club in Washington to discuss the problems. As a result, six recommendations were agreed upon: (1) the provision for the seven life directors should be eliminated and the previous system reinstated, "leaving the choice and election of all the Directors wholly in the hands of the members of the Association"; (2) in place of permanent directors, three permanent trustees should hold the AFA's endowment funds; (3) the president, vice presidents, and treasurer should be elected annually by letter ballot by the AFA members instead of by the directors; (4) nominations should be made by a representative committee and any group or groups of members numbering more than twenty-five; (5) the power of the directors to amend the bylaws should be eliminated, and only members should have that power; (6) a forester should be hired permanently to help shape the AFA magazine's editorial policy on forestry matters.[45]

All these recommendations were approved by the directors, including Charles, on August 30, 1921. By this time he had realized that this was no longer simply a power struggle between himself and Herman H. Chapman. All the directors, including those he respected and admired and had handpicked for the board, had one by one turned against him. Charles had lost his battle for control of the AFA, and there was nothing left to do but accept defeat graciously.[46]

One year later, Charles announced his resignation from the AFA effective December 1, 1922. In his resignation statement, Charles said that he would "continue to work in forestry ... largely in an educational way" and that "as the Association was now built up to a strong and effective organization" he could retire with the feeling that the association had accomplished a great deal for forestry.[47] Ridsdale and three of the directors, Charles F. Quincy, John Hays Hammond, and H. S. Drinker, also resigned.[48]

In accepting Charles's resignation Henry Graves said that "Mr. Pack's retirement would cause much regret among the members." He expressed for himself, the other officers, and the members earnest appreciation of Mr. Pack's work and his generous support of the association.[49]

CHAPTER 14

The War Gardener
Victorious

PART OF WHAT led to the ousting of Charles Pack from
the AFA was his involvement with politics—not just AFA
politics, but national politics as well. His war garden
work was one of the first things that caused him trouble
with Herman H. Chapman, who charged that Charles's main goal
in creating the privately funded National War Garden Commission was to promote his own name. Furthermore, Chapman
believed the war garden work detracted from Charles's work with
the AFA.

Some people agreed with Chapman, but Pack supporters
claimed that since Charles affiliated the AFA with the War Garden
Commission, the AFA benefited from the publicity. Indeed, his
War Garden Commission's mailing list helped recruit seven thousand new AFA members from 1917 to 1919, bringing membership
to a total of fifteen thousand.[1]

Yet even Charles's supporters wondered at times if his main
motive for creating the commission was not, as Chapman charged,
self-aggrandizement. It was obvious that Charles thrived on the
publicity generated by his war garden work, like being quoted
daily in the papers, seeing his name prominently displayed on the
many commission posters that were plastered in windows across
the country, and being favorably caricatured by editorial cartoonists supporting the movement. Yet when all is said and done, the

issue of whether Charles's motives were selfish or pure is beside the point. The fact remains that the National War Garden Commission did a great deal of good. In fact, it can be said to have helped, in no small way, to win the war.

In 1916, while suffering the rigors of war, Europe was hit with a massive crop failure. In the book that he wrote about his war garden experiences, *The War Garden Victorious*, Charles called this year "agriculturally, the most disastrous year the world has known, in recent times." Rationing was instituted across Europe, with meatless days and severe bread and sugar rations. In the French and Italian armies bread rations were reduced, which had a devastating effect on morale in the Italian army. "The soldier well knew that if his food was cut his family must be well-nigh starving to death."[2]

Americans also were suffering from the crop failure. Meatless and wheatless days went into effect, and sky-high prices for such basic staples as butter, eggs, and milk cut general consumption as well.[3]

One account of how Charles began his war garden work says, "Back in the World War days of 1917 Herbert C. Hoover, United States food administrator, summoned Charles Lathrop Pack of Lakewood. 'Mr. Pack,' he said, 'this country needs more vegetable gardens, and needs them badly. I wish you would organize a commission and see what can be done about it.'

"And so, as president of the National War Garden Commission, this noted Jerseyman undertook a tremendous task."[4]

But in *The War Garden Victorious*, Charles gives himself credit for originating the idea: "The author, therefore, realizing the need of developing latent resources of food supply, and after consultation with other men who were eager to do their duty in the circumstances, conceived and organized the Commission."[5]

"Lessened consumption," he wrote, "was not enough [to stop the famine]. There had to be increased production. Obviously Europe could not raise any more food than it was raising. . . . The war drums . . . had called 3,000,000 men from the farms of France. . . . Since America was the only country from which it was possible for Europe to draw food, it became necessary that we should enlarge our yields."[6]

At first America turned to its farmers to do this, but unforeseen problems, Charles wrote, hampered farm production:

For a decade or more, there had been a tremendous exodus from our farms [to the cities]. Our farmers cried for help, but their cry went unheeded until we found ourselves facing hunger. Then it was too late. It would have been as easy to put Humpty Dumpty together again as to bring back to the farm the thousand of boys and men who had been lured away by high wages in town and factory. . . . Every agricultural section of the nation was short-handed. When the crisis came, when the production of more food was absolutely imperative if the forces fighting for freedom were not to be starved into surrender and submission, our farms were stripped of helpers. Our agricultural system, weighted in the balance, was found wanting. . . . When the appeal went out to our farmers to produce more food they replied in a memorial to the President, that under existing conditions the previous rate of production could hardly be maintained, let alone increased—a prophecy which later proved true.[7]

Charles loved to solve problems. He loved to teach. And he believed in one basic fundamental law, a law which often eludes so many of us: the law of cause and effect. He knew from his experience in building and overseeing businesses that small things make up larger, more important things. At fifty-nine, he had rarely known failure and seems to have never doubted his abilities. He was a man who loved to make things happen.

In discussing the food shortage with his cronies, Charles became convinced that he and his friends could help save the world from starvation, and help win the war. Given the calibre of his friends, this was not such a farfetched idea.

They consisted of well-connected, well-informed, and highly influential men—men like his ever-present friend John Hays Hammond, the renowned mining expert who was also president of the National League of Republican Clubs and associated with some of the most important financial groups in the country; and Frederick H. Goff, president of the Cleveland Trust Company and vice chairman of a federal capital issues committee with a mandate to help conserve the country's monies and direct them to America's war efforts.

Charles also included among his friends Myron T. Herrick, the former ambassador to France; Frank Scott, a long-time Cleveland friend and a military-preparedness expert who now headed the federal Council of National Defense General Munitions Board and would soon run the War Industries Board; and James Garfield, former secretary of the interior, who was now a member of the Cleveland War Council.

Although Goff and Herrick were the only men from Charles's Cleveland crowd to become members of his War Garden Commission, it is not farfetched to imagine that he discussed the idea with all his Cleveland cronies while he was in Cleveland attending to other affairs and that the idea, at least, came out of these discussions. It is easy to envision Hammond, Goff, Herrick, Scott, Garfield, and Charles in the club chairs at the prestigious Union Club of Cleveland, wreathed in cigar smoke, drinking brandy or whiskey from fine crystal, and animatedly discussing the national savings in food, labor, and fuel that could be had by creating a nationwide war garden movement.

Given Charles's vibrant, outgoing, and determined nature, he could easily have led such a discussion, filling his friends' souls with his own enthusiasm. As Charles soaked up the statistics and economic projections provided by this council of economic and agricultural experts, his Vandyke beard, now turning white, would be vibrating with the "same unquenchable animation that caused his blue eyes to sparkle as he gesticulated with his ever present cigar"[8] and painted, in vivid verbal detail, the picture that was developing in their imaginations: "Little fountains of foodstuffs springing up everywhere, and the products of these tiny fountains, like raindrops on a watershed, united to form rushing streams which would fill the great reservoirs built for their compounding. The tiny fountains were innumerable back-yard and vacant-lot gardens."[9]

As his vision grew, Charles, always the enthusiastic optimist, might have leaned his small frame forward in his chair, stabbed his cigar in the air for emphasis, and exclaimed, "It can be done, by God, it can be done!"

The next morning, though, perhaps through a bourbon-and-cigar hangover, one question would have loomed large in Charles's mind: How would he pull this off? How would he convince one hundred million people that a war garden movement was not just a worthy cause but a critical cause, a cause that could make the difference between victory and defeat?

To make it happen, Charles first began recruiting "other men who were eager to do their duty," men "with that vision without which the people would perish." In 1917, they created the National Emergency Food Garden Commission, which became the National War Garden Commission in 1918.[10]

The original visionaries were Carl Vrooman, assistant secretary of agriculture; Luther Burbank, the renowned horticulturist and plant breeder and member of the Academy of Sciences; Dr. Charles W. Eliot, president emeritus of Harvard and a trustee of the Rockefeller Foundation; Dr. Irving Fisher, a Yale professor of political economics; Fairfax Harrison, president of the Southern Railway Company and chairman of the Railways War Board; Dr. John Grier Hibben, president of Princeton University; Emerson McMillin, a prestigious and powerful New York City banker; A. W. Shaw, editor of *System* magazine; Mrs. John Dickinson Sherman (Mary Belle King Sherman), an official parliamentarian, instructor in parliamentary law, and director of the American Civic Association; John Barber White, who, in addition to his work as a timber baron, was a member of the United States Shipping Board; James Wilson, who had served under Presidents McKinley, Roosevelt, and Taft as secretary of agriculture; P. P. Claxton, U.S. commissioner of education; and John Hays Hammond.

Charles became president of the commission and operated it out of the American Forestry Association offices at 1410 H Street, N.W., in Washington, D.C. In its first year, the Emergency Food Garden Commission printed across its stationery that it was "affiliated with the Conservation Department of the American Forestry Association." Later, after the commission changed its name to the National War Garden Commission, it gave its address as the Maryland Building, and did not mention the AFA on its stationery.[11]

Charles and his friends were not the first private citizens to conceive of war gardens. The U.S. secretary of agriculture received numerous letters from various individuals proposing similar plans, including a letter from the president of Hunter College suggesting that his institution create a volunteer garden extension service, and one from the president of the Pittsburgh Backyard Gardening Association suggesting a plan to induce "city and town people the country over to plant home gardens by working through mayors and local committees."[12]

Charles Pack's extensive political connections, together with his fortune, however, fairly guaranteed that his plan would win out over others in bids for governmental endorsement in the form of advice and cooperation. This was provided, most significantly, when Vrooman, the assistant secretary of agriculture, became a member of Charles's commission at its inception, although he did not remain a member of the commission throughout its existence.

As Charles recalled, he and his recruits decided "that if the mountain would not go to Mahomet, [we] would see that Mahomet went to the mountain." The mountain in this case was labor, and Mahomet the space necessary for the production of food.[13]

Charles wrote:

The difficulty was that the average American . . . lacked imagination. He could not visualize the collective contributions of millions of back-yard and vacant-lot gardens. He was like the little girl, who, when asked to save a slice of bread to help feed the army, replied: "Papa, I don't see any reason why I should save a slice of bread. It can't feed an army." Her father took her down to the harbor in New York City and showed her a great transport at the wharf, waiting for food to carry to Europe. He then told her that if every little schoolgirl in the United States saved a slice of bread a day, their combined savings would fill eight large transports every week. Her blue eyes opened wide as the great truth flashed upon her, and after that she didn't want to eat anything at all.

In his nursery days, the average American had learned that:

Little drops of water, little grains of sand,
Make the mighty ocean and the pleasant land.

Unfortunately, however, that infantile lesson had been put away with other childish things when he became a man. The task that the National War Garden Commission set itself was to make the average American feel the truth, the actual force, of that childhood jingle.[14]

Above, left: Lady Liberty is typical of the symbols that Charles used in his campaign to plant millions of war gardens. (Courtesy of the Library of Congress.)

Above, right: The infamous "Can the Kaiser" poster. (Courtesy of the Library of Congress.)

Charles knew that to make Americans feel his "truth" he must organize and launch a huge daily educational publicity campaign, larded with patriotic symbolism and slogans.

"Before the people would spring to the hoe as they instinctively sprang to their rifle," Charles observed, "they had to be shown, and shown conclusively, that the bearing of the one implement was as patriotic a duty as the carrying of the other. Only persistent publicity, only continual preachment, could convince the public of that."[15]

Tapping the substantial knowledge, connections, and finances of his fellow commissioners, Charles launched a massive, unrelenting publicity campaign, directed by his American Forestry aide-de-camp, P. S. Ridsdale, and executed by the newly recruited Russell T. Edwards. Between them, they created an incredible propaganda campaign. According to Arthur Pack, as late as the 1950s expert publicists were still referring to the commission's war garden campaign "as one of the most soundly effective educational propaganda campaigns ever created."[16]

The campaign was designed to do four things: convince Americans of the need for war gardens; show war gardeners what, when, and how to plant, through short, easy-to-read newspaper articles and booklets distributed by the commission; encourage and assist communities in organizing war gardening associations and groups; and equate war gardening with patriotism through the use of patriotic symbols and slogans.

Having worked successfully with editors before, Charles believed they would give him full cooperation, as they had in the past. Yet even he was overwhelmed by the reception the press gave his campaign. "The promptness of the editors in recognizing the vital importance of home food production," Charles recalled, "and their patriotic readiness in conveying the appeal to their millions of readers should be recorded in letters of gold among the nation's permanent records. . . . Almost unanimously, from one end of the country to the other, the newspapers daily published material furnished by the Commission. If this could be totalled it would run into tens of thousands of columns."[17]

Ridsdale and Edwards made it easy for the newspapers to cooperate by providing them with beautifully designed pages of copy, complete with articles and professionally drawn illustrations, that were put together in matrix form. All the editors needed to do was have the printers cast the stereotypes from which these pages would be printed. Thus it was easy to publish daily war garden material, including feature articles, succinct how-to articles, illustrations, comics, and even poems. One doggerel poem, given its old-fashioned humor and moralistic tone, may well have been written by Charles: "Little Miss Muffet will sit / on her tuffet / and giggle in merriest glee / for she'll not be needing to buy her stuff for feeding / 'I'll can it this summer,' says she."[18]

The commission's articles and illustrations were picked up by news services everywhere and reproduced in newspapers and magazines of all types, ranging from the small local dailies to such gray old ladies as the *New York Times*. "The most remarkable cooperation," Charles recalled, "was given in New York City when virtually every one of the big metropolitan dailies was running the Commission's garden hints and suggestions simultaneously." On Sundays some papers regularly ran an entire page or two of war garden material.

The information was prominently displayed. The *Philadelphia North American*, for instance, ran a war garden poster on nearly one-quarter of its front page, and the monthly *Garden Magazine* illustrated two of its covers with two different War Garden Commission posters. In addition, such magazines as *Good Housekeeping, Woman's World, Forbes, Country Gentleman*, and *Literary Digest* regularly printed the commission's articles.

Foreign-language dailies also published the commission's articles and even requested more information from them. The British food controller cabled a request for five thousand copies of the commission's book on gardening.[19]

The commissioners also wanted to link war gardening with patriotism and thereby bolster the war gardeners' spirits and incentive. The commission achieved this by creating grand, patriotic posters and slogans that equated war gardening with our Lady Liberty, and gardeners with the valiant American soldier. These posters were drawn by the leading commercial artists of the day: James Montgomery Flagg, Frank V. Du Mond, Maginel Wright Enright, and J. Paul Verrees.

The superstar of this group was Flagg, who had created the Uncle Sam image and the famous Uncle Sam "I Want YOU for U.S. Army" World War I recruitment poster. For the National War Garden Commission, Flagg created a graceful, heroic, color figure of Lady Liberty, dressed in a flowing robe made from the American flag, and striding across a field as she broadcasts seeds before her. This poster was circulated with various patriotic headlines ranging from "Will You Have a Part in Victory?" to "Sow the Seeds of Victory." Along the bottom of each version ran the inspirational quote from Charles Lathrop Pack: "Every Garden a Munition Plant."[20]

Du Mond also appealed to war gardeners' patriotism through

the Goddess of Victory, while Enright created a more playful and childish image with a poster of a young boy marching across the land with a hoe slung over his shoulder, leading an army of vegetables. This poster carried the headline "War Gardens Victorious."

Verrees created the infamous "Can the Kaiser" poster, which showed the German kaiser encased in a fruit jar and featured the line "Can Vegetables and Fruit and the Kaiser Too." A London version of this poster substituted the Britishism "tin" for "can" and thus missed the pun. This mistranslation caused a riot. When passersby saw the poster in a shop window, all they understood, according to Arthur, "was that Kaiser Wilhelm's picture was being displayed and this they greatly resented. A mob smashed the glass window and tore the poster down."[21]

Eye-catching posters appeared everywhere—on bulletin boards, in factories, libraries, railway stations, clubs, banks, and stores—and were an important part of spreading the war garden campaign.

The power of the press and patriotism made for a heady propaganda combination. Charles claimed, however, that the commission could not have succeeded without the help of local organizers who created state, county, and town war garden committees. These in turn organized plantings in school playgrounds, city lots, and neighboring fields and also served as information sources for the individual gardeners going it alone in their backyards. Charles rallied this type of local support by sending representatives to cities and towns to confer with the local chambers of commerce or other organizations on how to direct gardening campaigns.[22]

The results of the commission's efforts seemed almost magical. Charles claimed that he had hoped to produce 1 million war gardens, yet approximately 3.5 million gardens were planted in the 1917 season, and 5.3 million in the 1918 season. The commission also reported that in 1917 the food value produced was estimated at $350 million and that in 1918 the value rose to $525 million. It was estimated that the food canned and stored on pantry shelves exceeded 500 million quarts of fruits and vegetables in 1917, and 1.45 billion quarts in 1918.[23]

Charles calculated that the 1918 war gardens "grew food equal in body building power to the meat ration required by an army of

1,000,000 men for 302 days; the bread ration for 248 days, or the entire ration for 142 days."[24] In other words, gardeners freed this equivalent of commercially grown food to be sent overseas to the Allied soldiers and citizens.

Charles believed that there were other indirect benefits of the war gardens as well. "Cannon and shells and rifles and cartridges and uniforms and innumerable other articles were demanded in incomprehensible quantities," he said. "After taking four or five million men away from productive industry, obviously we should not have sufficient man-power left to create all that was needed of these various supplies. War gardening, by adding to the food supply, released for work on these lines men who otherwise would have been necessary on the farms. In short, war gardening conserved labor by making labor go farther."[25]

Furthermore, war gardeners released an "army of men which otherwise would have been needed to transmit this food from producer to consumer," and these laborers could be used for other work.[26] They also conserved transportation by releasing "thousands of freight-cars, motor-trucks, and wagons, for purposes other than the hauling of food, which also saved fuel.[27]

As president, cofounder, and primary funder of the National War Garden Commission, Charles Lathrop Pack was not only the leading figure in the war garden movement but the one personality most commonly associated with it. Cartoonists regularly featured him in pro–war garden editorial cartoons. A cartoon by J. N. "Ding" Darling, for instance, which ran in the *New York Tribune*, featured Charles dressed in a military officer's uniform with a hoe sticking out of his back pocket and wearing a sash identifying him as "Charles Lathrop Pack President of National War Garden Commission." He is reading a governmental order that states, "Uncle Sam expects every War Garden to do its duty."[28]

In the minds of many, Charles was the sole power behind this movement. Although Charles would have been happy to let people believe this, he was not the only national supporter of war gardens. The federal government promoted them as well, if not as efficiently. Charles gave only grudging credit to the government, however. In a statement that apparently came from information provided by the commission and was published in the *Country*

Gentleman, the following description was given of the government's and Charles's roles in the movement:

For a number of reasons—or for no reason at all—our Federal overseer of husbandry was asleep at the switch when the call for action came. It was necessary for a wealthy amateur to turn aside from his hobby of stamp collecting and understudy the Department of Agriculture. It took a private citizen . . . Charles Lathrop Pack, to make a food-raising noise that has reverberated in the back-yards from Maine to California and has caused most people to think that the United States Government was doing it.

"We can't turn over fast enough on this garden job," was the pathetic admission made by a high official of the Department last spring. "We are tied up with six kinds of tape. By the time we get out a bulletin on planting radishes it will be the season to bank up celery."

The Department of Agriculture did catch up with the campaign 'round canning time and helped to inform housewives what to do with food that private folks had shown them how to raise. Full credit must be given the Department for continuance and expansion of boy and girl club work, which applies chiefly to rural districts. And there is credit for individuals of the government staff who volunteered services and helped along the general campaign.[29]

After dispensing with the inefficient Department of Agriculture, the author then gave a brief account of the glorious work of Charles Lathrop Pack and his War Garden Commission.

Away back last March, before war was declared, and when national food shortage was a cloud no bigger than a man's hand, the National Emergency Food Garden Commission was organized and opened its office at Washington, D.C. Charles Lathrop Pack, President of the American Forestry Association, was the leader and chief motive force of the garden body, and he gathered round him as members of the commission such persons as Luther Burbank, Doctor Charles W. Eliot, Irving Fisher, John Hays Hammond . . . and others.

It is violating no secret and contains no reflection to say that some men lend their names to a cause and others put their whole energy into it. Many people would not have planted a garden if they had not been prodded thereto by names. A funny kink of human nature, that in order to feed ourselves we must be cheered on by celebrities.[30]

Celebrities indeed! The men on the commission, Charles included, were all highly successful, but as bankers, university presidents, engineers, and statesmen their names were hardly household words. If any name was well known it was that of Charles Lathrop Pack, since it had been in the press regularly in connection with his forestry work for the past few years. The "celebrities" statement goes far to support H. H. Chapman's claim that Charles's chief motive in forming the War Garden Commission was self-aggrandizement, for he either wrote this statement or provided the information for it, and in either case would be responsible for its contents and thus for the claim that the commission was made up of inspirational "celebrities."

This is not to say that Charles's work was unpraiseworthy. Indeed, it was amazing, patriotic work that was absolutely worthy of acclaim and celebrity. As Charles so poetically put it,

The war garden was found in tiny clearings beside the logging camps of Louisiana, in irrigated plots among the arid sands of New Mexico, in the rugged iron lands of Minnesota, and on the open, fertile stretches of the Middle West. Even the lighthouse-keeper at Santa Cruz, California, planted a little garden under the shadow of his protecting shaft. From coast to coast, from lake to gulf, little areas that had been barren as the desert suddenly blossomed like the rose. Behind each of these innumerable gardens was a heart animated by the desire to serve God and country.[31]

In one case, a group of teachers moved into a summer cottage in New Hampshire in the summer of 1918 in order to raise vegetables to supply the table of a large local hotel.[32]

Charles dreamed that war gardens would be planted here and abroad for decades to come. The government did, for a time, continue the program when the U.S. Bureau of Education took it over and enlisted a "school garden" army of 1.5 million boys and girls. The program died out eventually, enjoying only a brief revival during the Great Depression when various people, including Charles, supported local emergency garden campaigns. Charles created the Lakewood, New Jersey, Food Garden Commission in 1932 to help feed the poor, and Henry Ford also organized food gardens for the poor.[33]

Although war gardens failed to become a permanent part of American culture, their importance to the First World War did not go unnoticed. In 1918, Trinity College in Hartford, Connecticut, awarded Charles an honorary degree for his war garden work, and in 1919 he received the Great Medal of Honor from his National War Garden Commission.[34]

Charles published *The War Garden Victorious* that same year and sent copies to hundreds of statesmen, dignitaries, and scholars both in the United States and abroad. The letters of praise and acclaim that poured in to Charles from around the world must have overwhelmed him. If he had ever envied the praise heaped upon his father by the citizens of Asheville, dreaming of achieving even greater recognition himself, then he may have felt that at last he had achieved this goal. His father had aided the citizens of Asheville; he, Charles, had aided the citizens of the world.[35]

Despite being doubly occupied with his AFA and commission work, Charles still made time for his family. In 1917, Charles advised Arthur to accept a position as a "dollar a year man," working for Charles's friend Frank Scott, head of the General Munitions Board in Washington. Arthur became Scott's private secretary and general errand boy; one of his duties was to chauffeur visiting dignitaries.[36]

To ensure that Arthur made the proper impression in his new role, Charles insisted on buying Arthur a new car—a Hudson Super-Six Speedster—"to be more in accord with the status of its frequent passengers," as Arthur put it.[37]

In the fall of 1917, as the draft crept closer to Arthur's number, there were "talks and walks with the family, discussing the problems of what [Arthur] could and should do." The choice was between entering the navy pay corps and army ordnance. Arthur chose the latter, largely because some of his friends were already serving there. In May 1918, he said goodbye to his parents in Lakewood before shipping out to France:[38] "There were tears of pride in my father's eyes. I was the first Pack to serve his country in war as a soldier since Colonial days. . . . But to my family, I was already a hero."[39]

When Arthur sailed, Charles made sure he was equipped with a rubber survival suit in case of shipwreck. Embarrassed by the gift, Arthur kept it hidden during the voyage, and sold it to one of the ship's officers on his arrival in Europe.[40]

Arthur's entry into military service was just one of several milestones that the Pack family passed during 1917 and 1918. Charles and Gertrude became grandparents for the first time when Virginia Pack was born to Randolph and Georgia. Several months later, Charles's mother died suddenly at the age of seventy-nine, making Charles and Gertrude the new reigning monarch and matriarch of the Pack clan.[41]

In 1919, Charles and Gertrude celebrated the birth of their second grandchild, Joan Beatty Pack. Although Charles was unhappy that he still had no grandson, all else was right with the world. Arthur had returned home in February, and nine months later, on December 18, married a girl whose attentions he had long yearned for—Eleanor Brown. The two were married at her parent's home in Waterbury, Connecticut.[42]

By 1920, with his sons grown and married, one well entrenched in the family business, two grandchildren under his belt, and the promise of more to come, Charles could feel well satisfied as a family man.

Professionally, he was also riding a crest. As AFA president and the power behind the hugely successful National War Garden Commission, which ended its work in 1919, he was a man in love with his own power to achieve great and good things. By now he was virtually driven by his ability to dream dreams and make them come true. Although he had achieved what could well have been the greatest accomplishment of his lifetime with his war garden work, he was not about to rest.

After quitting the AFA in 1922, he immediately formed his own forest conservation association, the American Tree Association. This time he would teach, among other things, the importance of planting and conserving not food, but trees. Helping him achieve this task was none other than the team that had so beautifully brought off the National War Garden campaign—P. S. Ridsdale and Russell T. Edwards. As always, however, Charles would be directing the operation.

CHAPTER 15

The American Tree Association: The Start of an Empire

ESPITE THE CALM wording of his resignation statement, when Charles resigned from the AFA in 1922, there was little doubt that he was taking his ball and going home. As the forester Emanuel Fritz put it, "The fight got so hot that Pack just threw the whole thing in the scrap basket as far as he was concerned."[1]

Charles's friendship with Gifford Pinchot also landed in the scrap basket. Although Pinchot had backed H. H. Chapman, the final straw came when Charles refused to give Pinchot a copy of the AFA membership list. That confrontation ended the friendship. Pinchot would go on to serve two terms as governor of Pennsylvania, while continuing to work on forestry issues, but he no longer consulted Charles regarding this work.

Nor did Charles seem to need Pinchot any longer. In 1922, after leaving the AFA, he started two organizations—the American Tree Association and the American Nature Association. He was most closely associated with the ATA, however, and through it he accomplished his most impressive and influential conservation work.

The purpose of the ATA was "to further forest protection and extension, to increase appreciation of forests and natural resources essential to the sound economic future of the country."[2] It accom-

At the behest of Charles Lathrop Pack and his American Tree Association, America began planting trees for every occasion. Here, Charles and First Lady Florence Harding participate in planting an elm on International Avenue, facing the Lincoln Memorial, in Washington, D.C. (Courtesy of the Arizona Historical Society.)

plished this primarily through publicity—by using the press to encourage the planting of trees by the public, and by providing editors with popular and topical forestry news. When a major flood occurred, the ATA issued editorials on how tree conservation prevents flooding. When white pine blister rust was spreading, it sent out news items about this and other tree diseases. Later, the ATA also disseminated news on legislation and technical forestry information to the professionals in the field.

Through the ATA Charles did the kind of grass-roots publicity that he loved, but which got him in trouble with Chapman and his crowd. Now Charles could do all that he had done through the AFA—and more—with no interference. The ATA was a private organization. There was no board of directors, so Charles was free of any constraints a board might put on him. Nor could ATA members tell him what to do, since they paid no dues and thus had no power over the association. To become a member, individuals merely sent the ATA a form stating that they had planted a tree. In return, the tree planter received a certificate of membership in the ATA's "Tree Planting Army." By 1929, the association's membership had reached 129,000.[3]

Charles must have experienced a certain amount of "so there" glee when he left the AFA to set up the American Tree Association. The ATA was housed in the very same building that Charles had once promised to give to the American Forestry Association, which offer was scorned by AFA directors as an attempt to bribe and control that organization. Leaving the AFA to flounder in its inadequate offices, Charles set up the ATA in this spacious, elegant, three-story brownstone duplex at 1212–14 16th Street, N.W., in Washington, D.C., fully equipped with desks, chairs, conference tables, stationery, and all the other office equipment necessary to run his new empire.

The ATA was staffed by Charles's right-hand man, P. S. Ridsdale, ATA treasurer; Russell T. Edwards, director of the ATA's educational section; Arthur Pack, secretary; and Richard W. Westwood, assistant secretary. Later, William Savage joined the team to serve as a "field representative" for Charles, traveling to "every state in the union, and to several foreign countries, in promoting" the goals of the ATA.[4]

Although Charles may not have realized it at the time, creating the ATA was the most important move he would ever make. The association made unprecedented strides in educating the public about forestry and nature conservation. Along with Charles's American Nature Association, the ATA was the first of four Pack organizations to constitute a private conservation empire the likes of which had never been seen before nor has been seen since. Ultimately this empire would achieve numerous conservation firsts,

This editorial cartoon is typical of those issued by the American Tree Association, which were in turn printed by the press. *(Courtesy of Virginia Lathrop [Pack] Townsend.)*

both in educating and mobilizing the public to take forest conservation seriously and in funding groundbreaking forest conservation research and development.

Of these first two organizations, the American Tree Association was better known and accomplished more. Its success was due in large part to the fact that its publicity department, run by Ridsdale and Edwards, was modeled after that of the National War Garden Commission.

Just as they had done with the National War Garden Commission, Ridsdale and Edwards put the ATA's message across on a massive scale by regularly submitting broadsheets containing forestry-related news items, features, editorials, and cartoons to the nation's newspapers and magazines.

The press welcomed the ATA's forest and tree conservation campaign, and soon it was as popular as the war garden movement.

The difference was that the forestry campaign lasted not two years, as the war garden campaign had, but fifteen years, until Charles's death, and gained more and more momentum each year.

Thanks to the ATA's publicity efforts, newspapers began running forestry editorials and news stories daily. The syndicated columnist Frank Crane, for instance, regularly wrote forest conservation editorials that ran under such pointed headlines as "Now Is the Time to Plant Trees," and appeared in such papers as the *Boston American* and the *Washington Times*.[5]

Together Charles, Ridsdale, and Edwards made a formidable team. By 1930, Charles cautioned Henry Schmitz, then chief of the forestry division at the University of Minnesota, to whom he sent some clippings, "Do not return the enclosed clippings—we get thousands. The press carries more forestry today than ever before. We estimate that 150 daily papers are now carrying our stuff on an average day."[6]

The ATA's onslaught of forestry propaganda made Charles Lathrop Pack something of a celebrity. He was quoted in virtually every article or editorial issued by the ATA, and his picture frequently accompanied articles. He was a darling-looking little man, dapper in dress and sporting a neatly trimmed small beard and moustache, as well as an ever-present merry glint in his eye. In some pictures in which he appears at tree plantings, he resembles a benign wood elf giving a blessing to the ceremony.[7]

Charles also appeared in cartoon caricatures, some commissioned by the ATA and some created autonomously by independent cartoonists. One editorial cartoon, which ran under the heading "Uncle Sam Needs New Glasses," showed Charles handing Uncle Sam a pair of spectacles with the words "forest policy" written across the lenses. Uncle Sam is seated on a tree stump, one of hundreds in this drawing. In the background is a lone tree, upon which is nailed a paper bearing the statement "81,000,000 acres idle land $250,000,000 freight bill on lumber every year," signed by the American Tree Association.[8]

In addition to appearing frequently in cartoons like this, as ATA president Charles was regularly quoted as an authority on forestry conservation. Anyone who doubted that Charles craved the limelight could now put these doubts to rest; he clearly thrived on the attention.

But forestry and forest conservation thrived as well. Eleven years after Charles's death, the renowned forester Ovid Butler, who had opposed Charles's leadership of the AFA and who ran its magazine for twenty-five years after Charles left the organization, wrote a tribute to his work:

The American Tree Association ... issued during a period of almost two decades educational material running into millions of pieces which reached every section of the country and virtually every level of American life. Viewed in the light of passing years, there can be no doubt that this mass education leadership had a profound influence in the planting of thousands of acres of trees and in developing the conservation-minded America of today.[9]

Charles received acknowledgment of his achievements from outside the world of forestry as well. In 1926, Oberlin College awarded him an honorary doctorate for his educational work "on the need of reforestation and putting the millions of acres of idle lands in this country to work growing trees."[10]

As well as working with magazines and newspapers, the ATA published books on forestry conservation that were aimed at the general public. In addition to publishing books written by others, such as *Forestry in the Pacific Northwest,* by Hugo Winkenwerder, it published several books by Charles: in 1922, the ATA published *Trees as Good Citizens* and *The School Book of Forestry,* both written by him.

Aimed at adults, *Trees As Good Citizens* was written, according to Charles, "to simplify to some extent the problems of those who would grow shade trees." The book was probably one of Charles's less successful projects. To begin with, its audience was narrow, limited only to those people interested in planting shade trees. Furthermore, its style was uneven, switching between cleanly written technical advice on how to care for shade trees, and sweet, sentimental prose expounding upon the wonders of such trees:

It must be borne in mind, that for its friendly offices the shade tree is entitled to man's best care and protection. In its demands it asks nothing in selfishness. Its one aim is to thrive for man's benefit. Its sole purpose is to bless the world with its kindly gifts. . . .

The city with fine shade trees is the City Beautiful. . . . A city without an abundance of shade trees on its streets, on lawns and in parks is incomplete.[11]

The School Book of Forestry, on the other hand, was aimed at children and written in a clean, straightforward, unsentimental style. Charles explained his reasons for writing the book in the introduction, stating:

Our forest fortune has been thoughtlessly squandered by successive generations of spendthrifts. Fortunately, it is not too late to rebuild it through cooperative effort.

The work has been well begun, but it is a work of years, and it is to the youth of the country that we must look for its continuous expansion and perpetuation. A part of our effort must be directed toward familiarizing them with the needs and rewards of an intelligent forest policy.[12]

There is no record of how these books were received. Given Charles's penchant for self-promotion, if either book had had great success, Charles would have seen that this news was well publicized. Since it was not, one is left to assume that their reception was disappointing.

In 1926, however, the ATA published a book that had astounding success: *The Forestry Primer,* written by Charles. This slim, paperbound book featured fifteen two-page lessons in forestry, written in clear, short sentences. It totaled thirty-two pages. Despite its diminutive size, it had a huge reception: the *Pennsylvania School Journal* ran an article praising it, departments of education endorsed it, and requests for copies poured in for years from elementary schools around the country. Between 1926 and 1934, the ATA distributed 4.2 million copies of *The Forestry Primer,* including a revised edition in 1934 and special editions for Michigan, the Gulf States, and the Pacific Coast.[13]

This success was due largely to Charles's outstanding marketing instinct. When the book first came out, the ATA sent thousands of free copies to friends and associates in forestry to distribute as they pleased to schools. The schools responded with requests for hundreds of copies.[14]

But this publicity coup was nothing compared to one that

Charles and the ATA would pull off in 1930. That year, in anticipation of the 1932 celebration of George Washington's bicentennial birthday, Congress appointed a national committee to arrange bicentennial celebrations. According to Charles, this committee asked the ATA to "take charge of the memorial tree planting."[15]

Charles took on the assignment with characteristic energy and enthusiasm. He immediately created the Washington Bicentennial Tree Planting Association, to be run by the ATA. The association's sole purpose was to persuade millions of Americans to plant ten million memorial trees in honor of George Washington. Its slogan, written by Charles, was "If the nation saves the trees the trees will save the nation." Every individual, club, or association financing a bicentennial planting would be entered in the national honor roll of the American Tree Association.[16]

Charles explained to his friend Hugh Baker, then dean of the New York State College of Forestry at Syracuse University (now State University of New York College of Environmental Science and Forestry), that in taking on this project he hoped "to aid the American public in becoming 'forestry minded' and to gain more intelligent supporters for the cause of forestry in general. I hope we will succeed and it looks as if we might."[17]

In fact, Charles's plan succeeded beyond his expectations. His goal had been to see ten million trees planted. By January 1932, the ATA had registered more than fifteen million memorial trees, and would soon register twenty million. In the end, reported totals ranged from over twenty-five to over twenty-seven million; whichever number is correct, either is amazing.[18]

As usual, Charles owed the campaign's success to his own vision and the masterly skills of the ATA's publicity team of Ridsdale and Edwards. "Just see how the International News Service is handling our Washington Tree Planting," Charles wrote to Baker in the winter of 1932.[19]

Indeed, papers across the country were printing Washington memorial tree-planting editorials, cartoons, and features supplied by the ATA, as well as locally written articles reporting on tree-planting efforts closer to home. The *Cincinnati Enquirer*, for instance, reported:

It is . . . planned to spread through Cincinnati's parks generous planting of redbud and flowering dogwood, trees indigenous to this and to no other area, and quite as beautiful in blossom as the much-heralded cherry trees at Washington, which bring an annual pilgrimage.[20]

The response to the efforts of the Washington Bicentennial Tree Planting Association was especially impressive considering the fact that its campaign was going on in the midst of the Great Depression. It was hard for a club or organization to justify spending fifty or one hundred dollars to plant a George Washington bicentennial tree when banks were closing regularly and soup lines were growing by blocks at a time. Yet even city governments supported these expenditures. The news report of Cincinnati's tree planting, for instance, justified what may have seemed an extravagant waste by stating, "The tree planting will be done in part by labor supplied through the Welfare Department, and will, therefore, aid in giving employment to many who need it."[21]

Although Charles originally formed the ATA in order to sell the public on forestry conservation, he soon had the ATA serving forestry professionals as well. He took his first step toward this end in 1924, when he charged the ATA staff with the enormous task of compiling and publishing the first complete forestry reference book, the *Forestry Almanac*. He sold the book for one dollar per copy. Updated and republished periodically, this reference book, which later became the *Forestry Directory*, was a complete guide to forest-related activities and organizations. Published from the 1920s through the 1940s, it served foresters in much the same way as the *World Almanac* serves journalists today.

An equally valuable resource was the Forestry Legislative Survey, conducted and published by the ATA in 1926. The creation of this survey was typical of how Charles tended to take an idea and run with it. The idea originated at the World Forestry Congress in Rome, held in April 1926, where it was suggested that international forestry statistics should be collected. Charles did not attend the conference but sent a representative in his place, his cousin-in-law Frank Baldwin. Baldwin was an editor for *Outlook* magazine, as well as the cousin who lived in Lakewood with whom Gertrude was rumored to have been in love. When Baldwin told Charles about the desire for international forestry statistics, Charles immediately decided to help. Three months later he had compiled and published *The Forestry Legislative Survey*.[22]

The survey brought together in one source, for the first time, all the state forestry legislation that had been passed through June 1, 1926, and featured brief reviews of the legislative situation in every state. Copies were available gratis upon request, but Charles also sent advance copies to forestry professors and foresters of his acquaintance.[23]

"I was delighted with the Forestry Legislative Survey," Henry Schmitz, head of forestry at the University of Minnesota, wrote to Charles. "It condenses into one small volume a wealth of information which has been so scattered in the past that it was hard to lay one's finger on exactly what one wanted. You have rendered another great service to forestry and are to be congratulated."[24]

In 1925 the ATA launched another major contribution to forestry news when it began publishing a monthly forestry newspaper, the *Forestry News Digest*, which ran from August 1925 to January 1939. Subscriptions were free, and Charles claimed that the *Digest*'s average circulation was fifty-five thousand copies per issue. The *Digest* contained a lively mix of personal news, such as a professor's latest promotion, and factual information, such as reports on important forestry conferences. It also featured a state news section that covered everything from who spoke at an annual meeting of the Michigan Conservation Council to a new state forestry law in Idaho.[25]

The *Digest* also promoted the ATA's work. A lead article in the June 1926 issue, for instance, announced, "The Forestry Legislative Survey by States for 1926, prepared by the American Tree Association, is going to press. . . . Professional foresters in both National and State work, as well as private foresters, teachers, and others are awaiting with keen interest the appearance of this publication which contains most useful information."[26]

Such cases of self-promotion aside, the *Digest* filled a niche in the world of forestry, despite the fact that several forestry publications already existed, including the *Journal of Forestry* and *Ameri-*

can Forests and Life. An extension forester for the state of Ohio wrote,

I have been receiving the Forestry News Digest for several years, and I do not know of a better newspaper in the whole field of forestry that presents the forestry news more dynamic, crisp, and active [*sic*] than your publication does.

Not only is it informational to the professional foresters, but the average layman can readily absorb what is being done in the forestry field and apply it practically to his own work.[27]

A lumberman wrote the *Digest* a letter in which he claimed that the publication was "doing forestry and conservation a great deal of good and it is almost a text book in our organization. Several of us read it thoroughly and then spend considerable time discussing it. It is doing a great deal of good."[28]

D. S. Jeffers, dean of the University of Idaho School of Forestry, praised the *Digest's* coverage of a Society of American Foresters meeting in Portland, Oregon:

As one of those who were fortunate enough to be able to attend the meetings, I feel safe in saying that the way in which you handled the meetings should fully satisfy those who were not able to attend. . . .

I feel quite certain you have charted a safe course between the extremists on either side, which is a most difficult task in this generation.

If you are able to maintain the present policy of the middle of the road, present all sides of a controversy, and still give us national forestry news, I have no doubt but what the Digest will continue to be what it has been in the past—a welcome feature throughout the country.[29]

There were, however, foresters who were less than thrilled with the *Digest.* Royal S. Kellogg of the National Lumber Manufacturers Association, for instance, was infuriated by the same article on the Society of American Foresters meeting that the dean of forestry at Idaho had praised. The article featured the headline "Paper by Sherman Starts Word Battle at Society Meeting; Cronemiller and Jewett in Hot Defense of Timber Men." Kellogg complained, "When one reads the article he finds difference of opinion, it is true—But that was what the meeting of the Society, a technical organization, is for. The headline makes it look like a 'free for-all' fight, which it was *not*."[30]

But by stirring up controversy among some foresters, and gaining praise from others, the *Digest* was doing its job. Spreading news and creating discussion are two goals toward which all good newspapers strive.

In addition to serving foresters, the *Digest* became a reliable resource for the general press. In 1936, for instance, Charles reported to his friend Samuel Spring, dean of the New York State College of Forestry at Syracuse University,

The February and March issues of *The Forestry News Digest* have certainly made big hits. We are getting a great many editorials [published in other papers] based on material in those two issues. We recently had a very close inventory made of the number of editorials that appeared in the daily press during the year of 1935 that mentioned our work in some way. Probably nine-tenths of these editorials mentioned *The Forestry News Digest*—the American Tree Association—or Charles Lathrop Pack, and in many places they mentioned the whole three. How many editorials do you suppose have been authenticated? I was surprised—over 10,000 editorials in one year. More editorials than the newspapers have ever published on any subject except politics. You can now rest assured Sam that the American public is really to a considerable extent tree-conscious and forestry-minded. It is [*sic*] taken years of hard work but it looks as if we are really beginning to arrive somewhere.[31]

Thanks in large part to the *Digest*, the American Tree Association became a major clearinghouse of information for professional foresters and state and federal legislators, as well as the editors of the nation's dailies and magazines.

The greatest good the ATA did Charles, however, was to save his reputation among foresters. In creating a national clearinghouse and establishing himself as a master of forest conservation public relations, Charles regained his credibility among professional foresters. The distrust and dislike that had emerged during his last years with the AFA died down and was transformed into respect.

Considering the extreme sense of outrage and anger against Charles in 1921, this was quite an accomplishment, and one of which he must have been proud. It would have been easy for him to justify developing and holding a grudge, indeed a deep hatred, against the seventy-seven foresters who had signed their names to the petition protesting his "undemocratic" leadership of the AFA. Surely he must have especially loathed the men who had written and published the castigating articles and editorials in the *Journal of Forestry*. He could have easily said that he wanted nothing more to do with any of those men. Yet he chose to take what could be called, depending on one's point of view, either the higher moral ground of forgiveness, or the Machiavellian road of ingratiating himself with these men in order to further his own purposes.

However it is characterized, this decision must have been a difficult one, given the depth of Charles's anger. In the midst of the AFA controversy, when he learned about the articles and editorials that H. H. Chapman was putting together for publication in the *Journal of Forestry*, Charles had someone phone the editor of the *Journal*, Raphael Zon, threatening to sue for libel.[32] Although this threat might have contributed to Chapman's decision to suppress the one article in which he charged that Charles held stock in the Buchanan mills, the threat largely failed. The other articles that publicly exposed, humiliated, and embarrassed Charles were still published. Yet now Charles was cultivating his enemies—asking their opinions of his *Digest,* entreating them to send him news items for publication, and continuing to trumpet their cause.

The most bizarre reconciliation came in 1926, when Charles began a nine-year correspondence with Zon, the man who had published the series denouncing Charles and who had worked hand in glove with Chapman in planning and developing that scathing series. Most amazing of all, this correspondence is friendly, chatty, and candid, full of instances of Charles asking Zon's advice and Zon praising Charles.[33]

In the end, it might be said that the foresters who had tried to oust Charles from the AFA became friendly and cooperative with him in an attempt to use him and his resources to their benefit. After all, it happens every day that people are polite to someone they do not like, if there is even a small chance that that person will support a pet project. Given human nature, such a way of thinking probably occurred with many of the foresters Charles was in touch with, at least in the beginning of this period.

Yet years later, it seemed that Charles's true supporters out-weighed his detractors. If these supporters knew of his involve-ment with the Buchanan mills or his Canadian timber invest-ments, they ignored this information. Charles was doing too much good through his American Tree Association for anyone to allow these involvements to become an issue now.

CHAPTER 16

"Dragged into the Vortex": Arthur Pack and His Father's Empire

I N 1922, the same year that Charles started the American Tree Association, he also started the American Nature Association. Articles about Charles imply that the Nature Association was his idea, yet if Arthur's memoirs are correct, Charles launched it solely as a tax-free organization to support a magazine that Arthur and P. S. Ridsdale had dreamed up: *Nature Magazine*. Arthur was associate editor, then president and editor in chief. Ridsdale was managing editor.[1]

At first, Arthur was thrilled to be running his own magazine. "I had a job quite to my liking," he said, "for I could not only do as much writing as I wanted, but also work at the complicated problems of organization and circulation."[2] Nevertheless, he never forgot that the magazine depended not on his writing or managerial skills, but on his father's fortune: "Indeed," Arthur noted in his memoirs, "during the first few years of our project, generous donations by Charles Lathrop Pack rapidly ran up our so-called subscribing memberships to one hundred thousand and for a time we ran neck and neck with *Time Magazine* which was founded the same year."[3]

Since the magazine was circulated free, Arthur never really knew how well it was received. Yet he never considered trying to run the magazine independently. This was the crux of the relationship between Arthur and Charles: Charles's will, direction, and money always dominated Arthur. And Arthur always admired his father and struggled to please him.

"His influence to a most unusual degree shaped my own life," Arthur once recalled. "I tried to escape from it and failed. I know now that had I succeeded, I would have missed much in life." Arthur never said how he tried to escape his father's influence—perhaps he only dreamed of escaping it.[4]

He did have a short vacation from Charles during World War I, when he served as an army ordnance officer in France. But although this experience bolstered his confidence and sense of maturity, it failed to liberate him from Charles.

"On my return from France," Arthur recalled in his unpublished memoir, "From This Seed," "I found myself being dragged into the vortex of my father's irrepressible activity." Almost immediately Arthur went back to work for his father in Charles's Cleveland office. In his eyes, his one hope for independence was in marriage.[5]

After Arthur married Eleanor "Brownie" Brown in December 1919, the couple set off for British Columbia in January 1920 to live in Vancouver, where Arthur served as Charles's buyer of timber rights. Luckily for Arthur, the brown-haired, blue-eyed Brownie, who was noticeably taller than Arthur, loved the outdoors. Although Brownie was a doctor's daughter and had attended the boarding schools of the privileged set, her grandfather had been a farmer and veterinarian, her uncle had run the family farm, and her father was a true outdoor sportsman—a crack shot and avid trout fisherman. Brownie, too, had an adventurous spirit and thrived on camping, hiking, boating—in fact, all manner of outdoor living and exploration. She loved her new life exploring British Columbia forests with her husband.[6]

Although they lived far away, Arthur and Brownie were still close to Charles and Gertrude. "Three thousand miles of the nation's breadth lay between my father and me," Arthur wrote, "but we were 'partners' again."[7]

Arthur and Brownie returned east in October 1920, when it became obvious that the depression that was dragging the British

Columbian economy down was not going to lift in the near future. They bought a house in Princeton, New Jersey, thirty-five miles west of Charles and Gertrude's home in Lakewood. There Arthur fell even more deeply under his father's influence.[8]

"No sooner were we settled in Princeton," Arthur wrote, "than CLP came up with the idea of sending me to Europe to investigate and write articles [for *American Forestry*] about the tree seeds which he had sent as gifts to the various allied nations. He paid all the expenses for my wife and me as we toured nurseries and forests from Southampton to northern Scotland, from the battle-scarred trenches of northern France to the Pyrenees and across the Rhine into Germany."[9]

From this point on, Arthur devoted his life to nature conservation. "Without my realizing it," he later noted, "I was becoming committed to a pattern laid down by Charles Lathrop Pack." The independence he had dreamed of was not to be.[10]

Arthur wrote for *American Forestry* during his father's last two years as AFA president, before conceiving the idea of *Nature Magazine* and suggesting it to his father.

Arthur explained:

Writing articles for *American Forestry* magazine was equivalent to carrying coals to Newcastle. Mr. P. S. Ridsdale and I came up with the idea of a new publication to be called *Nature Magazine* and devoted to wild animals, birds, fish, flowers and all living things, and thus commanding a far larger audience than trees and forests only. It would take a generous supply of capital to launch such a venture, so we set out to sell my father on the proposition. He accepted it with highest enthusiasm and a non-profit corporation was organized under the favorable laws of the District of Columbia. Duly called 'The American Nature Association,' its incorporators and self-perpetuating board of directors comprised just the three persons involved.

These three were Charles, Arthur, and Ridsdale.[11]

Although Arthur believed that he and Ridsdale came up with the idea for *Nature Magazine,* it may have been his father's idea. Since the magazine was everything that Charles and Ridsdale had wanted the AFA's magazine to be, it is possible that Charles arranged for Ridsdale to suggest the idea to Arthur in such a way that Arthur would think it was their own inspiration. Considering how Charles had manipulated Arthur's decision to attend Harvard Business School rather than MIT, such a tactic would not be out of character.

Regardless of their origins, both the American Nature Association and *Nature Magazine* proved to be effective conservation vehicles. Dedicated to "the broad program of stimulating public interest in all forms of nature and to conservation of wild animal life as well as of forests," the Nature Association was a nonprofit organization that operated for thirty-seven years, even surviving the Great Depression. The association was set up so that anyone who subscribed to *Nature Magazine* would automatically become a member. The association used the magazine to further its fight "for the preservation of vanishing species" and the enunciation of conservation principles to the general public. To this end, it hired some of the country's leading conservationists to write for the magazine, including Professor E. Lawrence Palmer of Cornell, who contributed a column on natural science and nature-study teaching, and the wildlife conservationist William Lovell Finley.[12]

Bill Finley was an outstanding conservationist who also became a great influence on Arthur's life. Nineteen years younger than Charles, Finley may have been the first person in America "to approach environmental conservation and wildlife protection with an eye to teaching the general public on such matters." Finley and his wife, Irene, were among the first to make "remarkable still and motion pictures of wild birds and animals." When sound movies came into being, the Finleys' movies were distributed to the nation's schools and released by major motion picture companies to theaters around the country. Under the Finleys' direction, Arthur and Brownie began making nature films as well; soon Arthur, too, had carved out a career for himself on the nature conservation lecture circuit, in addition to writing for *Nature Magazine.*[13]

In 1935 the association began publishing an additional section of *Nature Magazine,* known as *Conservation,* which Arthur edited. The goal of *Conservation* was to show the connection between abuses of natural resources and the welfare of the people as a whole, and to promote the preservation of endangered species.[14]

Although the magazine also backed forestry issues, it was primarily pro-wildlife; for instance, it publicized the plights of the black bear, American antelope, and American eagle, which all faced extinction.[15]

In addition to publishing magazines, the Nature Association lobbied against public littering and to keep billboards and signs off scenic highways, produced the *Nature Almanac,* and created course outlines for nature study and reference material for educators.[16]

Ultimately, the American Nature Association became Arthur's baby, for Charles preferred his forestry work with the American Tree Association. In 1926, Charles resigned as president of the American Nature Association, continuing to serve only as its board chairman. Arthur became president and held that position until 1946, nine years after his father's death, when he became president emeritus. Arthur also stopped writing for the magazine in 1946, but it continued to be published until 1960, when it was absorbed into *Natural History,* a magazine published by the American Museum of Natural History. The American Nature Association was dissolved in 1959.[17]

Arthur's work with *Nature Magazine* offered him the chance to live out one dream, that of being an outdoorsman. No longer tied to an office, he traveled across the country with Brownie and the Finleys, photographing, observing, filming, and writing about all sorts of wildlife. During this time, Arthur and Brownie also produced a family, the grandson Charles had longed for, but who died twelve hours after birth, and two daughters, Eleanor and Margaret. They also adopted a son, Vernon.

Although Arthur was responsible for the Nature Association and its magazine from 1926 to 1946, Charles helped him decide what projects the association should take on. Usually these meetings took place at Lathrop Hall, with father and son ensconced in Charles's study. Charles sometimes urged the association to collaborate with a Tree Association project. During its first years, for instance, the Nature Association collaborated with the Tree Association's campaign to plant trees along highways and at roadside stops.[18]

Now Arthur and Charles were truly partners. Yet although Arthur had long dreamed of this arrangement, he now struggled with a dark side of that dream: "I think I have always envied those who were forced to earn their own living instead of having life served up with a silver spoon as I had," he once observed. "They at least have the satisfaction of struggle and of an occupation so demanding that there is certainly less time and opportunity for introspection. To be sure my venture with [*Nature Magazine*] . . . seemed a good idea. . . . Nevertheless it left a residue of dissatisfaction and restlessness."[19]

Arthur had wrestled with this "residue of dissatisfaction" for eleven years when suddenly he had the perfect chance to become independent. In 1933, the Arthur Packs were well settled in a lovely house in Princeton with a garden that rivaled Charles's Lakewood garden. That year, however, the family physician suggested that Arthur move his family to a drier climate for at least two years to help their daughter Peggy recover from the aftereffects of a bad bout of pneumonia. Arthur immediately moved the family to New Mexico, which he had fallen in love with while filming wildlife there. But this was also an opportunity to break away from Charles by putting nearly two thousand miles between them.[20]

Arthur took his family to a remote, nearly destitute twenty-three-thousand-acre dude ranch, Rancho de los Brujos, or Ghost Ranch, seventeen miles from the tiny rural town of Abiquiu, New Mexico, and some fifty miles north of Santa Fe. There he bought some land from the owner, built his family a new home, and soon after bought the remaining acreage, becoming the "patron" of Ghost Ranch.[21]

Arthur went through many personal changes after moving to New Mexico. Brownie left him for a man twenty years his junior, the archaeologist Frank Hibben; she obtained a divorce, took the two girls, Peggy and Norrie, with her, and left Vernon with Arthur at Ghost Ranch. In 1936, Arthur married Phoebe Finley, the daughter of William and Irene Finley. According to Arthur, Phoebe, fourteen years his junior, had blossomed from a "fat teenager" to an attractive young woman. Arthur and Phoebe had two children, Charles II (born one year after Charles died) and Phoebe. They ran Ghost Ranch as a dude ranch, where the young artist Georgia O'Keeffe lived for many years. She presented Arthur with a skull painting that became the logo for the ranch.[22]

Arthur and Phoebe moved the family to Tucson in 1946 so their children could get a better education than what was offered in Abiquiu and Espanola, the rural towns near Ghost Ranch.[23] In Tucson Arthur, like his father and grandfather before him, became a civic leader. He was an elder of the Presbyterian church and director of the chamber of commerce and many other institutions. He and Phoebe financed a new hospital in Espanola, and they later gave $1.5 million to St. Mary's Hospital in Tucson. In 1952, Arthur was named Tucson's first Man of the Year.[24]

That same year, Arthur financed the Arizona–Sonora Desert Museum near Tucson, an internationally renowned trailside museum still in existence today. In addition to nature displays, it features live animals in their outdoor environment, including a tunnel where subterranean desert animals can be observed going about their business. The remarkable part of the story is that Arthur created this museum as a way to give his friend, the naturalist William Carr, a new start. At that point Carr was at an impasse in his life, working in a bookstore rather than with nature. With Arthur's help, Carr happily planned and directed the Arizona–Sonora Desert Museum until health problems forced him to retire.[25]

In 1959, Arthur and Phoebe, with Carr's help, created the Ghost Ranch Museum, a smaller version of the Arizona–Sonora Desert Museum. They also donated Ghost Ranch land to the Presbyterian church to use as a conference center. Arthur and Phoebe retained a residence at the ranch and spent more and more of their time there, often participating in conferences by acting as unofficial hosts and hostesses to the visitors. Bill Carr lived at Ghost Ranch as well, and Georgia O'Keeffe kept the ranch house Arthur had sold her years before.[26]

Yet despite his having moved so far away from his father, despite all the projects he undertook on his own, Arthur never truly broke away from Charles. It is true that Arthur and Phoebe came up with the idea of the Ghost Ranch Museum and were very proud of it, but Charles's image still reached from the grave. In speaking about the first museum, the Arizona–Sonora Desert Museum, Arthur wrote, "I knew that it had really been Bill Carr, not I, who had conceived the idea of the Desert Museum and directed the work building it. I had merely supplied the money—money which I had not earned myself and the giving of which had required no personal sacrifice. This circumstance must have created what the psychologists call a guilt complex, and therefore led me into other civic enterprises."[27]

This sense of guilt no doubt overshadowed the Ghost Ranch Museum as well, for while this was Arthur and Phoebe's idea, it was still funded by Charles's fortune. Furthermore, its function was clearly an extension of Charles Pack's work: to educate the public about the importance of conservation.

Thus, despite the fact that Charles died years before the creation of Ghost Ranch, he was still dominating Arthur's life. "I lived and worked within the aura of my father's determination to become the greatest conservation leader of his time," Arthur wrote in his memoirs. "My young man's dreams of independence never died entirely, but receded into the background, adapting themselves to the day to day [sic] schedule of work wherein my function was primarily to serve as an extension of the personality and unflagging zeal of Charles Lathrop Pack."[28]

CHAPTER 17

The Charles Lathrop Pack Forestry Trust

I F CHARLES had done nothing more than create the American Tree Association and the American Nature Association, he would still have done more than anyone else to spread the word about forest conservation and convert the general public. He did not stop with this, however. Driven, perhaps, by an insatiable need to be known and loved by the public, or the adrenaline generated by the constant activity of his American Tree Association, or the need to find a tax shelter—or perhaps for all of these reasons—he created yet another organization: the Charles Lathrop Pack Forestry Trust, established in the amount of one million dollars, in 1924, with Arthur Pack as its official administrator.[1]

The history of the Pack Trust has been greatly clouded, since it was often confused with yet another of Charles's organizations, the Charles Lathrop Pack Forestry Foundation, created in 1930.

What documentation there is, however, shows several things: the trust was distinct from the foundation; the trust was created in 1924 and not 1927, as has been erroneously stated by numerous sources; its creation "seemed necessary and advisable on account of certain problems of taxation" that Charles faced; the trust would "secure the perpetuation of" Charles's work in the event of his death; it was to be operated by Arthur Pack, and its main function was to finance "other educational projects with the definite purpose of building up an enlightened forest consciousness on the part of the public." Or, as one description of the trust put it, "The fundamental idea of the Charles Lathrop Pack Forestry Trust is that forest-mindedness must be made to impinge itself upon the American consciousness by boring from within."[2]

To that end, Charles had the trust invest in a variety of conservation projects: demonstration forests, endowed chairs, research fellowships, and essay prizes. Two demonstration forests, one for the University of Washington and one for the New York State College of Forestry, were among the trust's largest contributions to forestry.[3] In addition, the trust gave Harvard a $100,000 grant to be equally matched by others. The resulting $200,000 paid maintenance, salaries, and research for Harvard Forest.[4] The Pack Forestry Trust also gave $5,000 toward the maintenance of Cornell's Arnot Forest.[5]

In addition, the trust established an endowment fund of $325,000 at Yale University for the creation of the Charles Lathrop Pack Forestry Foundation at the Yale School of Forestry. These funds were intended to support the Yale Forest (now known as the Yale-Myers Forest). Today, however, with the forest being self-supporting, the funds pay for a variety of Yale's forestry needs.

Charles also gave Yale ninety-four acres of forest adjacent to Yale's experimental forest, located near Keene, New Hampshire, and funds for a forester whose duties included the management and development of "various species adapted to the region, but especially White Pine."[6]

Demonstration forests show landowners and foresters how scientific forestry is conducted and how the best forestry practices can result in a well-managed forest and a sustained timber yield. In addition, forestry professors and students use the forests to conduct forest research.[7]

Although Charles was credited with being among the first to conceive of demonstration forests, he was not. Harvard Forest, for instance, was established in 1906. What is true, however, is that he invested more than anyone else in establishing demonstration forests and using them to sell the idea of sustained-yield forest management to the public.

Designed as "show windows of forestry," the Charles Lathrop

Pack Demonstration Forests that Charles established at the University of Washington and the New York State College of Forestry were situated along major highways and featured large, attractive signs announcing their existence and welcoming passersby to stop and visit, see forest management at work, and ask questions of forester guides.

The University of Washington's Charles Lathrop Pack Demonstration Forest, established through the Pack Trust in 1925, was the first of these "show windows." Its history and that of Charles's other forestry endowments shed light onto his personality.

The correspondence between Charles and Hugo Winkenwerder, then dean of forestry at the university's College of Forestry reveals Charles as a lively, humorous, slightly pompous, very determined, and hyperactive man. Charles's letters create a picture of a man who seems never to sleep, who at every moment is either gathering together and reading hundreds of wire service news clippings concerning forestry matters or arranging conferences with leading foresters and legislators, soliciting foresters like Winkenwerder to write books or articles to be published by the American Tree Association, or polling leading foresters about their ideas on the latest forestry issues, ranging from whether one federal department should be moved to another to how to increase flood control and flood control awareness.[8]

By this time, his American Tree Association and its *Forestry News Digest*, his American Nature Association and its *Nature Magazine*, and his astounding public-relations machinery had put Charles dead in the center of forestry activity. The end result was that he kept in almost constant touch with every leading forester, forestry professor, and forestry legislator. Through his hundreds of letters to these people, his impressive publicity machine, and his multimillion-dollar fortune, he managed to con, coddle, wheedle, praise, persuade, and otherwise convince the same leading foresters who had once despised him and tried to oust him from the AFA that he was their ally, a man worth knowing and trusting.

The story of how Charles gave a demonstration forest to the University of Washington is typical of how he operated, how he came up with ideas and how he used his contacts to make ideas come to fruition.

Charles had been wondering where to create his first demonstration forest for some time when he discovered that Winkenwerder was trying to establish a demonstration forest for his college. Typically, this discovery came to Charles via his news service: "I was much interested reading in one of the newspapers your idea of demonstration forests," Charles wrote to Winkenwerder, "—what I call window-dressing forests, being exhibitions of forestry along highways where they can be seen by the public and help to educate the public." Then, to explain how he could lay his hands on a West Coast paper and furthermore find the article by Winkenwerder, Charles explained in his inimitable, self-consciously self-deprecating, chatty style, "I take the service from a great many clipping bureaus and try personally to keep in some contact with what is really going on."[9]

By now, Charles was sixty-nine years old, and highly resistant to traveling beyond his usual New York–Washington, D.C.–Lakewood circuit. To get around this problem, Charles sent emissaries such as his field agent Russell T. Edwards, his son Arthur, and P. S. Ridsdale to call on people for him. In addition, he relied on professors or senators to serve as his messengers or advocates and report back to him in conferences at Lathrop Hall or in his Vanderbilt suite in New York.

To research the idea of the Washington demonstration forest, Charles first recruited Nelson Brown, a professor of forestry at the New York State College of Forestry, who was going to the West Coast anyway, to visit Winkenwerder for him. He instructed Brown to persuade Winkenwerder to write a popular book on Pacific Coast forestry, which the American Tree Association would publish, and to tell Winkenwerder more about Charles's interest in establishing a demonstration forest at the University of Washington.

In so doing, Brown would establish whether Charles and "Wink's" ideas about demonstration forests were compatible and report back to Charles on his findings. By this time Charles had given the New York State College of Forestry 964 acres of forest along Cranberry Lake in the western Adirondacks to use as an experimental forest.[10] Brown may have believed that the college would receive a demonstration forest as well if he cooperated with Charles.

After calling on Winkenwerder in the fall of 1925, Brown wrote to Charles assuring him that Charles and Winkenwerder had the same ideas about the value of demonstration forests. Charles wrote immediately to Winkenwerder, practically promising him the forest:

> After this forest is purchased, it should be put into shape to sell forestry. It would not be just a forest to grow timber, but a forest to aid in selling the idea to the public. Something of real educational value. . . . From what [Brown] writes, I should judge that your ideas and ours are practically identical. You will realize the value of selling forestry to the public. I, for some time, have realized that you have in mind to do the very sort of things that we are endeavoring to do. We want to help the foresters. We don't assume to compete with them. We simply want to aid the foresters in selling their goods and help to dignify the profession.[11]

The deal went through a few months later when Charles sent a check for $9,222 for the purchase, maintenance, and development of 334 acres of land near Eatonville, a small town in southern Pierce County, approximately sixty-five miles south of the University of Washington in Seattle.[12]

Two years later, Charles expanded the forest to 2,000 acres. Today, 4,250 acres of Douglas fir, hybrid poplar, old growth, and waterfalls in the foothills of the Cascades, twenty-five miles west of Mount Rainier, make up the magnificent University of Washington Charles Lathrop Pack Demonstration Forest. Located near the Mashel and Nisqually rivers, Pack Forest is a living laboratory for both University of Washington students and professors, whose work largely focuses on different ways to grow the most and best trees.

In addition to developing a variety of sustained-yield management techniques, ranging from new ways to use tree-thinning equipment to the breeding of what could be considered "purebred" types of trees, using outstanding "parent" trees, researchers have done important work in the application of municipal sludge as a remarkably effective tree fertilizer. These developments and others are being applied by professionals in the industry, ranging from the U.S. Forest Service to the Weyerhaeuser Company, as well as private, nonindustrial forest landowners.[13]

The forest is the site of a weather station, an acid-rain gauging station, a seismograph, and research on ozone and other atmospheric discharges. Although it took years to get this forest in shape, it is now so self-sufficient that it provides all but 5 percent of its biennial operating budget of $1.7 million.[14]

If, as he sold Winkenwerder on Charles's idea for a demonstration forest, Nelson Brown had thought that Charles might also give his college one, he was right. In 1927, two years after establishing the Washington demonstration forest, Charles gave the New York State College of Forestry at Syracuse University between two thousand and three thousand acres (reports of the acreage vary) of white pine, beech, birch, hemlock, oak, chestnut, and red cedar. These woods stretched along both sides of what was then the main Albany-Montreal highway, over which thousands of people motored daily, thus giving the public easy access to the demonstration forest.[15]

This Charles Lathrop Pack Demonstration Forest lies between Lake George and the upper Hudson River, with its southern boundary three miles north of the village of Warrensburg. The tract cost the Pack Trust "over $100,000." It included 240 acres of ancient white pine, "purchased at a great cost to prevent its being sold for lumber. It will be preserved as a museum to show what primeval forest looked like when our first settlers came to this country."[16]

The Pack Forest at Warrensburg also established white pine nurseries in which various growing practices were compared and contrasted for their effectiveness. In addition, an ecological reserve area of mixed woods was established, where no cutting was to be done and tree mortality was to be recorded for study and observation.[17]

Nearly five hundred acres of forest land that make up the Pack Forest at Warrensburg had been heavily cut over by timbermen by the time Charles bought it. The soil was believed to have been stripped as well, so that it was impossible "to obtain more than a meager return from the soil."[18]

Charles, however, believed that with proper planning he could bring back the forest. According to one report, "Nothing was done hastily. Crews of technicians surveyed the entire property, making records and classification of species and laying them out on detailed maps. Biologists, ecologists, and foresters, each in his own field, worked out a balance sheet of timber and wildlife resources." Today, thanks to both management of natural reforestation and the planting of trees, the once-barren area is a sea of green, as is the entire two thousand acres of land that make up the forest.[19]

Three-fourths of the forest's area were set aside for the practice of commercial forestry, using the best of forest management and sustained-yield techniques. Students were trained in these methods and taught other skills such as surveying, timber estimating, planting, and thinning. As part of the "show window" feature Charles insisted upon, their work was often conducted where the public could watch.[20]

"What a magnificent gift you have made," Brown wrote to Charles on February 11, 1927. "You are doing a wonderful work for forestry. You are way ahead of the foresters in the profession but their appreciation will roll up as a great cloud and your name will go down in history with much glory and real appreciation. You have already done so much that this seems quite enough. This will bowl them over in magnificent fashion. Many congratulations. You are certainly the Moses who is leading the cause of forestry out of the bulrushes of insignificance and mediocrity. More power and glory to you."[21]

These grand predictions of power and glory were premature, however. The main highways running through the Pack forests at both the University of Washington and the New York State College of Forestry were relocated, cutting back on the public-demonstration possibilities of the forests, since fewer people drove by the main entrances.

Nevertheless, the public did come. Although Yale's Keene Forest had only eleven hundred visitors in a five-year period, of these people many returned, "telling of applying certain practices to their own property." Newspapers covered the work of the two Pack demonstration forests, and both forests became popular centers for field days for private forest owners, where talks were given on particular subjects such as forest taxation; for regional meetings of the Society of American Foresters; and for special classes for such groups as 4-H clubs.[22]

An ongoing benefit of the demonstration forests is their teaching and research possibilities. Here professors train students in forest management fieldwork—tree thinning, planting, scaling, marking, and milling—skills they will need as foresters. Furthermore, the forests are living laboratories for experimenting with the best ways to grow and thin trees, match various trees to various soil types, control pests, or fertilize soils.

While Charles hoped the demonstration forests would convert clear-cutters, in the end, economics had a more powerful influence. As David Smith, professor of forestry at Yale, in charge of Yale's demonstration forests, observed,

These [the forests] were kind of missionary ventures, and I guess I'd have to say that they were somewhat premature. . . . Unfortunately, in the 1930s and up until just after the second World War, the economic climate wasn't really favorable [to forest management]. There was just so much timber [and] it was so cheap that it was very difficult trying to get private owners interested in this kind of thing. Also, the tax situation wasn't favorable . . . until 1944 when . . . [new] legislation was passed.[23]

Harry Burry, a former State University of New York College of Environmental Science and Forestry professor, who worked with private timber companies near the Pack Forest at Warrensburg for fourteen years, concurs. According to Burry, the private timber companies never "cared to emulate the practices of intensive management such as was being done at Pack Forest." When it was profitable to do so, timber companies clear-cut with no thought of leaving seed trees behind.[24]

Beginning in the mid-1940s, however, between new tax laws favoring sustained-yield forest management practices and incentive programs that paid foresters to replant their cutover acreage, the industry began practicing forestry management. Although corporations did not come directly to the demonstration forests to ask for help, foresters trained in sustained-yield management techniques at the Pack forests became industrial foresters and applied the knowledge gained at the demonstration forests. As professional foresters, they also came to the demonstration forests for conferences or technical advice to aid them in their work.[25]

Pack Forest research at Warrensburg has strengthened the basic science of forestry. Professor Svend Heiberg, for instance, found in his studies there that potassium was essential to good forest soil fertility. This discovery formed the cornerstone of knowledge about forest soil fertility requirements that is taken for granted today. Heiberg's successor, Albert Leaf, advanced knowledge of phosphorous and potassium in forest soils, and Edwin White used Heiberg's data on tree growth, now fifty years old, as the control in critical work on the effect of acid rain on tree growth.[26]

Furthermore, Cliff Foster, who managed the forest from its inception to the mid-1950s, developed techniques for cultivating and managing eastern white pine, a species that grows in several areas in the continental U.S. and Canada. Eastern white pine is difficult to grow. Today, the Pack Forest at Warrensburg is the place to learn how to manage and cultivate it. And the primeval eastern white pines that Charles had preserved in the Warrensburg Pack Forest are there to this day.[27]

Despite the fact that Route 9, the major highway that ran past the main entrance to the Pack demonstration forest at Warrensburg, was relocated away from the main entrance, several hundred visitors visit the forest annually to hike, fish, canoe, or learn.[28]

The two Pack forests were the first major gifts given by the Charles Pack Forestry Trust. In establishing these forests, Charles took one of his first steps in personally participating in the reforestation and forest management techniques he had preached—but never practiced in his businesses.

In 1929 the trust made another contribution to forestry when it gave two hundred thousand dollars to the University of Michigan to create the George Willis Pack Forestry Foundation.[29] Charles wanted the George Willis Pack Forestry Foundation "to advance practical forest land management in the broadest sense of the term" as well as make "a profit from wood and wood products,

The Charles Lathrop Pack Forestry Foundation made possible the planting of 200,000 white and Norway pine in Michigan. (Courtesy of the Denver Public Library Western History Collection.)

such as may be produced under silvicultural methods ... [since profit has an] important place in practical forest land management. The silviculture practiced on any given area must, therefore, be such as to eventuate in the profitable marketing of the products derived therefrom."[30]

The income from this foundation was to pay the salary of a George Willis Pack Professor of Forest Land Management at the University of Michigan, whose work would include the replanting of 3,330 acres of cutover and burned forest land in Cheboygan County, which had once been covered, in Charles's words, "with a fine stand of white and Norway pine" and was "now covered with scattering jack, white, and Norway pine and miscellaneous hardwoods." Since this area was "characteristic of millions of acres of similar land in the Lower Peninsula," Charles believed "its restoration to full productivity by planting and improvement cuttings would serve as an excellent example of the possibilities in this direction."[31]

If, in funding this work at the University of Michigan, Charles dreamed of one day undoing the damage his family's industry had wrought, he must have been overjoyed when, in 1937, shortly after his eightieth birthday, he received a letter from George Willis Pack Professor Willett F. Ramsdell. Written on May 7, Charles's birthday, the letter read,

Thanks to the George Willis Pack Forestry Foundation, we are in the midst of planting some 200,000 good old Michigan white and Norway pine, and it means not only a better Michigan for the future, but better than a week of good wages for these hard working young farmers, everyone of whom . . . knows about you and the "Pack Foundation" and sent personal best wishes. . . .

Our policy since we first started "Pack Forestry Work" here in 1930 has been to hire men from nearby farms for part time work, except one or two student assistants during the summer. It has gradually built up a strong feeling of "partnership" and friendly interest in this demonstration forest and [they] are enthusiastic about the success of our plantations. . . .

So you see, Mr. Pack, in how many ways your influence for a better world to live in is spread! As this spring season which carries your birthday unfolds, I wonder just how many trees are being planted, how many people are engaged in constructive conservation work, here and abroad, because of you and your vision? And under the George Willis Pack Forestry Foundation you have the satisfaction of knowing that men will be working and trees growing and forests developing in the Michigan pine woods every May 7th as long as there is a University of Michigan.[32]

Ultimately, Ramsdell planted most of the open land on this 3,330-acre tract in red pine and spent summers developing a timber management plan. Nevertheless, it was decided that the odds were against the tract becoming profitable and that the forest would best be used for research only. Ramsdell used the tract for a fifty-year study of carefully laid out sample plots. Today the tract is being left to grow as nature dictates and is the site of significant ecological research. Thus, Charles's goal of having profitable sustained-yield management was never carried out.[33]

Similarly, plans for the George Willis Pack professors to turn three thousand acres of forest on Sugar Island in St. Mary's River into a demonstration forest and acquire and develop seven thousand acres of virgin hardwood along Beaver Lake never came to be.[34]

One dimension of Charles's plan that did become a reality was that Pack professors would work with both private forest owners and the state and federal governments in developing solid forest management programs. Ramsdell worked as a consultant for private timberland owners, operators, and companies, particularly the Northern Hemlock and Hardwood Manufacturers' Association.[35]

After Ramsdell died in 1951, the Pack professorship was extended to include the study of forest economics. The next Pack professor was Gustav Robinson Gregory, one of only two or three forest economists in the country at the time. George Willis Pack Professor from 1952 to 1983, Gregory was handpicked by Michigan's dean of forestry, Samuel T. Dana, who felt the future of forestry lay not only in the physical properties of forestry, such as how to plant, but in the economics of forestry as well.[36]

Gregory was one of the key developers and promoters of the dollar curve, as opposed to the growth curve, in forestry. In the past, a forester might wait sixty years before cutting a crop of trees. Under Gregory's dollar curve theory, however, this same crop would be thinned several times, with the thinnings sold for pulp, until the forest was producing trees mature enough to be sold for lumber. While this means a smaller lumber output, it gives a more consistent usage and dollar return. Previously, by waiting for the entire forest to mature, timbermen had often lost money—by the time maximum growth had been reached, the market for that type of timber could very well be at a low ebb, making it unprofitable to harvest the timber. Under this dollar curve system of operation, however, Michigan timbermen cut a variety of timber at a variety of stages, thus expanding their economic returns.[37]

Gregory became one the leading forest economists in the world. His *Forest Resource Economics* became the standard forestry economics text and was translated into Chinese in 1985. He was recruited to work overseas several times, including consulting for the Ford Foundation and the United Nation's Food and Agriculture Organization. His research revolutionized numerous foreign industries, including India's teak industry.[38]

Gregory retired in 1983. The new George Willis Pack Professor, Gary W. Fowler, was appointed in the autumn of 1989. He specializes in statistical entomology and management of forest resources.

Six years after the George Willis Pack Professorship was established, the Pack Trust also established the Charles Lathrop Pack Professorship in Wild Land Utilization at the University of Michigan.[39] This was a onetime, three-year position that had as its objective "the development of some means of evaluating the different uses to which wild lands can be put, together with a careful analysis and interpretation of the economic and social factors involved."[40]

The Charles Lathrop Pack Professorship was held briefly by two professors, each of whom left the position to work elsewhere, before it was assumed by Willard S. Bromley. During his tenure Bromley produced numerous reports and studies, including "Trends in Land Use in Northern Michigan," which reported on land in Alpena County that had been heavily logged by Charles and his father. Bromley later had a long and successful career as executive director of the American Pulpwood Association.[41]

The work done by this professorship may have let Charles give back to the Michigan forests some of what he and his father had taken from them.

In addition to giving gifts to the University of Michigan, Charles threw himself into some behind-the-scenes politicking to ensure that the university would devote itself to forestry in the way that he, Charles, thought it should.

In 1926, three years before the George Willis Pack Foundation was established, the University of Michigan transformed its forestry department into a forestry school. Among the candidates for dean of the school was one of the university's own outstanding foresters and forestry professors, Samuel Trask Dana, who had also been a director of the Northeastern Forest Experiment Station, an assistant chief of the U.S. Forest Service Bureau of Research, and land agent forest commissioner of Maine.

Dana was one of the foresters who ousted Charles from the

AFA. But since starting the American Tree Association, Charles had established cordial, even highly productive, relations with almost everyone who had signed the petition against him. Now, Dana was being wooed. Charles agreed with Dana's views on forestry and his opinion of how Michigan's new school of forestry should be run. In his typical style of controlling and encouraging others, Charles campaigned to ensure that Dana would be the university's first dean of forestry, and that, as dean, Dana would have full control of the school in order to build it up. Charles wrote to Dana:

I want to say that I think you are one of the best men in the cause of forestry, and further than that, I do not think that forestry has a better friend; neither have I.

I hope you will have a plain understanding with Dr. Little [Clarence C. Little, University of Michigan president]. He has his troubles, with the Board of Regents. I had last week a good heart to heart talk with a man from Battle Creek, Michigan, who knows the situation. He says "Any high class man who is going to Ann Arbor to assume the head-ship [sic] of the Forestry School should have an ironclad contract."

Of course, you would not think of going there unless you were Dean . . . and reported directly to the President. The present arrangement has been the cause of a great deal of friction and criticism.

Now Sam, if you do go to Michigan, you can just bet we will cooperate with you.

Here are some things I have in mind. I want to get out the *Common Trees of Michigan* and, in fact, have decided to do so and we are at work on the job. If you take the new position, we would want you as Dean to write a little statement to be printed in the new book. We would also like to help you in various ways in connection with your schemes for extension work. It is possible we might go in for a show window in Michigan. . . . There are a good many things that later on we ought to talk about if the real story comes to pass. I think that the State of Michigan needs forestry leadership even worse than the University of Michigan needs a Forester-Dean.[42]

Charles also offered to write to Little on Dana's behalf. If Charles did so, the letter has been lost. One can only speculate on how much Charles influenced Little's decision to make Dana dean, or how much Charles's offer of support had to do with Dana's decision to accept the position.[43]

Charles, however, can take credit for Dana's longevity in this position. In 1929, the New York State College of Forestry tried to woo Dana away to become its dean. Charles immediately intervened. He threatened to withdraw the two hundred thousand dollars for the George Willis Pack Foundation unless Dana stayed at Michigan for several years and the university pledged to Charles that it would support Dana's School of Forestry and Conservation. Dana gloatingly reported to his wife that "the University won't get the money unless I stay."[44]

In the end, Charles got his wish. Dana stayed at Michigan; the School of Forestry and Conservation, later renamed the School of Natural Resources, as well as the George Willis Pack Forestry Foundation and the George Willis Pack Professorship in Wild Land Utilization were established. Thanks in large part to Dana's leadership and Charles's gifts, the University of Michigan's School of Natural Resources became an outstanding school of forestry.

Cornell University was another beneficiary of Charles's influence and the Pack Trust. Charles gave his first gift to Cornell in 1914, when he donated five hundred dollars "to be used in whatever way the Forestry Staff shall see fit." The staff decided to give the interest on this investment to the all-around best senior of each class. In 1924, Charles doubled the gift and the income was used for special departmental needs. That same year, the Pack Forestry Trust established a fund of one thousand dollars for a Charles Lathrop Pack Foundation Forestry Prize. The interest from this fund was awarded annually for the best essay on any forestry topic that, in Charles's words, would "arouse in the public an interest in forestry and an appreciation of what forestry means to the country, and so be of service in furthering the forestry idea." The contest was so selective that sometimes the award was withheld for lack of a first-rate entry. In other cases, however, winning essays were published by independent journals.[45]

Charles also established essay prizes at the New York State College of Forestry, the New York State College of Agriculture at Cornell, Oregon State College, Hanover College, Iowa State College, the Pennsylvania State Forest School, the University of California, the University of Michigan, the University of Washington, Yale

University, and the University of Minnesota. The essays were published in major journals, and the competition is still held today in many of the colleges. The original first prize ranged from fifty to sixty-five dollars. Today it is as high as five hundred dollars.[46]

In 1927, the trust gave Cornell $5,000 for the maintenance of its demonstration forest, the Mathias H. Arnot Forest. In 1928, it created Charles Lathrop Pack Fellowships in Nature Education and Forestry at Cornell. The fellowships were temporary, renewed only if Charles wanted to renew them. The awards ranged from $1,200 to $1,800. In its first year, the program awarded two two-year fellowships of $1,500 each. These were renewed in 1930, but at $1,250 each.[47]

Charles gave his most important gift to Cornell in 1927, when the trust endowed a forest soils chair. This was the first endowed chair in forest soils in any American university. The original $130,000 grant was supplemented by cash grants of $5,000 and $6,500 for research.[48]

Since there were less than a dozen forest soils researchers in the world at the time, the endowed chair was a major contribution to the field. In the United States, it was the first attempt at an in-depth study of the fundamental problems of forest soils.[49] The chemical laboratories necessary for soil research were only available in the agronomy department in the College of Agriculture, which housed chemical laboratories. The Pack Professor of Forest Soils was therefore located in the agronomy department.[50]

Dr. Lars Gunnar Romell held the forest soils chair from 1928 to 1934, when he resigned over a dispute with Charles about the type of research he was doing. Romell was focusing on organic decomposition in forests, but Charles wanted him instead to take on a nursery project which he submitted in detail to Romell. Romell refused, claiming there was already a great deal of research going on in that field and that, further, nursery methods did not have "much to do . . . with forest soils." Charles did not take well to Romell's rejection. "Your father's letter," Romell wrote to Arthur, "is so worded that I prefer not to answer it."[51]

Romell resigned and returned to his native Sweden. The chair was then held successively by soil scientists whose work became renowned: Robert F. Chandler and Earl L. Stone.

As Pack Professor of Forest Soils, Chandler coauthored one of the first books on forest soils, published in 1946. His studies of how the chemistry of trees alters the chemistry of forest soils for better or worse has been helpful in forest management and planning. His work in soil nutrients, especially the importance of nitrogen, resulted in fertilization standards that are now commonly accepted. In addition, he headed the first Forest Soils Society of America. He resigned in 1947 to become president of the University of New Hampshire. He later headed the International Rice Research Institute in the Philippines.[52]

Earl Stone, a graduate student of Chandler's, replaced him as Pack professor. Stone has been called the "most respected forest soil scientist of the past twenty years," a reputation based on a number of key scientific papers. Stone continued the work begun by Chandler regarding the importance of growing trees in the appropriate soil type.[53]

Their research, along with work done by the New York State College of Forestry professor Svend Heiberg at the Warrensburg Pack Forest, revealed the importance of both potassium and magnesium for soil fertility. According to Fred E. Winch, a Cornell professor emeritus, it exorcised "some demons in a sense—here the unknown, this thing that was affecting the trees, we now had an answer for." Fertilization practices that are taken for granted today are grounded in this research.[54]

Stone also studied the best ways to cultivate red, or Norway, pine, which has been used extensively by New York State as its prime reforestation species. This research saved the state thousands of dollars. In addition, soil science research into land use at Cornell's Arnot Forest, and forest management research funded by Charles, "had great impact on present-day land use of the State of New York."[55]

Today, Susan Riha is Pack Professor of Forest Soils. Riha's work includes examining the importance of acid rain in soil acidification processes, the effect of poor drainage on conifer seedlings (much of the forest soil in the northeastern states is poorly drained), the transport of water and nitrogen, and the transformations of nitrogen in forest ecosystems. The nitrogen studies, Riha says, are "aimed toward better management of nitrogen and toward understanding the effects of drought stress on growth and nitrogen uptake by plants."[56]

By funding key areas of forestry research, Charles helped the profession mature more quickly. To this end, in addition to pumping trust money into higher education, in 1926 he cofounded, with the Tropical Plant Research Foundation, of which he was a trustee, a three-year study of tropical forests in countries contiguous to the Caribbean.

This was the first study of these forests, and it is said to be the first time airplanes were used in tropical forest reconnaissance. The survey was directed by Tom Gill, a dashing, handsome young forester who also wrote novels that were made into movies and serialized by magazines, both in the United States and overseas. Gill had been a Yale forester and had worked in the U.S. Forest Service under Gifford Pinchot before becoming the Charles Lathrop Pack Forestry Trust forester.[57]

Through his tropical forest survey Gill mapped many forest areas whose content had been previously unknown. His work also expanded the knowledge of the range of several tropical tree species. The results of the study were published in 1931 as *Tropical Forests of the Caribbean*. The book was purchased by over forty foreign governments and institutions. Gill later became president of the International Society of Tropical Foresters, still in existence today, and a founder and executive director of the International Union of Societies of Foresters.[58]

By 1930, Charles was a central figure in nearly every aspect of forestry. His American Tree Association and American Nature Association were keeping forestry in the public eye. He used these organizations and his own stable of stenographers, sometimes as many as three a day, to help him lobby for or against forestry legislation, depending on the bill in question. In addition, his *Forestry News Digest* put him in the center of professional forestry activity.

Now, through the Pack Forestry Trust, he was the godfather of forest education as well, partially controlling, guiding, and backing a handful of the most promising forestry schools in the country. His demonstration forests strengthened public awareness of forestry, gave students better educations, and served as living research laboratories for educators and professionals. His fellowships furthered education and public relations as well, as did his essay prizes. His research grants created groundbreaking research. It is hard to imagine that Charles could have done anything else for forestry. But he did. He created the Charles Lathrop Pack Forestry Foundation and the Charles Lathrop Pack Forest Education Board, expanding his empire even further.

CHAPTER 18

Expanding the Empire

ERHAPS THE MOST impressive conversion of enemy
to ally among Charles's former detractors was that of Col.
Henry S. Graves, dean of the Yale School of Forestry and
former U.S. Forest Service chief. Graves had been the
third person to sign the petition against Charles when he was running the AFA back in the early 1920s. In fact, as dean of forestry at
Yale Graves was now the boss of H. H. Chapman, who had been
the driving force behind the uprising against Charles.

Nevertheless, Charles gave money to Yale—to further its demonstration forest work. In 1929 the Charles Lathrop Pack Forestry
Trust established a Pack Foundation at Yale to study "eastern and
southern forestry problems relating to small land ownership" as
well as "cooperative endeavors for the utilization of watershed
forests, demonstration forests, and private forests on an economic
basis."[1]

It is possible that Charles bought Graves's approval by giving
money to Yale. It is also possible that Graves was naturally con-
verted. All he had to do was pick up a newspaper to see that
Charles Pack's American Tree Association was getting regular,
daily publicity for forestry. Furthermore, he knew that Charles had
no problem writing checks. Yale had received funds from Charles,
Cornell was regularly receiving his financial backing, and the University of Washington and the New York State College of Forestry
at Syracuse had been blessed with Pack demonstration forests. In
addition, word must have been out that Charles had pressured the

University of Michigan to hire Sam Dana as its first dean, the carrot being Charles's promise of financial aid to the forestry school. In other words, it was clear to anyone involved with forestry that if a project could fill a need in forestry, Charles Pack would probably underwrite it.

As a staunch friend of forestry himself, Graves must have realized that he could do worse than to ally himself with Charles and enlist his aid for projects.

As an educator and professional forester, Graves believed that forestry standards needed raising. According to Tom Gill, "In those days especially, there were very few technically trained foresters . . . and even forestry graduates had not been brought far enough along in much of their technical training. Standards varied widely in the forestry schools and some were very low. Men were being graduated who in no way measured up to professional levels."[2]

Graves knew he could not raise the standards of every forestry school. But in addition to keeping up Yale's standards, he wanted to do something to develop "qualities of administrative and intellectual leadership within that profession." When Charles asked Graves and some other foresters how he could best support forestry, Graves suggested that Charles create both a foundation and an education board. Charles and Arthur immediately welcomed the idea "as a means of furthering their joint endeavors to advance the practical application of forestry throughout the Western Hemisphere."[3]

Thus, Charles created the Charles Lathrop Pack Forest Education Board in 1929. That same year, or a year later, depending on which source one believes, he also founded the Charles Lathrop Pack Forestry Foundation.[4]

Over the years, various statements have been made regarding the purpose of the foundation. According to the bylaws, its purpose was "to promote educational and scientific work in connection with a constructive policy of forest protection and extension, and the increase of appreciation of forests as natural resources as essential to the sound economic future of America."[5]

Yet another statement said its purpose was:

to encourage men who have shown unusual intellectual and personal qualities to obtain training that will best equip them for responsible work, either in the general practice of forestry, in the forest industries, in the teaching of forestry, in forest research, or in the development of public forest policy. It is hoped that the winning of a fellowship under this foundation will be recognized as a distinctive honor, and that the fellowships will stimulate forest students and professional workers of outstanding qualifications and will encourage men of marked ability and aptitude for leadership to enter the profession of forestry.[6]

The foundation's ten-year report states that in addition to training potential leaders in forestry, it hoped that "a body of relevant data might be amassed which in itself would aid the progress of forestry." Nevertheless, immediate results in either of these areas were not expected: "No illusions were entertained that any impressive body of facts would come into immediate existence or that two or three years of specialized training would create a group of professional supermen."[7]

Two clear objectives of the Pack Forest Education Board and the Pack Forestry Foundation emerge out of these three statements: to develop forestry leaders and to conduct excellent forestry research. These were the goals that guided the foundation from 1930 to 1937, while Charles was alive.[8]

In these seven years, the Pack Education Board held annual competitions for forestry fellowships. Applicants presented their résumés and summaries of the studies they wished to undertake. The board advised the foundation as to which applicants were worthy of support, and the foundation wrote the checks.

Although some accounts say that the board's original role was also to propose projects and find people to execute them, the board did not take such an active role until later, after Charles had died.[9]

Although Charles was neither the president of the foundation—Arthur held that post,[10] with Gill as secretary and P. S. Ridsdale as treasurer—nor a member of the Education Board, one can be sure that Arthur acted as his mouthpiece and that no forester received a fellowship without Charles's say-so.

Charles could afford to play a behind-the-scenes role, for his

Education Board was made up of some of the major figures in forestry, ranging from forestry deans to railroad foresters, on whose judgment Charles could rely. The directors of the first board, for instance, included an impressive collection of the country's leading foresters and educators. Graves was chairman (a post he would hold for fourteen years). The other members were Michigan's Samuel T. Dana; Washington's Hugo Winkenwerder; Raphael Zon, director of the Lake States Forest Experiment Station; and Ward Shephard, a former Pack essay prizewinner and a forest inspector for the U.S. Forest Service, who also served as board secretary. Membership changed every three years to ensure that "diverse forestry viewpoints—Federal, state, educational, private and industrial"—were represented. The awards that the directors made were called the Charles Lathrop Pack Forest Education Board Fellowships.[11]

These fellowships differed from the nature education fellowships at Cornell, which the Pack Trust funded in 1928. While the Cornell fellowships were limited to students, the Pack Education Board Fellowships were targeted beyond higher education: any American or Canadian, whether a student or working professional, could apply for a fellowship in any area of forestry or nature conservation. The board cautioned, however, that it preferred people with college degrees.[12]

Fellowships originally ranged from five hundred to twenty-five hundred dollars, although the board could authorize higher sums in special cases. During the Depression, however, the amounts decreased. In 1930 the limit was set at eighteen hundred rather than twenty-five hundred dollars, and in 1935 the ceiling dropped again, this time to fifteen hundred dollars.[13]

Fellows were expected to work full time and exclusively on their projects. From 1930 to 1937, thirty-seven fellowships were granted in general forestry, farm forestry, fire protection, aviation in forestry, industrial forestry, forestry entomology, forest pathology, forest ecology and soils, forest economics, wildlife, and wood technology. In selecting the recipients of these fellowships, it was conceded that "mistakes were inevitable" and that the results of some fellows' studies might be "unsatisfactory."[14]

By 1940, however, eleven of the thirty-seven Pack fellows had achieved leadership positions, including R. F. Taylor, who progressed from assistant forester in the U.S. Forest Service to senior silviculturist; W. W. Wagener, a consulting pathologist for the U.S. Forest Service who became senior pathologist at the U.S. Department of Agriculture; Bernard Frank, a graduate student in land economics who became principal forester for the U.S. Department of Agriculture Review Board for Flood Control; and A. J. Bailey, who graduated from the University of Washington College of Forestry and later became director of Lignin and Cellulose Research at that same university.[15]

Furthermore, as was pointed out in the ten-year report on the Pack Foundation, of eleven major articles in the October 1940 issue of the *Journal of Forestry*, "three were written by former Pack Forest Education Board fellows, one book review was written by a fourth, and the work of a fifth was the subject of another review. . . . Pack Fellows are increasingly seen in publications; they take their place on the roster of various professional societies; they are holding key positions in government and industry."[16]

The Pack fellows conducted an impressive number of acclaimed studies. One of the first, R. H. Rogers, studied farm woodland management near Cooperstown, New York, "with the objective of working out a plan of centralized management and marketing for the area." This plan was so successful that the Northeastern Forest Experiment Station used it to incorporate a cooperative association of woodland owners. The cooperative allowed the experiment station to use its woods for research into woodland management and marketing of forest products in return for technical assistance and advice.[17]

H. R. Hay used his fellowship to study and develop commercial applications for pentachlorophenol and its sodium salt. Hay was the first person to find semicommercial applications for these chemicals. Today they have found wide markets as wood preservatives, sap-stain preventatives, and control chemicals for pulp mill slime, among other applications.[18]

Another Pack fellow, G. S. Andrews, developed an inexpensive version of an aerial measurement tool and further evolved a method of calculating tree heights from aerial photos, both of which developments contributed to the science of air surveys.[19]

The Forest Education Board also funded a study to develop practical selective logging methods adaptable to various regions. The Pack Foundation then funded the publication of the findings, which were put into effect by one of the largest lumber and paper companies in the Pacific Coast region, and adapted by other groups both on the Pacific Coast and in the northern Rockies. The board and foundation backed similar studies in other regions.[20]

Charles wanted the fellowships to develop leadership in the field of forestry; the method of achieving this goal changed considerably in 1937, when Charles died and Arthur had become vice president of the foundation and Randolph president. That year, under Randolph's leadership, the foundation stopped its annual funding of individual fellowships, although it would "consider such applications as might be submitted from time to time." Instead, it chose to fund research into areas of forestry that the board felt were "most in need of strengthening through active leadership."[21]

Under this new policy, the Forest Education Board was renamed the Advisory Board. The board was responsible for deciding what studies should be done and recruiting top people to carry them out.[22] These researchers were also called Pack fellows, but under the new plan they worked directly for the Pack Foundation. Furthermore, fellows were not required to hold a university degree. They could qualify for a fellowship on the basis of their field experience.[23]

Under this program, from 1937 until 1957, the foundation sponsored an impressive series of major forestry studies in "every important forest region" and "virtually every field of forestry" in the United States and abroad. Fellowships lasted anywhere from several months to several years.

One study focused on Charles's former logging empire—the Lake States region—and created a system "embodying a compromise between destructive liquidation and sustained yield" for forests where sustained-yield cutting techniques would otherwise be impractical. According to one report, this system attracted a great deal of attention.[24]

In 1937 the foundation launched a three-year study of possible commercial applications of sustained-yield principles in the Pacific Northwest. The preliminary report alone, which detailed problems facing private forestry in that region, received widespread editorial comment from Pacific Coast papers, was discussed in the *Journal of Forestry,* and was included as text material for forest economics courses. The final report, "Management Possibilities of Douglas Fir Forests," was welcomed by practitioners.[25]

The foundation also initiated and funded a study of how owners of small sawmills obstructed forest management efforts in the South. This led to a three-year study on how to improve the relationship of these sawmill owners to forest conservation.

Another venture involved the foundation and the Society of American Foresters conducting a joint survey of state forestry administration in order to "define and establish standards necessary for the efficient administration of the forest resources within a state." The foundation also studied the limitations and possibilities of the forest farm, the results of which helped guide forest farmers.[26] In addition, it published other scientific and educational forestry studies as well as its own.[27]

It is important to note that the foundation's most prolific and productive period came about not through Charles, its energetic and visionary founder, or Arthur, its first president and Charles's alter ego. This leadership came from Randolph, who, before becoming foundation president, had shown little interest in forest conservation.

Although there is no record of Randolph's feelings for his father, his daughter Virginia recalls that although Randolph was proud of Charles, he nevertheless often resorted to "the filial put-downs of a son who, to bolster his own ego, jokes about his dad's foibles and idiosyncrasies."[28] Perhaps this was because Randolph, like Arthur, may have felt overshadowed by Charles in some way.

Whatever the case, one thing is clear: although Randolph became a vice president of the American Nature Association in 1923, there is no evidence that he was ever excited by his father's conservation work until he headed the Pack Foundation, after his father's death. One wonders if this enthusiasm came about because Randolph was now free of his father's shadow and psychically ready to be his own man. If so, this was a strange twist of fate, since Arthur, who labored a lifetime to so free himself, never succeeded in doing so.

Randolph may have become president of the foundation at this time simply because Arthur, its first president, lived in the Southwest. As an easterner, Randolph could easily meet with other foundation members and attend to business. But it is also possible that Randolph headed the foundation because he truly wanted to do so. He had developed a deep interest in world politics and economics. Through the foundation, he could launch forest management projects that would affect economics and politics in Asia and South America.

Randolph's devotion to international work was intense. He became a founder of the Mexican Institute of Renewable Natural Resources, which the foundation helped support. Ultimately, the institute became a central conservation organization for all of Mexico.[29] In addition, under Randolph the foundation helped create the United Nations Food and Agriculture Organization. Randolph's daughter Virginia says that he was more enthusiastic about his FAO work than about any other undertaking.[30]

Randolph had the foundation help the Department of Defense prepare a forest law for Japan, which that country put into effect. The foundation also helped the State Department formulate a forestry policy for Formosa. According to one report, Randolph supported this work because he believed that "effort expended in behalf of foreign forestry would create both good will and future markets for America in years to come."[31]

It is doubtful that Randolph could have accomplished so much for international forestry without the help of Tom Gill. Gill, the forester for the Pack Trust, was also the foundation's forester since its inception. Beginning with his tropical forest research, which had been cofunded by the trust, Gill carved out a reputation as a leading international tropical forester. He is credited with being the driving force behind the Mexican Institute of Renewable Natural Resources, which promoted integrated multiple-use land management in Mexico, and helped create a regional center for forestry education in Venezuela.[32]

Through the Pack Foundation, Gill became an international troubleshooter. According to James B. Craig in 1960, "When the Philippine people recently wanted somebody to 'really lay it on the line' to them for the mismanagement of their resources, they called on Gill to give them the business. Gill did so, minced no words about it, and the grateful Filipinos heaped praise upon him for giving them a badly needed shaking up." Ultimately, Gill helped formulate forestry policy for the Philippines, Formosa, and Japan.[33]

Gill is also credited with cofounding both the forestry division of the United Nations and the International Society of Tropical Foresters, of which he was the first president. In addition, he was the American delegate to the United Nations Commission for Food and Agriculture in 1947 and 1955, and an American delegate to the Third World Forestry Congress in Helsinki in 1949. He was chairman of the FAO Committee on Unexploited Forests, chairman of the American delegation at the Conference on Land Utilization in Singapore in 1951, and a member of the Far East For-estry Commission in 1952. He headed the U.S. contingent at the Fourth World Forestry Congress in India in 1954.[34] Randolph and the Pack Foundation made much of Gill's work possible.

Randolph Pack received many honors for his forestry work: Mexico made him an honorary member of the Mexican Society for the Protection of Nature, and in 1945 he became an honorary member of the Society of American Foresters, an honor shared at that time by only three living Americans, including Franklin Delano Roosevelt. He was also a director of the Northeastern Forestry Foundation, an honorary vice president and director of the American Forestry Association, and a member of the Boy Scouts National Conservation Committee. He helped organize and was a member of the American Citizens Committee for the United Nations Scientific Conference on Conservation and Utilization of Resources. In 1953, Randolph received an honorary degree from the University of Michigan in recognition of his conservation and land management work.[35]

By the time Randolph became president of the foundation he and Georgia had divorced; Georgia had retained custody of their two daughters. Randolph later married Maxine Wells of San Antonio and moved to Darien, Connecticut, where he and Maxine raised two daughters of their own.

Like his father, Randolph was an indefatigable talker who possessed a lightning ability to seize on ideas, develop them, and put them into effect.[36] An anonymous writer once said of him, "He tried always to find your point of view, he rejoiced in your successes, and he was sympathy itself when things went bad. There was about him a bigness in admitting his own errors, and a complete willingness to readjust his plans."[37]

Randolph died in 1956, at the age of sixty-six, after suffering for several months from a brain tumor. Following Randolph's death Arthur again became the foundation's president and spent the bulk of the foundation's endowment on a watershed development project in the Southwest. This project lasted three years. When it ended, so did the Pack Foundation.[38]

The Pack Foundation derived most of its funds from the Charles Lathrop Pack Forestry Trust. If the foundation was funded by the trust, why did Charles bother to even incorporate the foundation? Surely he could have simply carried out the same projects through the trust he had originally formed. The reason seems to lie in a description of the foundation, which states that it was exempt from the payment of federal income tax and District of Columbia sales tax.[39]

In addition to initiating and funding its own projects, the Pack Foundation maintained projects started under the Pack Trust, such as the demonstration forests. This created major historical confusion over which organization was started when and which funded what projects.[40]

This confusion was further complicated by the fact that the foundation worked with the trust on at least one project, the 1931 publication of Gill's tropical forest research study, which had been cofunded by the Pack Trust.[41] The foundation was credited with initiating and funding that study, despite the fact that it had been conducted three years before the foundation was incorporated. It is clear, however, that the foundation did fund projects started by the trust and may have replaced the trust, since the trust did not fund any projects after 1930, the year of the foundation's incorporation.[42]

To date there has not been another foundation quite like the Charles Lathrop Pack Forestry Foundation. As Gill once pointed out, the foundation was unique in that it could underwrite virtually any forestry project, unlike a university fellowship program, which must work within certain strictures. Thus the foundation's Education Board was able to respond to an unusual forestry research proposal, for instance, by saying: "This proposal may not fit into any existing pattern, but the man himself gives great promise. So let's give him some money." Gill explained, "We didn't care what school he went to, or even what country, provided [we were able to give him] the right kind of training."[43]

Furthermore, the foundation had the money and flexibility to meet immediate needs, such as when it published twenty thousand reprint copies of the *Third Report to Governments by the United Nations Interim Commission on Food and Agriculture*. This report had originally been published by the government, in a limited edition of three hundred copies. One day the Forest Service chief complained to Gill, "What in God's name can we do with a hundred copies? We need thousands." Immediately Gill asked Randolph to have the foundation print twenty thousand copies, which he did. "Otherwise," Gill pointed out, "this publication, the result of almost two years of work by a number of the world's leading foresters, would have had no distribution at all. It would have been practically buried."[44]

The one financial record that still exists regarding Charles Pack's forestry philanthropy shows that between supporting the work of the Pack Foundation, the Pack Trust, and the American Tree Association, he spent $2.8 million on forestry conservation. This is a low figure, however, for it does not include, and there is no record of, money issued by the American Nature Association as donations to conservation causes, the expenses incurred by Charles in running the Nature and Tree associations, or the total cost of publishing *Nature Magazine* or the *Forestry News Digest*.[45]

Considering that the figures for the trust, the foundation, and some of the Tree Association expenses total nearly $3 million, that

Charles must have spent in excess of that amount in paying employees and issuing his publications, and that he left $1.6 million in his will, his total fortune must have been at least $4.6 million. Having produced the bulk of his wealth from the American and Canadian forests, he was now reinvesting his profits in the salvation of American forests and forestry.

CHAPTER 19

Patriot Pack

S OME OF CHARLES'S descendants have the impression
that he was nonpolitical—that hehad no interest in running for office himself, and preferred to get things done
behind the scenes. It is true that he never ran for office. It
is far from true, however, that he was nonpolitical. He was in
touch with politicians throughout his career as a conservationist
and repeatedly tried to influence them. In the spring of 1928, for
instance, Charles wrote to Winkenwerder, "I entertained Governor
W. I. Nolan of the Minnesota Reforestation Commission at the
Vanderbilt Hotel in New York. We also had present various
foresters and economists to help answer their questions. They
seemed very much pleased."[1]

Charles was also involved in politics that went beyond conservation. World War I mobilized him as an active patriot concerned
with international peace. In 1915, he cofounded the World Court
League, which lobbied for the formation of a world court to settle
international disputes peaceably. Following British statesman Lord
Robert Cecil's 1916 proposal for a league of nations, however, the
World Court League quickly took up this cause as well,[1] with an
eye to establishing the court within the proposed league of nations. The World Court League's dreams were realized with the
establishment of the League of Nations in 1920, and the creation of
its World Court at The Hague in 1921.

The court was known as the Permanent Court of International
Justice until 1945, when it became the International Court of Jus-

tice. It is commonly referred to as the World Court, however. Composed of fifteen justices who serve terms of nine years, the court has little actual power, since it has no compulsory jurisdiction; rather, disputing international parties must voluntarily agree to submit their grievances to it and abide by its decision. Nevertheless, the court's power has grown; over the years hundreds of treaties have conferred "obligatory jurisdiction" on it and have referred disputes to it.[2]

Charles and his friends first drew national attention to the idea of a world court in May 1915 when the World Court League staged a World Court Congress in Cleveland. The congress was a national meeting in which the concept of the World Court League and its World Court were presented by such prominent speakers as former president William Howard Taft.[3]

The congress ran for three days, from May 12 through May 14, in Gray's Armory. The ideas for international peace espoused at the congress warranted daily coverage by the *New York Times*, and on May 13, 1,000 people attended a luncheon held in the Statler Hotel ballroom for the 250 honored delegates. Among the 100 members of the World Court League's general committee were Taft, Andrew Carnegie, and Alexander Graham Bell.[4]

Over the next several months, various state branches of the World Court League were established, and in December 1915 the charter of the league was issued by New York's secretary of state and the constitution was adopted. Officers were also elected, and Charles, already a director, became a vice president. His friend John Hays Hammond was elected president; Taft became honorary president.[5]

Two years later, Charles succeeded Hammond as president. Charles headed the league until February 1919 when he resigned, stating that he could not give the league the "virile" leadership it deserved. His reason for resigning was that he was overextended in his commitments: in addition to running the AFA and the National War Garden Commission, he was chairman of the Committee on French Agriculture of the American Society for Devastated France ("This work seems to be logical and I feel that I am really called to do it," he wrote). For his efforts on behalf of its country, the French government in 1919 awarded him the grand medal of honor of the Société National d'Acclimation and Le Mérite Agricole.[6]

Following the war, Charles continued his international political work when he sent millions of tree seeds to Europe to help reforest the Allied countries. In the aftermath of war, the rebuilding of cities is of primary importance. Yet forests, too, are devastated. As Henry S. Graves pointed out, during wartime forests make "natural positions for defensive works" and thus "become objectives for attack and come under heavy shell fire. Under such conditions they are utterly demolished."[7]

During World War I, the introduction of modern war weapons, combined with the long duration of the fighting, created major forest devastation. Artillery fire and cannon pounding throughout the long battle of Verdun, for example, reduced this once-verdant area to a barren and scarred landscape resembling the surface of a dead planet. In addition, forests were cut to make railroad ties, wagons, trench bracings, and temporary buildings. As Graves, who served as director of military logging operations in France, pointed out, "Cutting for war needs is [done] under great pressure and the woods operations can not be conducted as well as in peace times; often destructive methods of logging are employed."[8]

Charles was credited with leading the movement to reforest the Allied countries of Great Britain, France, Italy, and Belgium with American tree seeds. As AFA president, he arranged for the gathering and shipping of tens of millions of seeds that were sent to the Allies in January 1920. He also personally donated millions of tree seeds to the Allies in 1921, 1922, and 1923, for which he was awarded the Order of the Crown of Italy in 1924.[9]

The idea to help reforest the Allied countries came not from Charles, but from Graves, who in addition to being chief forester for the U.S. Forest Service was an AFA vice president and director when Charles was AFA president. Evidence that the reforestation plan came from Graves is found in an article in which he predicted,

After the war France ... must rebuild her forests. This will involve in many cases extensive seeding and planting, followed by careful protection and intelligent tending. Often times this will require annual outlays of money with material returns long deferred. The United States, joining France and her Allies in the fighting, will have required and used large quantities of materials from the French forests. The depletion of these resources in which, under the pressure of war, we have had to participate, presents to every American who appreciates the great sacrifices of France in this war a powerful appeal to ... contribute in some practical way to the rehabilitation of the French forests.[10]

Furthermore, a letter written to Graves in January 1919 by T. S. Woolsey, Jr., an American major stationed in Paris with the Comité Interallié des Bois de Guerre, indicates that it was Graves who first presented this proposal to the French government: "The principal species requested," Woolsey told Graves, "are Douglas Fir, 3000 kilograms & eastern white pine, 3000 kilograms." Woolsey added, "The French are counting on receiving this seed in time for spring sowing in 1920. They very much appreciate your cooperation in suggesting such a gift."[11]

The first seeds were collected by the AFA under Charles's leadership, paid for through an AFA European Reforestation Fund, and sent to a Boston nursery that tested and shipped them. Few of the seeds were white pine or Douglas fir, however, owing to a scarcity of these seeds.[12] Since Charles was AFA president, he was credited with leading this reforestation movement, probably to the chagrin of Graves.

Charles also threw himself into war activities unrelated to forestry. These ranged from creating his National War Garden Commission to dragging his son Arthur around the state of New Jersey to help sell the last issue of Liberty Bonds.[13]

He was an inveterate Republican campaign worker as well. In 1916, he and Arthur campaigned for the presidential defeat of Woodrow Wilson by Charles Evans Hughes. As Arthur put it later, Charles Lathrop Pack and his friends were "working openly for what they believed was a return to the principles which had made America great."[14]

Arthur noted in his diary on November 2, 1916, "Father has sent out all sorts of literature. He sent 100 or so posters here [to Charles's Cleveland office] which I today took around to Republican headquarters."[15]

On November 6, Charles also mailed a promotional piece, apparently composed by himself, celebrating what looked to be a Hughes victory. The title of this ditty was "Hughes Who!" and it went like this:

1.
Who leads all in the nation's news?
Who wins the fight without a bruise?
Who saw thru every clever ruse?
Who threw over the pirate crews?
Who? Why Hughes!

2.
Who gives the laboring man his dues?
Who, firm, fearless, fills Lincoln's shoes?
Who will not shirk when trouble brews?
Who, then, pray, did the voters choose?
Who? Why Hughes![16]

The reader may wonder whether Charles had lost his mind, for Hughes actually lost this election. While at first he seemed to have won by a landslide, when the western vote came in five days later, it was clear that Wilson was the victor.

In 1920, Charles again became involved in the presidential campaign. This time he suggested to the Republican National Committee that it make Charles's friend Stanley Washburn, the former war correspondent and Russian military and diplomatic aide who now lived in Lakewood, one of its main speakers for the Republican campaign. The committee soon put Washburn on the road.[17]

At first, the leading Republican candidate was Teddy Roosevelt's friend General Leonard Wood. Wood was someone whom both Washburn and Charles could back with a clear conscience. Their expectations that Wood would receive the nomination were defeated, however, when the Ohio lobbyist and political man- ipulator Harry M. Daugherty successfully lobbied to have Warren G. Harding nominated instead. Stunned by this turn of events, Charles sent Washburn a wire stating that he and his friends, including Myron T. Herrick and John Hays Hammond, thought Harding's nomination meant "certain defeat" of the Republican party in the presidential race. Two hours later, Charles and his cousin-in-law Frank Baldwin followed this telegram with another: "Only chance to win is to nominate Hoover for vice president."[18]

These fears proved false—Calvin Coolidge, not Hoover, was the vice-presidential candidate, and the Harding-Coolidge team won by a landslide. Despite his doubts, Charles backed this Republican team throughout the campaign by supporting Washburn's speaking tour.

Washburn's speeches on behalf of Harding and Coolidge were covered regularly in the daily press, thanks to Charles's formidable publicity team of P. S. Ridsdale and Russell T. Edwards. Ridsdale and Edwards also operated as publicists for the Republicans through a newsletter, the *National Welfare Union*. The *Union* was located in Washington, D.C., and its contributing editors were Charles, Hammond, Washburn, and Florence King, president of the National Women's Association of Commerce.[19]

In addition to swamping editors with material about Washburn's speeches, Charles arranged for a special publicity prop, the "Harding and Coolidge Flying Squadron of New Jersey," which operated under the auspices of the Republican National Committee and was affiliated with the "Harding & Coolidge Division of Clubs." The Flying Squadron consisted of a calliope followed by a flivver (an airplane body) mounted on a truck, accompanied by a bugler and "an excellent staff of speakers detailed by the Republican National Committee for this purpose."[20]

Apparently the Flying Squadron was designed to attract enough visual attention and noise to draw large crowds to hear the speakers.[21] Indeed, the sight of the flivver and calliope and the sound of the bugler seemed to pull impressive crowds. In one telegraphic report, Charles wired:

The Harding and Coolidge Flying Squadron of New Jersey closes the first week of its campaign with two meetings at Atlantic City tonight. In the last week we have held twenty-six meetings and our speakers have addressed approximately twenty thousand people, distributed fifty thousand pieces of literature and nearly ten thousand buttons. We expect to hold forty meetings within the coming week and our speakers will address at least fifty thousand people. We believe this is the most effective way to campaign wherever there is apathy or indifference in getting out the vote.[22]

Charles and Washburn were such close friends that Washburn once told Charles, "I would rather die in my tracks than fail to live up to your expectations." Charles later backed Washburn as a Republican candidate for Congress by making one of his own staff, William H. Savage, Washburn's campaign manager. Washburn was also backed by such diverse personages as the American diplomat and statesman Elihu Root, whom he had served as a diplomatic aide in Russia, and the former prominent socialist John Spargo. Nevertheless, Washburn lost his 1924 bid for Congress and lost again in 1932, despite Charles's backing.[23]

In 1924 Charles and Washburn again backed Coolidge. There is no record of Charles being directly involved with the Coolidge administration on any level after Coolidge became president.

In 1928, Charles became a presidential elector for Herbert Hoover.[24] Once Hoover was elected, Charles urged him to jump on the forest bandwagon. In 1929, he sent Hoover a memorandum, a "National Program for Forestry," that he had personally drawn up. The four-page paper presented a broad overview of the problems facing forestry and a detailed list of the solutions that had been tried to date—and their weaknesses. This was accompanied by a five-point forestry program created by Charles.

Charles wrote in the covering letter,

One of the most important economic problems requiring solution at an early date is that of forestry. It is essential that, before it is too late, adequate measures shall be adopted to enable this country to provide forest crops for future generations.

Having given many years' study—as a private citizen and as an official of forestry organizations—to this problem, I am taking the liberty of submitting herewith, for your consideration, suggestions for a National Program for Forestry.

It is based upon the plan of a commission, to be appointed by you, inquiring into major forestry problems and formulating definite recommendations looking toward a solution of them; and also upon a plan for furthering such existing necessities as fire protection, acquisition of land for demonstration forests, and for protection of watersheds, and for the planting of forest lands now idle and unproductive.

I hope to be in Washington in October and shall be glad to furnish you with information in addition to that summarized in the accompanying suggested plan, if you so desire.[25]

How presumptuous was Charles being when he tried to advise the president? Was he simply being incredibly naive and egotistical, or did he have an inside line to the president? There is no documentation indicating that Charles and Hoover had a personal relationship, but a 1932 letter to Hoover's secretary, Walter Newton, indicates that Charles had an inside line to Newton. In this rather chatty letter, Charles tells Newton of the progress of Stanley Washburn's congressional campaign, discusses the pros and cons of Prohibition—which he felt had backfired—and ends the letter on a personal note, saying, "You can tell me a lot of things, and I wish you could sit down and talk to me."[26]

Newton's answer, "Sometime after the conventions, I shall be glad if you will call, when we can talk matters over as you suggest," indicates that the two were on good terms and were probably friendly acquaintances if not actual friends.[27] But Newton did not—or could not—help Charles in his efforts to influence Hoover.

Hoover wrote to thank Charles for his forestry plan, but did nothing with it.[28] Nevertheless, Charles and other conservationists continued to try to get Hoover to come out as a conservationist, with only mild success.

In the fall of 1930, when an overproduction of lumber threatened the industry, Hoover responded to pressure from lumbermen and foresters to appoint a commission to investigate the industry and make recommendations for its improvement and stabilization. The resultant Timber Conservation Board was a privately funded commission of thirteen men, including the secretaries of commerce, agriculture, and the interior, and prominent lumbermen and foresters, including Charles. Charles helped finance the commission but was no doubt frustrated, despite claims to the contrary, by the futility of the commission's work: by the time the Timber Board presented Hoover with its recommendations in July

1932, Hoover was wholly involved in the upcoming campaign and ignored the report.[29]

That Hoover paid little attention to the recommendations is understandable. By that time he was trying to salvage an economy that was deep into the Great Depression. By July 1932, when the recommendations were made, the Depression had hit rock bottom and there were just four months to go before the presidential election.[30]

The 1932 Democratic nominee for president was the governor of New York, Franklin Delano Roosevelt, whom the Packs viewed as a "dangerous demagogue."[31]

With his vast and diversely invested fortune still intact, Charles was true to his Republican loyalties. He despised Roosevelt and continued to back Hoover despite the evidence that Hoover had lost control of the country and its economy. Charles realized, however, that given the desperate economic situation, others might not maintain party loyalties.[32]

In an effort to help Hoover win the 1932 presidential campaign, Charles again urged him to jump on the forestry conservation bandwagon, thinking this would, at least, gain Hoover thousands of votes among the special-interest group of foresters and conservationists. Charles hounded Hoover to take up this cause in the summer of 1932—shortly after FDR proposed that as president he could put a million men to work through a national reforestation program.[33]

Immediately after Roosevelt's announcement, Charles and Arthur began attacking his idea on the grounds that it would hurt the forests rather than help them. As dedicated Republicans, Charles and Arthur also opposed the plan simply because FDR was a Democrat whom they believed had dangerous leftist leanings. They launched their opposition by circulating a memorandum charging that FDR's plan was a dangerous "unemployment panacea" that would hurt the forest conservation cause by having unskilled workers do work that only trained foresters should do. They sent the memorandum to professional foresters around the country, with a cover letter asking for their opinions. Responses were mixed, ranging from a hearty "Amen!"

in favor of Charles's viewpoint to unequivocal support of FDR's proposal.[34]

Next Charles launched a nationwide survey of professional foresters to find out what tasks they believed unskilled workers could undertake, how many workers would be needed, and how long it would take to complete the work.[35]

Charles also wrote two short essays, "Forestry as an Unemployment Measure" and "Doctoring a Sick Nation Destructive Cants or Constructive Cures [sic]".[36] He sent these to Hoover on July 20 via Hoover's secretary. In his cover letter to Newton, Charles wrote, "I have been thinking out a plan that could be well adapted by Republicans. It would really steal Roosevelt's thunder, in my judgment. I believe it to be economically and socially sound."[37]

He assured Newton that he would be happy to come to Washington to discuss the plan and that he, Charles, had extensive publicity outlets to promote it.

This was followed by a letter to Newton from Stanley Washburn, in which Washburn enthusiastically endorsed the plan and Charles, whom he wrongly credited with starting the forest conservation movement.[38]

"Mr. Charles L. Pack of Lakewood whom you recall as the Father of the Reforestry movement and the most important man in the forestry [sic] and of the War Garden movement in the war, in the United States ... [wrote] a memorium on help for the unemployed thru reforestation. I am enclosing for your information a copy of the same memorium."[39]

Washburn then gave Charles his personal endorsement.

I am entirely familiar with Mr. Pack's methods, and his great capacity for giving publicity to his projects. He has a Washington office where he employs even in these hard times nearly sixty employees. I think I can safely and without fear of contradiction say, that within three months he can reach more than a million voters thru his publicity campaign if the President will make some definite, categorical statement in regard to the plan which Mr. Pack advocates.[40]

Urging Newton to allow Charles to present his idea personally, Washburn warned that "Roosevelt is preparing constructive plans on this subject and we should not let him get away with anything.

A statement by the President on this subject if it is definite will be used by Mr. Pack and given the widest possible circulation and directly and indirectly reach more newspapers and individuals than any publicity bureau that I know of . . . [for] he has an extra-ordinary [sic] competent staff which at times runs up to as high as 150 to 200 men and women handling the mail which comes in on these subjects."[41]

Newton thought enough of Charles's ideas to send the plan to Secretary of Agriculture Arthur M. Hyde. Hyde's response was mixed. "I suppose Pack and all other professional foresters ought to be forgiven for their zeal," he wryly commented. "They see in this unemployment emergency an opportunity to get, in the name of unemployment, a lot of work done in the existing forests which Congress has never hitherto seen fit to authorize."[42]

Despite this slightly disparaging comment, Hyde went on to say that he was "heartily in sympathy with a great deal that Pack says," including his ideas on fire prevention, and conceded that "much work could be and ought to be done in forests."[43]

He continued,

A great deal of land could, after proper survey and classification be refor-ested. I do not want to do anything or say anything which would get in the way of any such constructive moves.

But—and I notice with pleasure that Pack scrupulously observes this point without stating it, such a program is not self sustaining nor is it adequate security for a bond issue. It would yield large returns but those returns would have to be reckoned in other terms than money. The returns would lie in social values, recreational values, in conservational values. They would come in stoppage of erosion, in controlling (to some extent) floods, etc. etc. If the returns are reckoned in these values I am in sympathy with a lot that is set out in this memorandum.[44]

Despite Hyde's endorsement, nothing came of Charles's refor-estation-employment plan. There is no documentation indicating that Charles was invited to present the plan to Hoover, Hyde, or Newton in person, as Washburn had urged, nor is there evidence that Hyde or Newton passed the plan on to the president.

Charles, however, kept trying. In early September 1932, he sent Newton the manuscript of an article he had written, illustrating "some of the up-to-date changes in the forestry situation in this country."[45]

One of the most significant "up-to-date changes" was Charles's own attitude. He was now promoting the idea of easing unemployment through reforestation, an attitude which contrasted sharply with his earlier view that such a plan was merely a "political panacea."

"Through times of depression," he wrote, "European countries instinctively turn to the improvement of their forests as a sound public measure to engage unemployed resources of capital and labor. Up until this year we had not thought of forestry in those terms, but one need not seek far to find many avenues of useful employment that will result in increasing the productivity and value of our forest heritage."

This is quite a different point of view than the one first espoused by Charles and Arthur, when they claimed that forest protection and reforestation should be left to the professionals. What, then, was the reason for this about-face? Charles had charged his American Tree Association with conducting his forest employment survey of professional foresters, and the results had just come in. They indicated that seventy thousand men could be employed in unskilled fire protection and reforestation work for one year at a cost of fifty-two million dollars. Charles believed the figures were conservative.[46]

One week later, perhaps because Newton had not yet responded to his article, Charles wrote directly to President Hoover offering him a forestry statement to add to his platform, and again presenting himself as invaluable to the president and the success of his campaign:

Dear Mr. President:

I had hoped that you could find it desirable to make some sort of a statement in regard to forestry, and that you might possibly think it best to do so in some one of your speeches or statements.

I enclose a carefully drawn statement, which I trust will be of help to you, and I hope you will make this forestry statement in the near future.

You will recall that I am thoroughly in touch with the foresters of the country—not only the foresters of the Forest Service, but the state foresters, the educational foresters and many others. I have found that they are rather restless, politically, because of the splendid position they think Governor Roosevelt has taken in relation to forestry matters. Some of them are already "packing up their bags" and "skipping off" to his side.

A good forestry statement made by you would be helpful to you, and it would be particularly helpful to me in helping along our case. The election in Maine shows that we have got to be awake and make the fight on all fronts.[47]

The two-paragraph forestry statement accompanying this letter, however, said nothing new, offered no concrete plans, and was thoroughly general:

We need no longer fear any immediate national timber famine. That ogre at least has been banished from the conservation stage. Recent studies show that we have ample forest-producing area for all our wood needs. Nevertheless these studies also show that our forests are far from being in satisfactory condition, from the standpoints of both location and reproductivity. The great bulk of our remaining commercial timber lies in the Pacific Coast States, and the great centers of consumption are located among the massed population of the Eastern Seaboard. The result is *that* wood products must continue to bear the burden of high transportation charges over long distances until we secure better forest distribution *through reforestation, chiefly east of the Mississippi River.*

Fire has ravaged great areas, reducing the growth rate *of our forests* to a fraction of their capabilities and seriously deteriorating the value of the products. We need to set our face squarely against this fire menace. We need to increase the efficiency of our fire *prevention* system and of our fire suppression methods. The best proof that forest fires can be controlled lies in the fact that 90% of the area burned over by forest fires is land without organized fire protection. Federal, state and private managers of forest lands must cooperate toward better fire protection and toward better forms of forest management that will ultimately lead to cutting our woodlands upon a basis of perpetually sustained yield.[48]

This statement did elicit a response from Hoover, but not the response Charles wanted. On September 20, 1932, Hoover wrote to Pack, "I have your kind letter of September 17th. Some time in the campaign I hope to have a chance to say something about forestation. At the present moment the public mind is concentrated on more emotional things."[49]

Clearly, Hoover was primarily concerned with the economic

trauma being wrought by the Great Depression and felt forestry was a side issue, or merely a minor part of the much bigger economic picture.

Having failed to push Hoover onto the conservation-employment bandwagon, Charles wrote and complained petulantly to Newton about the president's response:

I am greatly disappointed because until the President says something on the subject, it is impossible for me to carry out my plan for work on his behalf. Now he may think the number of foresters is not important, but you must know that these foresters see great quantities of people all over the United States, and have a far-reaching influence. . . . It is really extremely discouraging to me, Mr. Newton, to have nothing done, when there is such a great opportunity for a gesture that could be used to produce votes.

With this letter Charles enclosed a copy of the results of his forest employment survey, which had just been compiled.[50]

His survey caught both Hoover's and Newton's attention at last. The president sent a copy of it to the Reconstruction Finance Corporation, the agency empowered to issue funds for the purpose of bolstering the economy, and Newton sent Hyde, the agriculture secretary, a memorandum requesting that they discuss the survey.[51]

But nothing came of Hoover or Newton's interest in the survey. By late October, Charles had resigned himself to the fact that Hoover would not act upon any of his suggestions.

He wrote to Newton on October 26, 1932,

Mr. Hoover lost a lot of votes by not coming out squarely for forestry. There are ten thousand foresters in the United States and most of them have already been lost to Mr. Roosevelt, and have started to work for him. Mr. Roosevelt made a splendid speech on forestry on October 24th at Atlanta. The ideas that he presented were well-conceived and well-expressed, and he came right to the front as the only candidate for the Presidency who has so ardently and so favorably spoken for forestry, and has gone on record in so definitely a manner in favoring the proper forestry development of this country.

It is just too bad that President Hoover has never really been interested in forestry. Forest workers travel all over the country and see many people. It makes me sad to see the President losing the support of so many of them.[52]

Charles's disappointment was short-lived, however. With Roosevelt's election, Charles joined the ranks of foresters supporting his conservation platform. Thus began the last energetic phase of his conservation career. Backing Roosevelt's effort to end unemployment through reforestation and conservation work, he threw himself, his *Forestry News Digest,* and his American Tree Association behind Roosevelt's national conservation-employment program, the Civilian Conservation Corps.

CLP and the CCC

ARTHUR PACK once observed that his father "was one of those rare individuals who always had the ability to adapt to circumstances and to do so promptly and without useless regrets." This ability was clearly evident in the late fall of 1932. With Roosevelt as president-elect, Charles gave no hint that he had ever viewed FDR as a "dangerous demagogue." Instead, he switched from criticism to wooing Roosevelt with remarkable alacrity.[1] He was, after all, a practical man. As he told Hoover's secretary, Walter Newton, two weeks after FDR's election, "While Mr. Roosevelt may be very weak on many subjects, he is strong on forestry." Lest Newton wonder whether Charles was a turncoat, however, Charles hastened to add, "I am sorry we could not do better for Mr. Hoover, who is one of the finest men that this country has ever produced."[2]

By this time Charles was actively courting FDR. In November he sent him a copy of a highly flattering article he had written for the American Tree Association, where he praised FDR's forestry views.[3] His cover letter indicates that by then he had already allied himself with the president-elect:

My dear Governor Roosevelt:

I am indebted to you for your good letter. I shall certainly be glad to cooperate with you and, from time to time, be of any possible help with forestry matters that may come up during the days that are ahead.

If you have time, you will be interested in glancing at the enclosed "News Sheet"—the last one sent out by our American Tree Association.

This "News Sheet" shows the effectiveness of your forestry talks during the campaign; also how wonderfully the newspapers have commented on these forestry talks, and also how they have approved our "Forest-Employment Survey," which was designed, of course, to help.[4]

The letter from FDR that Charles refers to has been lost. Another, however, dated a year earlier—December 29, 1931—reveals that, contrary to all that Charles had indicated during the 1932 presidential election campaign, Charles and FDR had been on good terms while FDR was governor:

Dear Mr. Pack:

Mr. Bowman [possibly Isaiah Bowman, who later became president of Johns Hopkins University] came to see me the other day and I had a nice talk with him about forestry and the uses of wood. He told me that he had recently seen you—and that reminded me that I should much like to have a talk with you some of these days with regard to the general forestry situation throughout the country. Perhaps sometime in the next month or two you can run up to Albany and see me.[5]

Evidently at some point the two had agreed on conservation issues. Now, following FDR's election, Charles began building on that understanding. From the end of November through December 1932, via Roosevelt's private secretary, Guernsey T. Cross, he sent the president-elect favorable clippings relating to FDR's reforestation-employment plan. These were either written and issued by the American Tree Association or inspired by it. In case FDR knew that Charles had once opposed his plan, Charles was now trying to convince FDR that he supported him.[6] Whether Roosevelt was baffled by this change of heart is unknown. Being a political animal himself, he no doubt understood such fence-jumping. If Charles's November 1932 letter to Roosevelt is any indication, the president-elect welcomed Charles's cooperation early on. Encouraged by this response, Charles began acting as though he now had direct daily contact with Roosevelt. He wrote to Henry Schmitz, dean of forestry at the University of Minnesota, on January 24, 1933:

President-Elect Roosevelt is very much interested in forestry, and he is keenly interested in the question of forestry and unemployment. I have had considerable correspondence with him and expect, a little later on, to have a conference, which he has suggested. He certainly is deeply interested in forestry, but my my! what a load he has on his shoulders. If he can get Congress to go ahead and pass two or three constructive bills, I think he will be blessed by the whole country.

Later on he will no doubt take up the question of forestry in a constructive way. I only trust that his physical and mental health holds out. He is a very hard worker, is a most delightful man to talk to and work with, but I am wondering whether he will have the strength to go through with it all. I hope so.[7]

What is interesting about this letter is that Charles states that he and FDR are in correspondence with each other. In fact, while Charles had sent the president-elect favorable articles throughout the month of December, it was FDR's private secretary, Cross, to whom Charles actually addressed this correspondence. There is no record of Roosevelt ever responding to these overtures. Nor is there any indication that he invited Charles for a conference at this time. The only record of FDR asking to confer with Charles is in the December 29, 1931, letter he wrote to Charles asking him to come to Albany for a conference sometime.

In February 1933, Charles wrote to FDR offering him the services of his American Tree Association staff.

Dear Mr. President:—

I understand that at the White House one of the subjects you will consider is that of forestry and unemployment.

We have a good deal of information at our Washington Office on this subject. The American Tree Association's building is at 1214 Sixteenth Street, N.W. Mr. Percival S. Ridsdale is the manager of our work. He and Mr. Tom Gill, one of our foresters have a great deal of information on the subject of forestry and unemployment.

Possibly you would like to invite Mr. Ridsdale to make a short talk before the House of Governors on this subject, or at least to furnish you the information which we have. This is only a suggestion. I don't want to burden you—I only want to be of help to you if I can and may.[8]

Charles also sent Roosevelt a copy of a forestry editorial, explaining that it had appeared in "some three hundred to four hundred medium and small-sized daily papers, from the Atlantic to the Pacific." He offered to send him more clippings on forestry and unemployment if he wished to see them, stating deferentially, "You have so much to do at present that I would rather not bring these subjects up until you wish to have them."[9] Headlined "Jobs on Trees," the editorial implied that Charles had always supported FDR's plan to solve unemployment through reforestation:

During the presidential campaign, Mr. Roosevelt suggested that the government could put a good many men to work by embarking on a large scale reforestation program. Charles Lathrop Pack, president of the American Tree Association, has conducted a survey of the whole project, and he now announces that jobs could be provided for fully 200,000 men in the various state forests.

In addition, he points out that the U.S. Forest Service estimates that 110,000 more could be put to work in the national forests.

Any program which would put upwards of 300,000 men to work is bound to commend itself pretty strongly these days. One hopes that when Mr. Roosevelt gets into the White House he will not forget the program he mentioned during the campaign. It seems to have real possibilities.[10]

The writer made no mention of the attacks Charles had previously made on this "political panacea" of Roosevelt's.

For his part, Roosevelt seemed pleased to have Charles as an ally. "I am delighted to see that editorial and to know of its wide distribution," he told Charles. "Before you and I get through we will make people understand something about trees."[11]

A few weeks later, Ridsdale sent FDR's assistant secretary, Stephen T. Early, a copy of the 1933 edition of the American Tree Association's *Forestry Almanac,* stating in the accompanying letter, "When the President's reforestation employment projects are taking form . . . it may be of some assistance to you. . . . We, in our organization, very greatly appreciate the interest that you have shown in this reforestation project."[12]

Roosevelt was inaugurated on March 4, 1933. The next week, Charles received a note from FDR's secretary stating that Roosevelt "hopes Mr. Ridsdale will get in touch immediately with the Secretary of Agriculture."[13]

Early in 1933 Roosevelt created the New Deal in an effort to relieve the massive unemployment that was sweeping the nation. Among the major New Deal programs was the Civilian Conservation Corps, which embodied Roosevelt's idea of easing unemployment through reforestation work. The CCC, as it was known, was a remarkable program. It depended upon the cooperation of four federal agencies, the Department of Labor, the Department of Agriculture, the Department of the Interior, and the Army Corps of Engineers. Together they recruited, trained, and supervised millions of men in various forms of reforestation and other forest work, ranging from planting to fire protection. In all, more than three million men worked in the Civilian Conservation Corps, from 1933 to 1942, accomplishing an amazing 730,000 man-years of forest work.[14]

The overtures from Charles and Ridsdale must have convinced Roosevelt that he could use Charles and the American Tree Association to good effect. With Roosevelt's sanction, Charles Lathrop Pack became a vital advocate and watchdog of this program.

His involvement with the CCC began as soon as Roosevelt created the corps in April 1933. In May, Charles wrote to Hugo Winkenwerder, dean of forestry at the University of Washington, that he was "receiving reports of the progress made in the development of the C.C.C. work program" from Washington, D.C. Charles and his American Tree Association staff communicated the results of these reports to the rest of the country via press releases to newspapers and magazines. In addition, Charles also sent personal missives on the CCC's progress to his forestry friends.[15] When the program first started, for instance, he advised Winkenwerder: "If your state has already met the Government requirements, and if you propose to request other camp sites, there is obviously little time left for you to do so.

"I am informed that the White House is entirely agreeable to an altogether informal agreement from your governor, such for instance, as a telegram stating that your Governor is willing to comply with the requirements demanded by the Federal Government."[16]

Over the next few years, Charles generated an impressive amount of such letters, offering the deans and foresters running the camps insights into what they could expect from the CCC.

In November 1933, for instance, Charles assured Henry Schmitz,

The C.C.C. work will undoubtedly continue for another twelve months after the present enlistment period of the second six months has expired. That is, the camps will run anyway until the spring of 1935.

Congressman McReynolds of Tennessee is preparing to introduce a Bill into Congress to make the work a permanent conservation relief work. . . . I don't know how far he will get with this, or how practical he is likely to make it. . . .

The educational plans for the winter in the camps have been what they call "perfected" and it is expected that the order will go out just as soon as they get the signature of General MacArthur's War Department. . . .

If this information has not yet reached you, I think you may like to have it.[17]

In 1934, he told Samuel Spring, assistant dean of forestry at the State University of New York College of Forestry at Syracuse University,

It is the belief that the camps next spring should be allocated to the places where there is the largest amount of forestry work to be done. If this idea is carried out, it will be difficult to find applicants for new camps to secure what they want. That's the way things look at present. We have recently had conferences with both Mr. [F. A.] Silcox [chief of the U.S. Forest Service] and Mr. [Robert] Fechner [CCC director].—What I have said is just between you and me.[18]

Charles was extremely proud of his connection with the CCC. In the summer of 1933 he told Winkenwerder,

Perhaps you don't realize how close our organization is to this whole employment forestry proposition. We have been close to the President in this matter from the very beginning. One of our men is at the White House every day. We are in close touch with Mr. Fechner's office and with the Chief Forester at Washington right along.

I frequently hear right from the President direct. This is simply private between us.[19]

The foresters running the CCC camps appreciated having an inside line to the program's administration. Schmitz, for instance, told Charles, "I very much appreciate the way in which you have kept us informed of new developments in the Emergency Conservation Work Program. The information contained in your letters and printed material is always 'hot off the griddle' and we very much appreciate receiving it."[20]

By June 1933, realizing what the vast American Tree Association publicity network could do for the CCC, Roosevelt asked Charles to devote the majority of the *Forestry News Digest* to coverage of the program; Charles agreed immediately. The press, very interested in the corps's progress, began using the *Digest* as the authoritative source on CCC news.

Charles chattily confided to Schmitz:

> I have to laugh sometimes about "The Forestry News Digest." When it was suggested, from the White House, that we devote "The Forestry News Digest" to the C.C.C. Camps, we of course were very glad to do so, and it has turned out well. That little publication is the most frequently quoted newspaper in the whole United States. An editorial staff representative of the "New York Herald-Tribune" told me so. . . . We knew it already, but were glad to have our knowledge confirmed. The newspapers of the country are full of stuff reprinted from the "Digest" and we have quantities of editorials from the daily press that are founded on material that they find in the "The Forestry News Digest." It is very interesting, isn't it?[21]

As *the* voice of the CCC, Charles was in his element. He had the ear of the White House and was at its service. It is hard to imagine receiving a higher sanction than this. Charles's letters indicate that he was having a grand time and reveling in his own importance.

The attention paid to Charles by the White House seems to have imbued him with an almost superhuman energy. He continued to travel from Lakewood to Washington and New York for conferences with such people as Fechner, who greatly impressed Charles. "He is a man of large executive ability," he confided to Schmitz, "a pusher and a go-getter. I think we will all like him."[22]

Charles occasionally went into the field to investigate camps himself. Most of his energy, however, went into planning and overseeing CCC articles. In August 1933, he told Winkenwerder that he had "different inspectors . . . going over practically all the camps of the country, or at least most of them," in order to get the information that he wanted for articles and reports on the CCC program.[23] And on June 27, 1933, he wrote to Schmitz, "Our Mr. William H. Savage will shortly be in the Lake States to inspect both the Forest Service and state C.C.C. Camps. He will call on you. . . . We are going over the camps in all the principal states and finding out just how they are and what they are doing on the ground. . . . The newspapers right now are all favorable to the CCC Camp idea."[24]

In publicizing the CCC, Charles pulled out every stop he could. In addition to devoting the *Digest* to CCC work, he wrote articles himself—"I am preparing articles all the time for the magazines"[25]—and recruited top foresters, ranging from E. W. Tinker, the U.S. Forest Service forester for Region Nine, to Joseph S. Illick, head of the State University of New York College of Forestry's Department of Forest Management, to write them as well.

"We . . . have in the *New York Times,* and other papers, an article, under the name of Joseph S. Illick, about the C.C.C. Camps of New York State," Charles bragged to Winkenwerder in August 1933. "We are trying to push this thing right along and help the President and the country all we can to the extent of our modest ability."[26]

While promoting the CCC, Charles also managed to promote himself. The press releases issued by the ATA and reprinted by newspapers invariably quoted Charles Lathrop Pack, president of the American Tree Association, as the major source of information. In 1935, for instance, from August 17 through August 20 the newspapers carried a variety of articles, ranging in length from a few inches to a quarter of a page, that quoted Charles as the authority on the problem of finding good men to work for the CCC. (By this time American businesses were recovering and better job opportunities were taking the cream of the crop of men who had previously been employed at the CCC camps.)

In Lowell, Massachusetts, a brief article in the *Evening Leader* began:

President Charles Lathrop Pack of the American Tree Association hopes that the CCC will be retained, not as an emergency relief agency, but as a permanent organization for conserving and developing the nation's forest resources. He praises the work that has been done and regards the CCC as one of the most helpful of the New Deal agencies. . . . He thinks that in the forest conservation and development work there is a field of endeavor that ought to attract young men. . . . If they are to be induced to take up this sort of work as a career, there will obviously have to be some such organization as Mr. Pack suggests to insure their employment.[27]

The Nashville, Tennessee, *Banner* announced:

Men are leaving the CCC camps in droves for other work and new enlistments are 160,000 short of the desired quota. This moves Charles Lathrop Pack, president of the American Tree Association, to make an appeal for the continuation of the forestry and conservation work of the corps.

He thinks that the movement should not be a relief measure to help out the needy, but be placed upon a permanent basis. It is his belief that, instead of forcing enlistments by changing the regulations and taking in a poorer quality of young men, the public interest would be served by concentration on efficient supervision and working personnel in fewer camps.

President Pack says the quality of the boys now coming into the CCC is far below that of previous enlistments.[28]

And, from the *Providence* (Rhode Island) *Journal:*

In the *Forestry News Digest* for September [1935] Charles Lathrop Pack, president of the American Tree Association, pleads for a Government policy toward the Civilian Conservation Corps which will henceforth preserve this agency as a means of conserving and developing the nation's forest resources rather than as a means of helping the needy.

Mr. Pack makes no assertion to the effect that the CCC has failed up to now to accomplish both of these objectives. Indeed he praises highly the work the organization had done. . . .

Nevertheless he asserts that improvement in business has created for capable young men opportunities for private employment which make CCC enrollment less attractive than heretofore, with the result that men are leaving the camps in droves. . . . He does not feel that the recruiting of less desirable men under revised regulations is a proper remedy.[29]

Although Charles certainly loved to promote himself, as president of the American Tree Association he was perceived by the press and the public as an objective and legitimate source of praise and criticism of the program. Comments such as the above would be better received coming from him than from the director of the CCC program, or even the president of the United States, who were both directly involved in running the program.

In his press releases Charles sometimes quoted higher authorities as well. In December 1935, for instance, he obtained from FDR a statement on the importance of forestry, honoring the sixtieth anniversary of forestry conservation—which was being traced back to 1876, when "the first inquiry as to our forest resources was authorized." This two-hundred-word statement first appeared in the *Digest* and was then reprinted in newspapers across the country.[30]

Swept up in the excitement of promoting the CCC, Charles's enthusiasm sometimes verged on the fanatical. It was not beyond him to chastise foresters he felt were not pulling their weight in publicizing the good that the camps were doing. "I have been trying to get you, or somebody, to write a real honest-to-goodness article about what the C.C.C. work will mean to the Pack Demonstration Forest in terms of forestry, in terms of economics, and in terms of human service," Charles wrote to Winkenwerder in the summer of 1933. "If I had had such an article from you I might have gotten it in one of the magazines. By this time it may be too late, but I hope not."[31]

Charles Pack's tenacity in publicizing the work of the CCC camps was based on a fear that the program could backfire and at the same time discredit the forestry conservationists. As Charles warned Winkenwerder in August 1933,

Let me call your attention to the fact that the Assistant Secretary of Agriculture, at the initial organization meeting of the C.C.C., held in Washington, said as follows:—

"I have always had a high respect for the members of the profession of forestry. You men now have a wonderful opportunity to do what you have been for many years saying you wanted to do. That is all I have to say except that I hope at the end of this year that my respect for the members of the forestry profession will be no different than what it is now."

In other words, "Wink," he told the foresters that it was up to them to do a thorough job and a worthwhile job with the 300,000 men who were going to be placed in their charge. I want to tell you, "Wink," that the sentiment of the people throughout the country is such that if the foresters believe that nobody will ever be foolish as to check up on what real forestry work has been done—I feel certain that the public will blame the foresters.

Well my job just now is examining what real forestry work has been done and will be done, through my field agents, and I am trying to get facts and more facts.

I would like to make this prediction. There is going to be an [outside] investigation of the kind of forestry work that has been done and if the work is not satisfactory the men who are going to be blamed for it are the foresters, both National and State. The President has given them the money, the men and the supplies, and its [*sic*] certainly up to them to make good.[32]

Charles need not have worried. Over the next nine years—the corps was dissolved in 1942—CCC men planted 2.25 billion trees, built nearly 6 million erosion-check dams, improved 4 million acres of forest stands, built truck trails totaling nearly 122,000 miles, and fought tree and plant disease, such as white pine blister rust, on 21 million acres of forest. In addition, they handled emergency situations, such as flood and fire. It was a remarkable job of strengthening forests and forest resources.[33]

The program also expanded the national forest reserves. In May 1933, FDR allocated twenty million dollars for the purchase of additional forest lands in the eastern states. This included buying cutover lands, "scarred with logged and burned slopes and eroding fields on poor hillside farms," such as the land that would become the Great Smoky Mountains National Park. Further acquisitions over the years resulted in sixty purchases of land totaling 7,735,000 acres of national preserves. That, as Sam Dana observed, was "two and a half times as much as during the preceding twenty-two year period."[34]

The CCC offered its men an impressive variety of jobs. There were over 150 major lines of work under the general headings of reforestation, forest protection and improvement, soil conservation, recreational development, range rehabilitation, aid to wildlife, flood control, drainage, reclamation, and emergency rescue activities.[35]

There were social benefits as well. When the program started, between and thirteen million and fifteen million Americans were unemployed. Teenage boys from the cities, with no jobs to offer them money, prestige, or even something to do with their time, often joined street gangs. Older men or men with families looked endlessly for work. Young or old, these men were often in poor physical condition, if not downright sickly. As Charles remarked to Winkenwerder, "Quite a number of the C.C.C. boys come from families where there is tuberculosis [a major health threat at that time]. They haven't got it but they are 'subjects.'"[36]

The CCC gave many men their health and happiness as well as a livelihood. As Charles would write in his article "Auditing the C.C.C. Ledger," "Reports from the camps [show] the physical improvement of the men, their increased appreciation of organized endeavor and, generally, a sounder mental outlook. Betterment in physical conditions alone is represented by an average gain in weight of eight pounds for each boy who has passed through one of the camps, while the gain in mental outlook, the increased cooperation, the general attitude of greater cheerfulness have been apparent to many."[37]

Charles could not paint an entirely rosy picture of the social side of the CCC, however. "Some of the boys did not like it," he wrote. "Some of them left of their own accord, and some left at the request of the camp authorities. . . . There have been, of course, a natural proportion of cases of moral and social lapses. There always are when any body of men are gathered together, whether it be in a conservation army or at a convention of the Amalgamated Order of This or That."[38]

That the CCC experience was an extraordinary one for most of the workers, though, is evidenced by the existence of the National Association of Civilian Conservation Corps Alumni, which to this day holds regular meetings, nationally and regionally, and publishes a monthly newsletter.

Although the CCC did great good for both human and natural resources, it did not escape criticism. Some argued that the gain of employing three million men over a nine-year period was not worth the $2.5 billion cost. Some said the "quality of the work was not always topnotch," that some of it was "busy work" at best, and destructive at worst. For instance, Harold Titus, a member of the Michigan Conservation Commission, observed, "As much as 50 per cent of CCC firebreaks" built in Michigan were unnecessary, and a program to combat mosquitoes, involving ditchdigging and swamp draining, was so badly planned that "thousands of ducks and muskrats were dispossessed with no other place to go."[39]

But as Sam Dana, head of forestry at the University of Michigan put it, "What else could be expected of an emergency program, directed largely by inexperienced supervisors and carried out by unskilled youths many of whom had never been in the woods before, the primary aim of which was relief of unemployment? The marvel is not that the program had its technical and financial shortcomings, but that these were not more serious. Taking everything into consideration, both the quantity and the quality of the work accomplished were impressive."[40]

Charles Lathrop Pack's contribution to the CCC included not just his publicity efforts, but also his educational efforts. By August 1933, Charles had printed and issued a CCC edition of his *Forestry Primer*.

"We have been making excellent use of these [primers] in the past," Winkenwerder wrote Charles upon receiving a new shipment of them, "and will see that this lot is properly distributed where these valuable little booklets will do the most good. It is about the only thing available that covers the subject completely and at the same time is so simply written that the ordinary human being has no difficulty in getting the picture."[41]

Charles also took it upon himself to act as a long-distance supervisor of some of the camps. For example, he wrote to Winkenwerder,

I was sorry to learn from one of our inspectors that the Camp on the Demonstration Forest is not very well run; that there is lack of coordination between the camp superintendent and the camp commander. My field agent thought it was largely the fault of the camp superintendent because he was not used to handling men, and not used to [not] getting his own way some way somehow. These military officers are usually good fellows and can be handled all right by a man who is experienced in dealing with business affairs and with men.

I was also informed, for the first time, that the boys in the C.C.C. Camp on the Pack Forest are only partly used at work in the forest—that a goodly portion of them work far away from the Camp and the Forest and a good deal of time is wasted coming and going. . . .

I hope your camp can be continued through the winter. BUT, why don't you get a larger number of men working on the forest, and why don't you get better coordination in that Camp. It is far from one of the best. It should be managed as well as any.

Of course, I understand this is not your business, but sometimes a little diplomacy will turn the trick.[42]

The problem was solved when the commander was transferred.[43]

Charles later urged his forestry friends who were operating camps to be sure that the supervisors were trained foresters. "I have your interesting letter of April 27," Winkenwerder wrote to Charles, "and want to compliment you on your efforts to see that the work in the CCC camps has some supervision by men who are real foresters." His directive was nevertheless ineffective. Even Charles could not force foresters to surface who did not exist. By now, trained foresters had good jobs and were not about to leave them for CCC work, which paid less and could end at any time.[44]

In reviewing Charles's work for the CCC, it is amazing that he began this work at the age of seventy-five. For five more years this intense, bossy, contradictory, funny little man showed no signs of slowing down as he became more and more involved with the CCC—publishing the *Digest*, gathering news, ordering articles, even helping to arrange a huge party in honor of F. A. Silcox, who, as chief of the U.S. Forest Service, was a key actor in coordinating CCC efforts. Charles threw himself into his CCC work as intensely as he had ever done anything. Then, in 1937, at the age of eighty, Charles's energy at last began to ebb; and his rich, full, contradictory, and fruitful life at last began to draw to a close.

CHAPTER 21

The End of "A Superb Life"

C HARLES LATHROP PACK died of a kidney ailment at 12:30 in the morning of June 14, 1937, at Doctors Hospital in New York City.[1]

Although his health had been failing for the past year, he had stayed active almost to the end. From his Vanderbilt suite he continued to hold conferences with his staff and colleagues and to dictate letters. These letters gave the impression that Charles was as energetic as ever. For example, he told Hugo Winkenwerder on January 26, 1937 that, "Due to the very large amount of valuable forestry material received as a result of the Society of American Foresters and Western Forestry and Conservation Association, we are coming out immediately with another issue [of the *Forestry News Digest*] and maybe another after that. Of course you know I personally devote a great deal of time in the selection and dramatization of the material used in *The Forestry News Digest*."[2]

If family recollections are accurate, however, the energetic tone of this letter belies the fact that Charles was at last succumbing to age. Although he was still making the Lakewood–New York City commute—working out of his suite at the Vanderbilt during the week and spending weekends in Lakewood—he was now accompanied by a live-in nurse and appeared, to visitors, to be tired and

Grover Page, one of the great editorial cartoonists of the day, sent this original illustration in honor of Charles Pack's eightieth birthday. (*Courtesy of Virginia Lathrop [Pack] Townsend.*)

frail. Certainly, the fact that the number of letters from Charles on record for 1936 through 1937 are few, and that some are written on his behalf by his field agent William Savage, indicates that Charles's remarkable energy level may have indeed begun to sink.[3]

Yet even with his health and powers waning, Charles Pack's ego was still in full flower. In January 1937, he sent a calendar featuring a portrait of himself to Winkenwerder as a holiday gift.[4]

He was also able and willing to socialize during the last year of his life. When he met Arthur and his wife, Phoebe, for dinner at the Vanderbilt during this time, he was accompanied by "an elderly girlfriend." According to Phoebe, Charles had asked Gertrude for permission to have this girlfriend, and she had given it. Unfortunately, her identity is unknown; Phoebe Pack is the only living relative to have met this woman, and since she only met her once, she has long since forgotten her name.[5]

Charles's waning energy gave way to illness one week after his eightieth birthday, when he entered the hospital for what was to be a week-long stay. On Sunday, June 13, the day before he died, Charles's doctors warned his family that the end was near. In Lakewood, the congregation of the First Presbyterian Church, where Charles and Gertrude were members, rose and prayed in silence for his recovery. On June 14, they learned their prayers had been in vain.[6]

The news of Charles's death spread so quickly that the Lakewood telegraph office had to stay open all night in order to handle the flood of telegrams of consolation.[7]

If Charles did not die happily—it is impossible to imagine this feisty, energetic man welcoming death—he must have at least died content in the knowledge that he had achieved the sort of fame and recognition he had always sought. Ten years earlier, in honor of his seventieth birthday, he had received hundreds of letters from foresters, editors, professors, and statesmen honoring him and his work.

"Your name is as thoroughly identifed with forestry and tree planting in the minds of one hundred and ten million Americans as was the name of Hon. J. Stirling [Sterling] Morton, 'the father of Arbor Day,' in the minds of forty million Americans in his day," wrote Carl Bannwart, shade tree superintendent for the Newark, New Jersey, Department of Parks and Public Property. "Henry Ford stands for flivvers and Thomas A. Edison for electric lights; Charles Lathrop Pack stands for the tree 'That looks at God all day, and lifts its leafy arms to pray.'

"Your life reminds me of a great tree; it has been so strong, so steadfast, so deeply rooted, so close to the living water, so well-rounded, so wide in the circle of its influence, so lofty in the reach of its uppermost branches, and I say, what a superb life."[8]

C. B. Waldron, a forestry professor at North Dakota Agricultural College, wrote, "I recall very vividly the first Conservation

Congress that I attended in Washington many years ago, and the two men that I most remember in connection with that nation-wide movement are yourself and Mr. Gifford Pinchot.... Even then I did not deem it possible that you would be able to accomplish so much in the years which have intervened.... [I] trust that you may long be spared to carry on a work that seems to be dependent largely upon your own efforts."[9]

Even the bishop of the diocese of Harrisburg, Pennsylvania, wrote to congratulate Charles on his work: "Your name is a tower of strength to all who believe in the outdoor life, and the plans you have perfected to recover our slashings and cuttings of timber all over the country, and to teach the youth of our land the necessity of replanting a tree, for everyone [sic] that is cut, has made your name a household word among all good citizens, young and old."[10]

And so it went. The accolades poured in from editors, congressmen, and even the director general of waters and forests in the French ministry of agriculture.[11]

The New York Times published an editorial and notice alerting the public that "Mr. Pack will be 70 on May 7" and which began with the following statement: "The ancient Greek gods, as the author of 'The Bride of the Mistletoe' has related the story, were all 'tethered' each to a different tree, Jupiter to the oak, Apollo to the laurel, Bacchus to the vine, Minerva to the olive and Juno to the apple. But no one of them ever gave so much thought to the nurture of the trees as the President of the American Tree Association and founder of the Forestry Trust that bears his name—CHARLES LATHROP PACK."[12]

Ten years later, this flood of praise was repeated on Charles's eightieth birthday, just two weeks before his death: "WHERE would the forestry movement be," wrote the German forester Carl Schenck," had it not been for this Godsent mission of C L [sic] Pack? There is the Forest Service,—and nothing else but C L Pack. And the Forest Service does not have that measure of independence which allows of real leadership. Officialdom here, Pack there. And there is no third alternative."[13]

Even Gifford Pinchot, who had otherwise disappeared from Charles's life, wrote to Charles on both his seventieth and eightieth

Alice Gertrude Pack with her son Randolph, granddaughter Virginia Lathrop (Pack) Townsend, and great-grandson Jim Townsend. (Courtesy of Virginia Lathrop [Pack] Townsend.)

birthdays to congratulate him for his protection of American trees and forests, and assure him that his work "will not be forgotten."[14]

These tributes certainly must have thrilled Charles, who had spent his life striving to achieve such acclaim. If, after he died, his soul could have lingered to glimpse the June 22 issue of the *New York Herald-Tribune,* it might have been able to leave this earth at last content, for this paper called Charles "one of the foremost apostles of forest conservation."[15]

Alice Gertrude Pack outlived Charles by thirteen years. She stayed in Lathrop Hall with a companion. As a leading Lakewood citizen, she continued to attend and support the First Presbyterian

Church of Lakewood, go to concerts, walk in her flower garden alone or with grandchildren, and have friends and neighbors over for tea or supper. A lively conversationalist, she loved to discuss books and music, was very interested in news of foreign lands, and enjoyed relating her own adventures abroad. Yet people who spent time with her once she was a widow remember that she spoke rarely of Charles or his work. Although she was pleased by and interested in many of his projects, such as the highway beautification program, she was never a boastful person. But despite her reserve, at least one grandchild sensed Gertrude had real pride in and fondness for Charles.[16] Today Gertrude is buried with Charles beneath a stand of white pine in the Charles Lathrop Pack Demonstration Forest at Warrensburg, New York, a site of his own choosing.[17]

Charles was buried under a stand of white pine in the Charles Lathrop Pack Demonstration Forest in Warrensburg, New York, in 1937. Thirteen years later, his wife, Gertrude, was buried there as well. (copyright © 1989 Nicolas Eyle.)

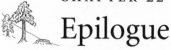

CHAPTER 22

Epilogue

WHEN CHARLES DIED, he left behind an estate valued at $1.6 million. Of this he bequeathed $50,000 to his forestry trust fund, to be used by the Pack Foundation for the "purpose of promoting the study and practice of scientific forestry, the scientific protection, development and use of forest resources, and the promotion of the study and practice of tree planting."[1] In addition, he gave $2,000 to the Society of American Foresters, and $5,000 to the state of New Jersey for the acquisition or maintenance of a forest tree nursery, or for forestry planting and work on the state forests.[2]

His employee William H. Savage received $10,000; the Walter Hines Page School of International Relations at Johns Hopkins University and the Institute of International Education, Inc., of which Charles was a director, each received $5,000. This amount was also given to the Lakewood Lodge of Free and Accepted Masons, of which Charles was a member. In addition, the Lakewood Community Service, Inc., received $10,000.

Gertrude, and in the event of her death, Beulah, were named heirs to Charles's house and personal possessions, including furniture, paintings, and sculpture. They received no other financial provisions since Gertrude was financially independent and Charles had already made provisions for Beulah. The remainder of the estate was divided between Randolph and Arthur.[3]

The Charles Lathrop Pack Forestry Foundation operated until May 1961, when the last of the foundation's money was spent.[4]

The American Tree Association became inactive during the 1950s. There is no record of the exact year of its dissolution.[5]

Following Arthur's retirement from the presidency of the American Nature Association in May 1946, the ANA was run by Richard W. Westwood, who was its president until its dissolution in 1959. The decision to end the ANA may have been related to a decline in membership, which might be attributed to the fact that its programs had become indistinguishable from those of the American Tree Association, and to the similarities of its policies to those of the Izaak Walton League of America.[6]

Arthur Pack died at his home on December 6, 1975, at the age of eighty-two. The Arizona–Sonora Desert Museum is still in existence and continues to be renowned internationally as a unique and outstanding example of a "living museum." It is run by a paid director and elected board of trustees, of which Arthur's widow, Phoebe Pack, is honorary chairman.[7] The Ghost Ranch Museum is also still in operation.

Charles Lathrop Pack's reputation as a leader in forest education and conservation did not live on following his death. Although Luther Halsey Gulick remarked in his book *American Forest Policy* that "the conservationists, led on by men like Gifford Pinchot, Theodore Roosevelt, Charles Lathrop Pack, and others, gradually mobilized public opinion and, step by step, led the federal and state governments into a series of activities designed to conserve the forests and safeguard the timber heritage of the nation," Charles Pack's name and the names of his organizations rarely appear in conservation books. When they do, they are mentioned in only the most general terms.[8]

It is safe to say that outside of his family, Charles Lathrop Pack is known today only to those people who benefited from him directly—the professors who held or hold his endowed chairs, the graduates who held a Pack fellowship, and the students and teachers who work or have worked in his demonstration forests. With few exceptions, even these people have no idea how much he accomplished during his lifetime, or contributed to their field.

Notes

Copies of all the archival documents cited below are housed in the Charles Lathrop Pack Collection, Terence J. Hoverter Archives, State University of New York College of Environmental Science and Forestry. All original sources of these documents are cited here, however, and should be cited by future scholars as well.

Introduction

1. *Saint Mary Academy 1898–1973* (Lakewood, N.J.: Saint Mary's Academy, 1973), unpaginated. The history of the academy, which once owned the Pack estate, states that Charles was one of the five wealthiest men in America prior to the First World War.

2. Elroy McKendree Avery, *A History of Cleveland and Its Environs* (Chicago: Lewis Publishing Company, 1918), vol. 3, 541–42.

Chapter 1

1. "Notes from Mrs. McNairy in Asheville," Charles Lathrop Pack Collection, Western History Department, Denver Public Library, Denver, Colo., p. 2.

2. "CLP Materials: Recollections of Charles Lathrop Pack," Pack Collection, Denver, drawer 4, pp. 1–2; Thomas Harvey Gill, unpublished biography of Charles Lathrop Pack, undated, Thomas Gill Collection, Forest Hill Society, Durham, N.C., box 1, p. 2.

3. "Pack, George 1800–1875," Bible of George Pack, Charles Lathrop Pack Collection, Terence J. Hoverter Archives, State University of New York, College of Environmental Science and Forestry, Syracuse, (henceforth cited as SUNY-ESF), drawer 4, 1.

4. Sanilac County Historical Society, *Portrait and Biographical Album of Sanilac County* (Chicago: Chapman Brothers, 1884), 185; Jane Miller, with assistance from Madeline Felker, "The George Pack Story," an unpublished manuscript produced under the auspices of the Sanilac County Historical Society, Port Sanilac, Mich., Pack Collection, SUNY-ESF, drawer 4, p. 2.

5. Gill, unpublished biography, 2; "Notes from Mrs. McNairy in Asheville," 2.

6. Maria Lathrop Pack to Abraham Lathrop, Feb. 20, 1849, Pack Collection, SUNY-ESF, drawer 4.

7. *Ibid.*

8. Frances White Field, notation on the Pack family tree, Pack Collection, SUNY-ESF, drawer 4.

9. Sanilac County Historical Society, *Portrait,* 185; Miller, "George Pack Story," 2.

10. Lawrence Rakestraw, "Michigan Forests," in *Encyclopedia of American Forest and Conservation History* (New York: Macmillan, 1983), vol. 2, 422; *History of Iosco County* (Iosco County Historical Society, East Tawas, Mich.: undated), 124.

11. *History of Iosco County,* 123.

12. *Ibid.*

13. *Ibid; Portrait and Biographical Album of Huron County* (Chicago: Chapman Brothers, 1884; reprint, Sebewaing, Mich.: Red Flannel Underwear Press, 1976), 362; "Verona," an unpublished, uncredited article, Bad Axe Public Library, Bad Axe, Mich. I am grateful to Helen M. Kerr of Bad Axe for drawing this article to my attention.

14. 1876 Wall Map of Sanilac County Washington Township, Sanilac County Historical Society; Miller, "George Pack Story," 2–3.

15. Walter Romig, *Michigan Place Names* (Grosse Pointe: Walter Romig, 1972), 426.

16. Neva Dumond, *Thumb Diggings: Adventures into Michigan's Thumb Area* (Lexington, Mich.: Neva Dumond, 1962), 193; Miller, "George Pack Story," 1.

17. Dumond, 193; *Michigan State Gazetteer and Business Directory for 1875* (Detroit: Tribune Printing Company, 1875), 606; Miller, "George Pack Story," 3; "Notes from Mrs. McNairy in Asheville," 1.

18. Dumond, *Thumb Diggings,* 193; Sanilac County Historical Society, *Portrait,* 185.

19. *Ibid.*

20. Virginia Lathrop (Pack) Townsend interview, audio tape, 1987, Pack Collection, SUNY-ESF, box 10.

21. *Portrait and Biographical Album of Huron County,* 175; Florence McKinnon Gwinn, *Pioneer History of Huron County* (Bad Axe, Mich.: Huron County Pioneer and Historical Society, 1922), 93.

22. *Portrait and Biographical Album of Huron County,* 121; Jim Coufal, personal communication, July 1989.

23. *History of Lake Huron Shore, with Illustrations and Biographical Sketches of Some of Its Prominent Men and Pioneers* (Chicago: H. R. Page, 1883), 188; *History of Iosco County,* 189.

24. *Portrait and Biographical Album of Huron County,* 175, 121, 303, 362; *Michigan State Gazetteer and Business Directory 1899* (Detroit: R. L. Polk & Co., 1899), 1333.

25. Edna M. Otis, *Their Yesterdays: Au Sable and Oscoda 1848–1948,* (Edna M. Otis, 1948), unpaginated.

26. Harry R. Solomon, "Historical Sketch of Oscoda and Au Sable," in *Homecoming Week on the Sable,* (Evansville, Ind.: Unigraph, Inc., 1979), unpaginated; "At the End of the Journey," *American Lumberman,* Sept. 8,1906, 1; *Cleveland Leader,* Oct. 10, 1901, Thomas Gill Collection, box 1; Solomon, "Historical Sketch."

27. "CLP Materials," 1.

28. "At the End of the Journey," *American Lumberman,* 1.

29. Solomon, "Historical Sketch," and *History of Iosco County,* 115, say 1894. Typewritten notes in the Gill Collection, box 1, dated 1901, state that "At half past three o'clock Wednesday afternoon the last log that will ever go up the logway into Pack, Woods & Co.'s mill was run through the mill and came out in the shape of lumber at the other end, and the work of what has been one of the greatest sawmills in the world was done. . . . [In] February 1893 . . . upon the death of Greene Pack, Mr. Charles Pack of Cleveland was made president and Arthur Pack made general manager." Neil Thornton, however, in *Along the Historic River Aux Sables* (Tawas City, Mich.: Printer's Devil, 1987), 99, says Greene Pack died in 1895.

30. William B. Greeley, *Forests and Men* (Garden City, N.Y.: Doubleday, 1951), 51.

31. *Ibid,* 50.

32. Thomas R. Cox, "Lumberman's Frontier," in *Encyclopedia of American Forest and Conservation History,* vol. 1, 387.

Chapter 2

1. Gill, unpublished biography, 1; *Portrait and Biographical Album of Huron County,* 362; "Verona," 2.

2. Townsend interview, 1987.

3. Gill, unpublished biography, 3.

4. "Notes from Mrs. McNairy in Asheville," 1.

5. "Notes from CLP," Pack Collection, Denver, 1.

6. Charles Lathrop Pack (hereafter CLP in all correspondence references) to P. S. Ridsdale, Feb. 7. 1934, Virginia Lathrop (Pack) Townsend family album, Pack Collection, SUNY-ESF, drawer 4; Charles J. Phillips, "Charles Lathrop Pack: Forester, Economist, Philatelist," *Stamps* 1, no. 4 (1932):117–18; "The Passing of Two Great Philatelists," *The London Philatelist* 46, no. 546 (1937):125–26; "Collectors' Club Gets Stamp Gift," *New York Times,* June 5, 1927; Charles J. Phillips, "Charles Lathrop Pack: An Expression of Appreciation on the Occasion of His 80th Birthday—May 7th 1937," *Stamps* 19, no. 6 (1937): 227; Arthur Newton Pack, *We Called It Ghost Ranch* (Albuquiu, N.M.: Ghost Ranch Conference Center, 1979), 83–84, 86; William H. Carr, "Three Distinguished Conservationists," *American Forests* 82, no. 6 (1976):8–9; Gill, unpublished biography, 4; "Notes from CLP," 1.

7. "Notes from Mrs. McNairy in Asheville," 4; Gill, unpublished biography, 4.

8. *History of Lake Huron Shore,* 188.

9. "CLP Materials," 1; *The Progressive Weekly,* East Cleveland (Ohio) Grammer School newspaper (unpublished), 1, nos. 2, 3, 5, in Charles L. Pack Family Papers, Arizona Historical Society, Tucson, ms. no. 640.

10. C. Pack, "Gun Powder," *The Progressive Weekly,* 1, no. 2, (1871):1, in Pack Family Papers, Tucson.

11. C. Pack, *The Progressive Weekly,* 1, no. 3 (1871):5, in Pack Family Papers, Tucson.

12. C. Pack, "The City Boy and the Lumber Woods Boy," *The Progressive Weekly,* 1, no. 3 (1871):1–2, in Pack Family Papers, Tucson.

13. Gill, unpublished biography, 5, states, "All during his early teens, Charles

Pack's summers were spent at Oscoda, where one of the Pack mills was located." Although there is no question that Charles spent summers at a Pack mill, he could not have been at the Oscoda mill during this time, because the firm that ran the Oscoda mill, Pack, Woods & Company, did not come into existence until 1876, when Charles was nineteen, and did not build its Oscoda mill until 1878, when Charles was twenty. Thus, he must have spent his summers at his father's Port Crescent mill, operated by his Uncle Greene Pack, from 1870–1876.

14. C. Pack, "Riding Logs," unpublished school essay, Pack Family Papers, Tucson.

15. "Notes from Mrs. McNairy in Asheville," 3.

16. "CLP Materials," 2; Gill, unpublished biography, 9–10.

17. C. Pack diary, "Impressions of Europe, 1874," Pack Family Papers, Tucson.

18. *Ibid.*, Aug. 7, 1874

19. *Ibid.*, Aug. 19, 1874

20. *Ibid.*, Sept. 9, 1874

21. *Ibid.*, Sept. 23, 1874

22. Cox, "Lumberman's Frontier," 387–88; David Smith, "Lumber Industry: Northeast," in *Encyclopedia of American Forest and Conservation History*, vol. 1, 374.

23. C. Pack, "Success," Pack Family Papers, Tucson, 5–7.

24. C. Pack, "Tree Oration," Pack Family Papers, Tucson, 10.

25. *Ibid.*, 1–2.

26. Cox, "Lumberman's Frontier," 387–88; Smith, "Lumber Industry," 374.

Chapter 3

1. Gill, unpublished biography, 11.

2. Hazel Mellick, "A City is Born," *A Wind Gone Down: West-Running Brook* (Lansing: Michigan Department of State, History Division, 1978), 25–27.

3. Gill, unpublished biography, 12.

4. Philip Mason, *Michigan Historical Commission: Lumbering Era in Michigan History 1860–1900* (Lansing: Michigan Historical Commission, 1956), 9, 13.

5. Gill, unpublished biography, 12.

6. C. Pack diary, April–Aug. 1878.

7. *Ibid.*, July 8, 1878.

8. *Ibid.*, July 9, 1878.

9. James B. Morrow, "No Sentiment, Just Plain Common Sense Made Him the First Active Worker for Forest Conservation," *Sunday Plain Dealer*, Jan. 5, 1913, editorial and drama section, 3.

10. Morrow, "No Sentiment;" "CLP Materials," 5.

11. "CLP Materials," 5; "Charles L. Pack," *The Cleveland Leader*, Sept. 1, 1901.

12. "CLP Materials," 5.

13. "Notes from Mrs. McNairy in Asheville," 5.

14. C. Pack diary, April-Aug. 1878.

15. Gill, unpublished biography, 12–13; "CLP Materials," 4.

16. *History of Lake Huron Shore*, 189.

17. "CLP Materials" 4; Gill, unpublished biography, 12; David D. Van Tassel

and John J. Grabowski, eds., *The Encyclopedia of Cleveland History* (Bloomington: Indiana University Press, in association with Case Western Reserve Univ., 1987), 982.

18. Gill, unpublished biography, 13.

19. "CLP Materials," 4.

20. Morrow, "No Sentiment."

21. George Alwin Stokes, "Lumbering in Southwest Louisiana: A Study of the Industry as a Culturo-Geographic Factor" (Ph.D diss., Louisiana State University, 1954), 31–32.

22. Ed Kerr, "History of Forestry in Louisiana," in *Tales of the Louisiana Forests* (Baton Rouge, La.: Claitor's Publishing, n. d.), 1. Claitor's says that as of 1989 this book was at least five years old.

23. Anna Burns, "Louisiana Forests," in *Encyclopedia of American Forest and Conservation History,* vol. 1, 363.

24. Burns, "Louisiana Forests,"36; Stokes, "Lumbering in Southwest Louisiana," 36.

25. The year 1881 is cited by Morrow in "No Sentiment" and by Gill in his unpublished biography. However, in an interview just two months before he died, Charles told Gill that the year was 1882. Because no other records have been found that can clarify this discrepancy, and because the interview was given when Charles was eighty years old and may have had a failing memory, I am using the earlier account of 1881.

26. Morrow, "No Sentiment."

27. Gill, unpublished biography, 13; "CLP Materials," 4; "Notes from CLP," 5. Charles would claim that he bought largely longleaf pine, but John Tarver, an editor for *Louisiana Agricultural Magazine,* says he may have been mistaken. It is difficult from the vantage point of the ground to tell the difference between short and longleaf pine simply because the branches start so high in the trees; needle lengths are therefore difficult to measure. Also, longleaf pine was more valuable than shortleaf, thus providing Charles a vested interest in believing—and saying—that that was what he had bought. On the other hand, by the time he was describing his holdings, Charles would have already sold much of his land to Buchanan, and once it was cut and milled, its identity could not be questioned. John Tarver, correspondence and telephone interview with the author, July 1989, Pack Collection, SUNY-ESF, letters, drawer 4; audiotapes, box 10.

28. "Notes from Mrs. McNairy in Asheville," 1, 4.

29. "Pack, Charles Lathrop," *Dictionary of American Biography* (New York: Scribner's, 1958), vol. 1, sup. 1,. 507.

30. "Pack, Charles Lathrop," *National Cyclopedia of American Biography,* vol. 28 (New York: James T. White, 1940), 125–26.

31. Gill, unpublished biography, 18.

32. "Save the Forests," Oct. 14, 1894, from an unknown newspaper, Pack Collection, SUNY-ESF, drawer 3.

33. "A Plea for Trees of City," *The Cleveland Leader,* March 20, 1902.

34. "Importance of Planting Forests, Trees," *New York Daily Tribune,* Oct. 30, 1903.

35. *The Forester* 5, no. 6 (1899):140; interview with Dorothea Hammond, a clerk with the Status and Research Department of the British Columbia Ministry

of Forestry, Pack Collection, SUNY-ESF, drawer 1; interview with Eleanor Brown Pack Hibben, the first wife of Arthur Pack, who lived in Vancouver when Arthur bought Canadian land for his father; Archer H. Mayor, *Southern Timberman: The Legacy of William Buchanan* (Athens: University of Georgia Press, 1988), 35, 161.

36. Cox, "Lumberman's Frontier," 388–99.

37. J. H. Foster, Bulletin 114:*Forest Conditions in Louisiana* (U.S. Department of Agriculture Forest Service, 1912), 7–8; "General Index to Real Estate Conveyances—La Salle Parish, La.—Vendees," (1883–1931), cites the first sale by Charles Pack to Josiah Prestridge in 1892, 65; "Notes from CLP," 6; Morrow, "No Sentiment"; Kerr, "History of Forestry in Louisiana," 6.

38. Mayor, *Southern Timberman*, 31.

39. Kerr, "History of Forestry in Louisiana," 3, 5-6.

40. Morrow, "No Sentiment."

41. Kerr, "History of Forestry in Louisiana," 5-6; Mayor, *Southern Timberman*, 31; Arthur Newton Pack, "From This Seed," (an unpublished autobiography) undated, Pack Collection, SUNY-ESF, drawer 1, p. 28.

42. Kerr, "History of Forestry in Louisiana," 6.

43. Herman H. Chapman, "The American Forestry Associaton Versus Charles Lathrop Pack," unpublished article, Gifford Pinchot Papers, Manuscript Division, Library of Congress, Washington, D.C., box 240, p. 4; H. H. Chapman, "Has the American Forestry Association Lost Its Former Usefulness? Reflections of a Life Director," *Journal of Forestry* 19, no. 4 (1921):347; David M. Smith, *The Practice of Silviculture* (New York: Wiley, 1962), 29, 354, 366.

44. Tarver to the author, July 20, 1989, 3; Burns, "Louisiana Forests," 364.

45. Mayor, *Southern Timberman*, 119.

46. "Planting Pine Trees on Cut-Over Lands Has Solved the Problem of a City's Permanency—The Town That Was Built to Satisfy the Life-Long Dream of Its Founder," Sept. 1923, Chapman Papers, box 20; *The Butt of the Log of the Sinnemahoning, Being the Record of a Trip to New Orleans in January, 1905*, a privately printed, unpublished booklet by Philip A. Rollins, the husband of Charles Pack's sister, Mary Pack, Pack Collection, SUNY-ESF, drawer 1.

47. Chapman, "American Forestry Versus Charles Lathrop Pack," 4.

48. Mayor, *Southern Timberman*, 161.

49. Morrow, "No Sentiment."

50. Galloway, "John Barber White: Lumberman," 187–89.

Chapter 4

1. Wilfred Henry Alburn and Miriam Russell Alburn, *This Cleveland of Ours* (Cleveland: S. J. Clarke Publishing Company, 1933), vol. 1, 640–41.

2. Van Tassel and Grabowski, *The Encyclopedia of Cleveland History*, 58.

3. Alburn and Alburn, *This Cleveland*, 918–19.

4. Gill, unpublished biography, 15–16.

5. Ella G. Wilson, *Famous Old Euclid Ave.* (Cleveland: 1932), vol. 2, 24; Alburn and Alburn, *This Cleveland*, 374–75; James B. Morrow, "Cleveland Man War Gardener's General," *Cleveland Plain Dealer*, Sept. 23, 1917, editorial and drama section, 10; A. Pack, "From This Seed," 2.

6. Morrow, "No Sentiment"; Gill, unpublished biography, 16.

7. *Ibid.*

8. Morrow, "No Sentiment."

9. Van Tassel and Grabowski, *Encyclopedia of Cleveland History,* 379–80.

10. Alburn and Alburn, *This Cleveland,* 375.

11. A poster of the mansion and other historic houses in the Pack Collection, SUNY-ESF, drawer 2; A. Pack, "From This Seed," 1; "CLP Materials," 3.

12. Gill, unpublished biography, 17; Thornton, *Along the Historic River Aux Sables,* 102.

13. "Notes from CLP," 5.

14. "CLP Materials," 4.

15. "Notes from CLP," 5.

16. "At the End of the Journey," *American Lumberman,* Sept. 8, 1906, 1, Harry A. Garfield, *The Cleveland Trust Company: A History* (Cleveland, undated), 62–63.

17. Solomon, "Historical Sketch"; Morrow, "No Sentiment."

18. "Charles Pack, Conservation Expert, Dies," *Cleveland Press,* June 14, 1937; Alburn and Alburn, *This Cleveland,* 44.

19. "Notes from Mrs. McNairy in Asheville," 8.

20. "CLP Materials," 3.

21. *Ibid.*

22. Gill, unpublished biography, 15.

23. "Notes from Mrs. McNairy in Asheville," 6; Garfield, *The Cleveland Trust,* 33.

24. *Ibid.*

25. "Notes from Mrs. McNairy in Asheville," 6.

26. Letter from Elizabeth Boggs to the author, April 19, 1988, Pack Collection, SUNY-ESF, drawer 1, p. 1.

27. Garfield, *The Cleveland Trust,* 35, 37.

28. *Ibid.,* 33–34.

29. *Ibid.,* 34.

30. *Ibid.,* 36–37.

31. *Ibid.,* 41–44.

32. *Ibid.,* 45.

33. *Ibid.,* 46–47.

34. "Some Significant Dates in Ameritrust History," provided by Monica M. Martines, Ameritrust Company National Association, Pack Collection, SUNY-ESF, drawer 1, p. 1; Garfield, *The Cleveland Trust,* 47.

35. Garfield, *The Cleveland Trust,* 57.

36. Boggs interview with the author, Pack Collection, SUNY-ESF, drawer 1, p. 3.

37. Gill, unpublished biography, 19.

38. *Ibid.*

39. Untitled, undated newsclip fragment, Pack Collection, SUNY-ESF, drawer 3; Avery, *A History of Cleveland,* 542.

40. C. L. Pack, "1,000,000 Population," April 17, 1901, Pack Collection, SUNY-ESF, drawer 1.

41. "Why Cleveland Will Have Population of 1,000,000 in 1925," *Cleveland Leader,* Jan. 11, 1903, Pack Collection, SUNY-ESF, drawer 1.

42. "Mr. Pack to Give a Dinner," *Cleveland Town Topics*, Oct. 12, 1912, 15; Lease No. 543504, v47, Dec. 2, 1910, in Cleveland Record of Leases, vol. 47, 532.

43. Lease No. 543504, Cleveland Record of Leases; William Ganson Rose, *Cleveland: The Making of a City*, (Cleveland: World Publishing Co., 1950), 614.

44. "City's New Hotel Host to Hundreds," *Cleveland Plain Dealer*, Oct. 20, 1912, 12; "Hotel Statler," *Cleveland Town Topics*, Oct. 26, 1912.

45. "Mr. Pack to Give a Dinner." *Cleveland Town Topics*, Oct. 12, 1912, 15

46. "In Society," *Cleveland Town Topics*, May 4, 1901, 13; Morrow, "No Sentiment."

47. "Cheers for Chas L. Pack," *Cleveland Plain Dealer*, April 23, 1902.

Chapter 5

1. C. L. Pack, *Thomas Hatch of Barnstable and Some of His Descendants* (Newark, N.J.: The Society of Colonial Wars in the State of New Jersey, 1930), 167–68.

2. Eleanor Pack Liddell interview with the author, 1987, transcript in the Pack Collection, SUNY-ESF, drawer 2, p. 11.

3. Phoebe Finley Pack, interview with the author, 1988, tape 3, transcript in the Pack Collection, SUNY-ESF, drawer 4, p. 5.

4. Liddell, "Grandmother," undated, Pack Collection, SUNY-ESF, drawer 2.

5. Townsend letter to author, Sept. 27, 1989, Pack Collection, SUNY-ESF, drawer 4; Liddell interview, 7.

6. Charles Pack, *Thomas Hatch*, 165–66; Townsend letter to author, Sept. 27, 1989.

7. Alice Gertrude Hatch diaries, May 28, 1879 to May 16, 1880; July 2, to June 18, 1885 (London); 1885 (Egypt); Pack Family Papers, Tucson.

8. *Ibid.*, June 3, Aug. 18, 1885.

9. *Ibid.*, June 9, 1879.

10. *Ibid.*, Feb. 15, 1885.

11. *Ibid.*, Feb. 17, 1885.

12. "Notes from CLP," 5.

13. Hatch diary, 1885.

14. Hatch to Frances Farman Pack, February 1886, Pack Collection, SUNY-ESF, drawer 1 (provided by E. Boggs).

15. *Ibid.*

16. *Ibid.*

17. Hatch to CLP, no date, Pack Collection, Denver.

18. Liddell interview, 6.

19. Townsend interview, 1987.

20. Liddell, "Grandfather's Laugh," undated, SUNY-ESF, drawer 2.

21. Townsend interview, 1987.

22. C. L. Pack, *Thomas Hatch*, 165–66.

23. A. Pack diaries. Dec. 25, 1908; Dec. 19, 22, 25, 28, 29, 31, 1909; April 9, 11, 10, 1910; May 31, 1915; and Feb. 27, 1916, are just some of the dates on which Arthur records socializing with the Baldwins; in Pack Family Papers, Tucson.

24. Townsend to the author, July 9, 1992, Pack Collection, SUNY-ESF, drawer 4.

Chapter 6

1. C. L. Pack, *Thomas Hatch*, 167; *Cleveland Town Topics*, Dec. 24, 1887.

2. "Beautiful Euclid: The Noble Avenue Handsomely Decorated from Erie Street to Lake View," date and newspaper unknown, Pack Collection, SUNY-ESF, drawer 3 (provided by Virginia Lathrop [Pack] Townsend).

3. "CLP Materials," 3.

4. A. Pack, "From This Seed," 2.

5. *Ibid.*, 1; "Ivywall and Norway Lodge" photo album, Pack Collection, SUNY-ESF (donated by Elizabeth Boggs).

6. A. Pack, "From This Seed," 2.

7. *Ibid.*

8. Correspondence between the author and Boggs, Dec. 7, 1989, and undated reply, Pack Collection, SUNY-ESF, drawer 1.

9. Boggs to the author, April 19, 1988, Pack Collection, SUNY-ESF, drawer 1; A. Pack, "From This Seed," 2.

10. C. L. Pack, *Thomas Hatch*, 165–66.

11. Pack Collection, SUNY-ESF, drawer 1 (provided by Virginia Lathrop [Pack] Townsend).

12. *Ibid.*

13. A. Pack, "From This Seed," 4.

14. *Ibid.*, 5.

15. *Ibid.*

16. *Ibid.*, 6; Muriel Pullen interview, 1988, transcript, Pack Collection, SUNY-ESF, drawer 4, pp. 5, 6, 11.

17. A. Pack, "From This Seed," 4–5.

18. *Ibid.*

19. *Ibid.*, 6.

20. "Memorandums for Mr. Tom Gill," Pack Collection, Denver, 1.

21. A. Pack, "From This Seed," 6–8.

22. "Memorandums for Mr. Tom Gill," Pack Collection, Denver, 2.

23. *The Golden Years of Lakewood: Pictorial Album of Lakewood*, compiled by The Ocean County Historical Society (Lakewood, N.J., 1971, unpaginated); Liddell interview, 4; Townsend interview; and Phoebe Pack interview, transcript of tapes 1 and 2, drawer 4, p. 3, and transcript of tape 3, drawer 4, p. 1.

24. *Lakewood in the Pines: A Backward Glance* (Lakewood, N.J.: Lakewood Heritage Commission, 1987), 2.

25. *Lakewood In the Pines*, 27, 30; *Golden Years of Lakewood.*.

26. A. Pack, "From This Seed," 7.

27. *Ibid.*, 8.

28. "Notes from CLP," 4–5; *St. Mary Academy, 1898-1973* (Lakewood, N.J.: St. Mary Academy, 1973), unpaginated; Townsend interview, 1988.

29. Postcard provided by Virginia Townsend.

30. *St. Mary;* Townsend to the author, Feb. 6, 1992, Pack Collection, SUNY-ESF, drawer 4.

31. Morrow, "Cleveland Man War Gardener's General"; Townsend interview, 1988.

32. A. Pack, "From This Seed," 8, 9, 19; Stanley Washburn correspondence with CLP, Stanley Washburn Papers, Library of Congress, boxes 1, 2, 3, 4.

33. Gill, unpublished biography, 14.

34. A. Pack, "From This Seed," 8; C. Pack, *Thomas Hatch*, 168; Townsend interview, 1988.

35. "The Collectors Club, New York. A Noble Gift from Mr. C. L. Pack," *Philatelic Classics* 1, no. 4 (1927):15; Phoebe Pack interview, transcript (tape 4), drawer 3, p. 1.

36. "Stamp Collecting Hobby Has Many Notable Riders," *New York Times*, Feb. 10, 1924.

37. A. Pack, "From This Seed," 8.

38. *Ibid.,* 9.

39. *Ibid.*

40. *Ibid.,* 6.

41. *Ibid.,* 4, 6.

Chapter 7

1. A. Pack, "From This Seed," 3.

2. Donald Gillis to CLP, September 5, 1906, Pack Collection, SUNY-ESF, drawer 4 (provided by E. Boggs).

3. Resolutions signed by Locke Craig, J. C. Pritchard, C. A. Webb, M. L. Reed, and J. D. Murphy [1906], Pack Collection, SUNY-ESF, drawer 4, pp. 1–2 (provided by E. Boggs).

4. S. Lipinsky, Retail Merchants Association memorial statement [1906], Pack Collection, SUNY-ESF, drawer 4, p. 1 (provided by E. Boggs).

5. Maria Brown, president, Flower Mission Board memorial statement [1906], Pack Collection, SUNY-ESF, drawer 4, p. 1 (provided by E. Boggs).

6. Charity Rusk Craig, Asheville Free Kindergarten Association memorial statement [1906], Pack Collection, SUNY-ESF, drawer 4, p. 1 (provided by E. Boggs).

7. Greeley, *Forests and Men,* 54.

8. *Ibid.,* 55–58.

9. *Ibid.,* 58.

10. *Ibid.,* 59; Gifford Pinchot, *Breaking New Ground* (New York: Harcourt, Brace, 1947), 49, 69.

11. Gill, unpublished biography, 19.

12. J. A. Larsen, "Carl Alwin Schenck and Biltmore Forest," reprinted from *The Ames Forester* 48 (1961):15–19.

13. Elwood R. Maunder, "Dr. Carl Alwin Schenck, German Pioneer in the Field of American Forestry," *The Paper Maker*, September 1954, C. A. Schenck Collection, Forest History Society, Durham, N.C., box 25, p. 21.

14. CLP to C. A. Schenck, April 29, 1934, The Biltmore Forest School, C. A. Schenck Collection, North Carolina State University Archives, Raleigh, N.C., drawer 1.

15. "Notes from CLP," 5.

16. Henry Clepper, "American Forestry Association," in *Encyclopedia of American Forest and Conservation History,* vol. 1, 17.

17. Greeley, *Forests and Men,* 64.

18. Clepper, "American Forestry," 17.

19. *Proceedings of the American Forest Congress Held at Washington, D.C., January 2 to 6, 1905, under the Auspices of the American Forestry Association* (Washington: H. M. Suter Publishing Company, 1905), 446–47.

20. Barry Walsh, note to the author, July 1989.

21. CLP to Messrs. Hardtner & La Croix, Feb. 18, 1898; Kerr, "History of Forestry in Louisiana," 6.

22. "CLP Materials," 4.

Chapter 8

1. Townsend interview, 1988; Eleanor Brown Pack Hibben to author, July 3, 1988, drawer 2; Hibben interview, transcript, drawer 2, pp. 1–2, 3; Barry Walsh to the author, July 26, 1989, drawer 4; all in the Pack Collection, SUNY-ESF.

2. Pinchot, *Breaking New Ground,* 1.

3. *Ibid.,* 1–3.

4. *Ibid.,* 2.

5. *Ibid.,* 5.

6. *Ibid.,* 3.

7. Harold T. Pinkett, "Gifford Pinchot," in *Encyclopedia of American Forest and Conservation History,* vol. 2, 528–29.

8. *Ibid.,* 529.

9. Greeley, *Forests and Men,* 70.

10. Paul Russell Cutright, *Theodore Roosevelt: The Making of a Conservationist* (Chicago: University of Illinois Press, 1985), 229.

11. Henry Clepper, "Conference of Governors," in *Encyclopedia of American Forest and Conservation History,* vol. 1, 98; Wayne Hanley, *Natural History in America, from Mark Catesby to Rachel Carson* (New York: Quadrangle, The New York Times Book Co., 1977), 284.

12. Clepper, "Conference of Governors," 98.

13. Avery, *History of Cleveland,* 542; C. L. Pack, "Jersey Pioneers" undated, Pack Collection, SUNY-ESF, drawer 3; Gill, unpublished biography, 21.

14. Pinchot, *Breaking New Ground,* 344.

15. Gary Craven Gray, "Conservation Movement," *Encyclopedia of American Forest and Conservation History,* vol. 1, 109; *Bulletin No. 4 (National Conservation Commission) Presenting the Report of the National Conservation Commission and a Chronological History of the Conservation Movement* (Washington, D.C.: The Joint Committee on Conservation, n.d.), National Conservation Committee papers, Pinchot Papers, box 514, p. 1.

16. Gray, "Conservation Movement," 109.

17. Samuel Trask Dana, *Forest and Range Policy* (New York: McGraw-Hill, 1956), 162–63.

18. *Ibid.,* 163.

19. Gray, "Conservation Movement," 109.

20. Dana, 164.

21. *Ibid.*

22. Gray, "Conservation Movement," 109.

23. *Ibid.*, 110.

24. R. W. Pullman, "National Conservation 1914–1916," James R. Garfield Papers, Library of Congress, box 118, p. 9; Pinchot, *Breaking New Ground,* 326.

25. Gray, "Conservation Movement," 110.

26. "For Immediate Release from the National Conservation Association," Garfield Papers, box 148, pp. 2–3.

27. CLP to Gifford Pinchot, April 4, 1913, Pinchot Papers, box 482.

28. "Report of the Secretary, Read at the Meeting of the Board of Directors, National Conservation Association, at the University Club, New York City, January 19, 1916," Garfield Papers, box 148, p. 5.

29. *Ibid.*, 6.

30. *Ibid.*, 7.

31. Gray, "Conservation Movement," 110.

32. Thomas R. Shipp, "Statement of the National Conservation Congress, 10 February, 1910" Pinchot Papers, box 514; Gray, "Conservation Movement," 110.

Chapter 9

1. Arthur W. Greeley interview with the author, October 1987, transcript in the Pack Collection, SUNY-ESF, drawer 2, p. 2.

2. CLP to Gifford Pinchot, Dec. 1, 1913, Pinchot Papers, box 169, p. 2.

3. Gray, "Conservation Movement," 110.

4. "Fair Play for Forests to Be Urged," *The Cincinnati Enquirer,* Nov. 15, 1913.

5. W. R. Brown to Robert P. Bass, June 6, 1913, W. R. Brown Collection, Sterling Memorial Library, Yale University, box 1; *Fifth National Conservation Congress* (Washington, D.C., 1913), Ralph Sheldon Hosmer Collection, Department of Manuscripts and Archives, Cornell University Library, archive number 20/1/560, box 15. The following five letters are from Pinchot Papers, box 169, all from the year 1913: CLP to Pinchot, June 5(a), June 5(b), June 6, June 9; Pinchot to CLP, June 13. D. P. Simons to Hugo Winkenwerder, July 25, 1913, Hugo Winkenwerder Correspondence, University of Washington Archives, Seattle, box 1.

6. CLP to Pinchot, Jan. 22, 1913; Pinchot to Pack, Jan. 24, 1913; Pinchot Papers, box 169.

7. "For Use at Your Pleasure," undated press release from the National Conservation Congress, Pinchot Papers, box 514.

8. "From the National Congress, Released for Publication," press release, October 13, 1913, Pinchot Papers, box 514.

9. "From the National Conservation Congress, 619-622 Woodward Building, Washington, D.C.," press release, stamped as recv'd Oct. 29, 1913, Pinchot Papers, box 514.

10. "From the National Conservation Congress," press release, Aug. 26, 1913, Pinchot Papers, box 514, p. 1.

11. CLP to Pinchot, June 5, 1913, Pinchot Papers, box 169.

12. CLP to Pinchot, May 16, 1913, Pinchot Papers, box 169.

13. CLP to Pinchot, Oct. 13, 1913, Pinchot Papers, box 169, p. 2.

14. Pinchot to James R. Garfield, Oct. 23, 1913, Garfield Papers, box 117.

15. "Report of the Committee on Water Power," Pinchot Papers, box 514, pp. 3–4.

16. W. L. Stoddard, "The Mad Hatters of Conservation," *Boston Evening Transcript,* Nov. 22, 1913.

17. *Ibid.*

18. *Ibid.*

19. *Ibid.*

20. *Ibid.*

21. *Ibid.*

22. *Ibid.*

23. *Ibid.*

24. Garfield to Pinchot, Nov. 25, 1913, Garfield Papers, box 117.

25. CLP to Pinchot, Nov. 14, 1913, Pinchot Papers, box 169.

26. "Conservation Row over State Rights," special to the *New York Times,* Nov. 19, 1913.

27. Pinchot to Garfield, Dec. 4, 1913, Pinchot Papers, box 117, p. 1.

28. *Ibid.,* 1.

29. "Oh Gifford, I Am Through," Nov. 20, 1913, *New York Sun.*

30. Pinchot to Garfield, Dec. 4, 1913, Garfield Papers, box 117, p. 1.

31. *New York Sun,* Nov. 22, 1913.

32. *New York Press,* Nov. 21, 1913, Pack Collection, Denver.

33. Gifford Pinchot, "Released for Publication," Nov. 22, 1913, Garfield Papers, box 117.

34. CLP to Pinchot, Nov. 25, 1913, Pinchot Papers, box 169.

35. C. L. Pack, "What the Conservation Congress Accomplished," press release, Pinchot Papers, box 169.

36. Pinchot to CLP, Dec. 1, 1913, Pinchot Papers, box 169.

37. Pinchot to Garfield, Dec. 4, 1913, Garfield Papers, box 117.

38. "Release for Use at Your Pleasure," press release, Pinchot Papers, box 514.

39. These activities are all documented in Charles's correspondence with Gifford in 1913: CLP to Pinchot, Dec. 1; Pinchot to CLP, Sept. 18, Oct. 8, Oct. 16(a), Oct. 16(b), Pinchot Papers, box 169.

40. CLP to Pinchot, Nov. 14, 1913, Pinchot Papers, box 169.

41. CLP to Pinchot, May 11, 1914, Pinchot Papers, box 182.

42. Pinchot to CLP, Dec. 13, 1916, Pinchot Papers, box 199.

43. "Interview Gifford Pinchot given Newspaper Men re: Conservation Congress, May 3, 1916," manuscript, Pinchot Papers, box 514, p. 1.

44. Pinchot to Harry A. Slattery, Feb. 14, 1916, Pinchot Papers, box 489.

45. Pinchot to CLP, May 2, 1916, Pinchot Papers, box 199.

46. Slattery to CLP, Feb. 25, 1916, Pinchot Papers, box 489, p. 2.

47. Pinchot to CLP, Dec. 18, 1915, Pinchot Papers, box 489, p. 2.

Chapter 10

1. A. Pack, "From This Seed," 9, 13.

2. *Ibid.,* 11–13.

3. *Ibid.*

4. *Ibid.,* 9–11.

5. *Ibid.,* 13–14.

6. *Ibid.,* 16.

7. *Ibid.*, 21.

8. "Randolph G. Pack, 1890–1956," Gill Collection, box 4, p. 1; "Randolph G. Pack Is Dead; Leader in Conservation," Pack Collection, SUNY-ESF, drawer 4; *Who Was Who in America 1951–1960*, vol. 3 (Chicago: Marquis– Who's Who Inc., 1960), 659; Tall Timber Lumber Co. Minute Book 1912, Directors' Meeting at Texarkana, Miller County, Ark., Dec. 10, 1912, in Pack Collection, SUNY-ESF, box 8, pp. 1–2 (provided by Archer H. Mayor).

9. "Fuller-Pack Wedding," *Cleveland Town Topics,* April 25, 1914, society section, 5.

10. "Entertaining for Miss Fuller and Mr. Pack," *Cleveland Town Topics*, April 18, 1914, society section, 10.

11. "Fuller-Pack Wedding," 5–6.

12. "Fuller-Pack Wedding," 5–6; Townsend interview, 1988; "Randolph G. Pack Is Dead," *New York Herald Tribune*, Dec. 26, 1956, in Gill Collection, box 5.

13. A. Pack, "From This Seed," 26.

14. A. Pack diary, March 15, 1914.

15. A. Pack, "From This Seed," 15, 27; "Trout Creek Lumber Co. of La., Inc., Minute Book, 1917–1941" (extracts), Pack Collection, SUNY-ESF, box 8, p. 3 (provided by A. Mayor); land sale deed listing Francis Dana as River Land and Lumber Co. president, Feb. 25, 1907, La Salle Parish Clerk of Court, Jena, La., book 10, p. 586; CLP listed as River Land and Lumber Co. president in land sale deed filed July 11, 1910 (recorded July 12, 1910), La Salle Parish Clerk of Court, Jena, La., book A, p. 291; A. Pack diary, Oct. 12–20, 1915; Edwin C. Eckel, *Iron Ores, Fuels, and Fluxes of the Birmingham District, Alabama, Dept. of the Interior United States Geological Survey, George Otis Smith, Director, Bulletin 400* (Washington: Government Printing Office, 1910), 55–93; Ruffner District map no. 4-99, Jan. 30, 1924, Ruffner District map no. 4-315, April 20, 1936, and United States Geological Survey, Ruffner District topographical map, 1959, Special Collections, Sanford University, Birmingham, Ala. (provided by Elizabeth Wells).

16. A. Pack diary, Sept. 23, 1916.

17. *Ibid.*, April 10, 1916. The entries of June through November 1915 document Arthur's early work responsibilities.

18. *Ibid.*, Oct. 11, 1915.

19. Map created by Beth Dinatelli Johnson, Pack Collection, SUNY-ESF, box 1; A. Pack diary, Nov. 11, 1915; A. Pack, "From This Seed," 29.

20. A. Pack diary, Oct. 20, 1915.

21. *Ibid.*, May 2–6, 1916; Oct. 24, 1915.

22. *Ibid.*, Dec. 4, 1915.

23. Arthur's diary entries for 1915–1916 extensively document his social life during this year.

24. A. Pack diary, May 20, 1915, 6.

25. *Ibid.*, April 29, 1916.

26. *Ibid.*, July 2, 1915.

27. *Ibid.*, Aug. 23, 1915.

28. A. Pack, "From This Seed," 63; Phoebe Pack interview, drawer 4, p. 6.

29. Interview with Phoebe Pack, pp. 1, 3–5; Townsend interview, 1988.

30. A. Pack, "From This Seed," 28.

31. A. Pack diary, April 11–17, 1911; April 12, 1911.

32. *Ibid.*, April 14, 1911.

33. A. Pack, "From This Seed," 29.

34. A. Pack diary, March 21, 1916.

35. *Ibid.*, March 22, 1916; "Cash Deed River Land and Lumber Co. to Trout Creek Lumber Co. of La., Inc., Good Pine Lumber Co. of La., Inc., Tall Timber Lumber Co., of La., Inc.," filed for record Sept. 24, 1925, recorded Oct. 2, 1925 as No. 2298 by La Salle Parish Clerk of Court, Jena, La., p. 6.

Chapter 11

1. Canadian timber leases TL137P, TL8887P, TL8888P, TL9477P, TL9484, TL2338P, Broughton Island; TL12919P–TL12924P, MacKenzie Sound; TL5499P, Toba Inlet; TL12786P, TL3856P–TL3861P, Vancouver Island; TL959P, TL960P, TL2004P–TL2008P, Gordon Pasha Lakes; TL12804P, TL12805P, Marion & Huaskin Lakes; TL12881P, TL12883P, Horseshoe Lake, Canadian Ministry of Forestry, Record Services, Victoria, B.C., Pack Collection, SUNY-ESF, box 9 (provided by Dorothea Hammond, Canadian Ministry of Forestry); Hibben to the author, July 3, 1988, Pack Collection, SUNY-ESF, drawer 2; A. Pack diary, July 23–Aug. 28, 1919; A. Pack diary, April 20–Sept. 9, 1920, provided by Margaret Pack McKinley, Santa Fe, N.M., excerpts on file, Pack Collection, SUNY-ESF, drawer 3; A. Pack, "From This Seed," 49–50.

2. Peter Gillis and Thomas R. Roach, *Lost Initiatives: Canada's Forest Industries, Forest Policy and Forest Conservation*, (New York: Greenwood Press, 1986), 129–90; H. N. Whitford and Roland D. Craig, *Forests of British Columbia* (Ottawa: Commission of Conservation, Canada Committee on Forests, 1918), 10.

3. Gillis and Roach, 129; Whitford and Craig, 10.

4. Lawrence, Joseph Collins, "British Columbia," *Encyclopedia Britannica Macropedia*, vol. 3 (Chicago: Encyclopedia Britannica, 1983), 297; Asa S. Williams, "Logging in British Columbia," *British Columbia Magazine* 7, no. 4 (1911):270–71.

5. Lawrence, 297.

6. Gillis and Roach, 130, 131.

7. Lawrence, 297; Whitford and Craig, 165.

8. Gillis and Roach, 133–34, 150–51.

9. *Ibid.*, 135–50.

10. A. R. M. Lower, *The North American Assault on the Canadian Forest*, (Toronto: Ryerson Press, 1938), 237.

11. A. Pack diary, Oct. 12–13, 1916; Rollins, *The Butt of the Log of the Sinnemahoning*, privately printed, undated, Pack Collection, SUNY-ESF, drawer 2 (provided by Virginia Townsend), 17 and cover page.

12. A. Pack diary, Oct. 13, 1916.

13. *Ibid.*, Oct. 19, 1916.

14. *Ibid.*, Oct. 20, 1916.

15. *Ibid.*, Oct. 21, 1916.

16. "British Columbia Distribution of Western White Pine," map in Whitford and Craig, *Forests of British Columbia*, 207; A. Pack, "From This Seed," 50; Whitford and Craig, "Forest Stand Types of British Columbia," Canadian Commission of Conservation map, 1917.

17. A. Pack diary, July 26, 29, 1919.

18. *Ibid.*, Aug. 24, 1919; Attorney General, Province of British Columbia, "Registrar of Company," call no. B 4402, file 335, pp. 17, 34, 42–3, 45, 49, Ministry of Provincial Secretary and Government Services, Provincial Archives, Province of British Columbia, reg. no. 88-1949, in Pack Collection, SUNY-ESF, box 9 (provided by D. Hammond).

19. "Registrar of Company," 43; A. Pack diary, August 25, 1919.

20. A. Pack, "From This Seed," 50; A. Pack diary, Aug. 15, 1919; A. Pack diary, Feb. 19, 1920, June 16, 29, 30, 1920, July 1, 1920, Aug. 5, 1920, Sept. 24, 1920, provided by McKinley.

21. A. Pack, "From This Seed," 50; A. Pack diary for 1919; A. Pack diary, October 1919 to May 1920, provided by McKinley.

22. A. Pack, "From This Seed," 50.

23. *Ibid.*

24. *Ibid.*

25. The distribution of the acreage is documented in the timber leases listed in note 1, chapter 11.

Chapter 12

1. Dana, *Forest and Range Policy*, 89.

2. Clepper, "American Forestry Association," 16; Herman Haupt Chapman, "Has the American Forestry Association Lost Its Former Usefulness? Reflections of a Life Director," part 3, *Journal of Forestry* 19, no. 4 (1921):327.

3. Clepper, "American Forestry Association," 16–17; Dana, *Forest and Range Policy*, 395.

4. Clepper, "American Forestry Association," 16–17; Gray, "Conservation Movement," 110.

5. Chapman, "Has the American," part 1 no. 3, 289.

6. Charles F. Quincy to H. H. Chapman, Nov. 27, 1915, and Alfred Gaskill to Chapman, March 2, 1916. Chapman Papers, box 41, p. 1.

7. Henry Clepper, "Crusade For Conservation: The Centennial History of the American Forestry Association," in "The Voice of Conservation," part 6, under heading "Gains on All Fronts," *American Forests* 81, no. 10 (1975): unpaginated.

8. Chapman, "Has the American," part 1, 287; Henry S. Drinker, review of George Fillmore Swain, "A Work on the Conservation of Water by Storage," *American Forestry* 21, no. 7 (1915):818–21.

9. Chapman, "Has the American," part 3, 328.

10. Clepper, "Crusade," in "The Voice of Conservation," part 6, under heading "Bonds For Sale."

11. Chapman to Charles F. Quincy, Nov. 23, 1915, 4, 1, Chapman Papers, box 41.

12. Chapman to E. A. Sterling, Nov. 23, 1915, 2, Chapman Papers, box 41.

13. Quincy to Chapman, Nov. 27, 1915, Chapman Papers, box 41.

14. Chapman to Alfred Gaskill, Dec. 15, 1915; Chapman to Sterling, Nov. 23, 1915, 1, Chapman Papers, box 41.

15. Chapman to Gaskill, Dec. 15, Chapman Papers, box 41.

16. "The Association's New President," *American Forestry* 22, no. 266 (1916):86.

17. Clepper, "Crusade," in "The Voice of Conservation," part 6.

18. *Ibid.*

19. Chapman, "Has the American," part 3, 330.

20. Clepper, "Crusade," under heading "Years of Stress and Strain," part 7.

21. Chapman to CLP, Feb. 5, 1916, 1, Chapman Papers, box 41.

22. *Ibid.*, 1–2.

23. Gaskill to Chapman, Feb. 14, 1916, 1; Chapman to CLP, Feb. 29, 1916; Chapman to CLP, Feb. 5, 1916, 2, in Chapman Papers, box 41.

24. Gaskill to Chapman, Feb. 14, 1915, 1; March 2, 1916, 1, in Chapman Papers, box 41.

25. "Meeting of the Executive Committee of the American Forestry Association at New York City, 90 West Street, March 2, 1916," Chapman Papers, box 41.

26. CLP to Chapman, July 5, 1916, Chapman Papers, box 41, pp. 1–2.

27. Chapman, "Drinker" (typescript), July 5, 1916, p. 1, and Chapman to Henry S. Graves, June 24, 1916, in Chapman Papers, box 41.

28. Chapman to CLP, July 7, 1916, p. 1, Chapman Papers, box 41.

29. Clepper, "Crusade," under heading "Years of Stress and Strain," part 7.

30. "Financial Statement of the American Forestry Association for 1919," *AFA Minute Books for 1920*, AFA Archives, box B6, Forest History Society, Durham, N.C.; Chapman, "Has the American," part 3, 330.

31. "Charles Lathrop Pack's Donations," in "Annual Meeting of the American Forestry Association at New York City, January 13, 1920, at 2 P.M.," *AFA Minutes 1920–1940*, AFA Archives, p. 1, AFA Archives, box B6, Forest History Society.

32. Gaskill to Chapman, Oct. 17, 1919, Chapman Papers, box 41.

33. Chapman, "Has the American," part 3, 330.

34. "American Tree Seeds in Italy," *Nature Magazine* 1, no. 1, (1923):61–62; "American Tree Seeds for Europe," *Nature Magazine* 1, no. 6 (1923):58.

35. Gaskill to W. R. Brown, April 21, 1919, 1, Chapman Papers, box 41; "Tree Seeds Sent Overseas," *Forestry Almanac* (Philadelphia: Lippincott Press, 1924), 42–44.

36. Gaskill to W. R. Brown, April 21, 1919, Chapman Papers, box 41, p. 1.

37. *Ibid.*

38. Clepper, "Crusade," under heading "Years of Stress and Strain," part 7.

39. *Ibid.*

40. Chapman, "Has the American," part 3, 329.

41. "Charles Lathrop Pack's Donations," 2; "Financial Statement of the American Forestry Association for 1919"; Chapman, "Has the American," part 3, 330.

42. CLP to Chapman, Feb. 9, 1917, Chapman Papers, box 41.

43. Chapman, "Has the American," part 3, 327.

44. *Ibid.*, 328.

45. *Ibid.*

46. *Ibid.*, 330.

47. Clepper, "Crusade," under heading "Years of Stress and Strain," part 7.

48. Joseph Persico, formerly a speechwriter for Governor Rockefeller, told this story to Michael Korda, editor-in-chief of Simon & Schuster. Persico claimed to be present when Rockefeller said this and swore that it was true (Korda, personal communication, Oct. 3, 1989).

49. Chapman, "Has the American," part 3, 335.

50. *Ibid.*, 334.

51. "Annual Meeting of the American Forestry Association at New York City, Jan. 13, 1920, at 2 p.m." *AFA Minutes*, Forest History Society, Durham, N.C.; Chapman to H. S. Graves, Dec. 19, 1919; F. W. Besley to Chapman, Dec. 29, 1919; Chapman to E. O. Siecke, Jan. 2, 1920; Chapman to Henry Hardtner, Jan. 2, 1920; Chapman to C. R. Pettis, Jan. 7, 1920; Chapman to CLP, Jan. 15, 1920, in Chapman Papers, box 41.

52. Chapman to Clifford A. Pettis (Chapman was mistaken; should be Clifford R.), Dec. 12, 1919, Chapman Papers, box 41.

53. C. R. Pettis to Chapman, Dec. 18, 1919, Chapman Papers, box 41.

54. Chapman to Graves, Dec. 19, 1919, Chapman Papers, box 41; "Annual Meeting of the American Forestry Association at New York City January 13, 1920, at 2. p.m."

55. Chapman to William B. Greeley, Jan. 28, 1920, p. 1; Chapman to A. S. Houghton, Feb. 6, 1920, Chapman Papers, box 41.

56. Gaskill to CLP, March 2, 1920, Chapman Papers, box 41.

57. Gaskill to Ralph S. Hosmer, March 22, 1920, Chapman Papers, box 41.

58. HHC to Raphael Zon, Jan. 21, 1920, Chapman Papers, box 41, p. 2.

59. Chapman, "Has the American," part 4, 339.

60. Chapman to C. R. Pettis, Feb. 27, 1920, 1; Chapman to Capt. J. R. Coolidge, Feb. 13, 1920, 1, Chapman Papers, box 41.

61. Chapman to J. R. Coolidge, Feb. 13, 1920, 1, Chapman Papers, box 41.

62. Chapman to Albert L. Webster, Feb. 20, 1920, Chapman Papers, box 41.

63. Chapman to CLP, April 22, 1920, and CLP to Chapman, May 8, 1920, Gill Collection, box 1; Chapman to CLP, July 7, 1920, Chapman Papers, box 41, p. 4.

Chapter 13

1. Chapman, "Has the American," 340.

2. "Meeting of the Board of Directors of the American Forestry Association at New York City, Dec. 16, 1920," *AFA Minutes*, Forest History Society, Durham, N.C.; Chapman, "Has the American," part 4, 340.

3. CLP to Chapman, Oct. 1, 1920, Chapman Papers, box 41; Chapman, "Has the American," part 3, 330, part 4, 340.

4. *Ibid.*, 340–41; "Meeting of the Board of Directors, Dec. 16, 1920"; Chapman, "Has the American," part 4, 341.

5. *Ibid.*, 341–42; Chapman (unsigned), "The American Forestry Association Versus Charles Lathrop Pack," Pinchot Papers, box 240, p. 2.

6. Chapman, "Has the American," part 6, 453; J. G. Peters, "Statement of Main Features of the American Forestry Association Meeting at the New Willard Hotel, Washington, D.C., February 25," dated March 7, 1921, Chapman Papers, box 41, 1.

7. Joseph Kittredge, "Report of American Forestry Association Meeting on February 25, 1921 (by an eye witness)," March 8, 1921, 1; Harris A. Reynolds, "Report to the Executive Committee of the Massachusetts Forestry Association, of the Adjourned Annual Meeting of the American Forestry Association at the Willard Hotel, Washington, D.C., February 25, 1921," one-page manuscript, March 8, 1921. Both from Chapman Papers, box 41.

8. "Meeting of the Board of Directors of the American Forestry Association at Washington, D.C., Feb. 25, 1921," Chapman Papers, box 41; Kittredge, "Report of AFA Meeting," 1.

9. Kittredge, "Report of AFA Meeting," 1; Peters, "Statement of Main Features," 1–2.

10. Peters, 2; Kittredge, 1.

11. Peters, 2.

12. *Ibid.*

13. Peters, 3; Kittredge, 2; Reynolds.

14. Peters, 4; Kittredge, 2.

15. Reynolds.

16. "Meeting of the Board of Directors, Feb. 25, 1921."

17. Reynolds.

18. CLP to Calvin Coolidge, March 8, 1921, Chapman Papers, box 41, pp. 1–2.

19. Henry S. Graves, "Editorial Comment: The American Forestry Association Turns a New Leaf," *Journal of Forestry* 19, no. 3 (1921):315; "To Foresters," April 1, 1921, Chapman Papers, box 41; W. B. Greeley to "Committee of Investigation, American Forestry Association," May 22, 1921, Chapman Papers, box 41, p. 9.

20. Graves, "Editorial Comment," 315.

21. Graves, "What Is to Be Done?" (editorial), *Journal of Forestry* 19, no. 3, (1921):316–17.

22. T. S. W., Jr., "After the Meeting of the A. F. A.—Ruminations of a Forester," *Journal of Forestry* 19, no. 3, (1921):317–18.

23. Chapman, "Has the American," part 4, 347.

24. Chapman, "Has the American," part 8, 465.

25. Chapman to Pinchot, Oct. 12, 1921, Chapman Papers, box 41; Chapman to Pinchot, May 27, 1921, Pinchot Papers, box 240.

26. Chapman, "The American Forestry Association Versus Charles Lathrop Pack," 4.

27. *Ibid.*, 4–6.

28. *Ibid.*, 6–7.

29. *Ibid.*

30. Chapman to Pinchot, Oct. 4, 1921, Pinchot Papers, box 240, p. 2.

31. Extracts from the following documents were provided by Archer Mayor and are on file in the Pack Collection, SUNY-ESF, box 8: "Grant Timber & Manufacturing Co. Minute Book 1905–1917," for 1906, 1908, 1917; "Grant Land & Lumber Co. Minute Book 1905–1910," entries for 1907, 1908, 1910; "Trout Creek Lumber Co., Minute Book 1904–1917," for 1909, 1911, 1917; "Bodcaw Lumber Co., Minute Book no. 2, Feb. 10, 1906–May 7, 1917," for 1911, 1912, 1913–1917; Tall Timber Lumber Co. Minute Book 1912–1917," for 1912, 1917; "Winn Land & Lumber Company, Feb. 20, 1912"; "Good Pine Lumber Co. of La., Inc. Minute Book 1917–1941," for 1917; "Tall Timber Lumber Co. of La., Inc. Minute Book 1917–1941," for 1920; "Trout Creek Lumber Co. of La., Inc., Minute Book 1917–1941," for 1917; "Pine Woods Lumber Co., Minute Book 1897–1930," for 1916, 1919, 1920–1923; Bodcow Co. "Stockholders Meeting," for 1918–1924, 1938, 1941.

32. From the year 1921: Chapman to Pinchot, April 16; Pinchot to Chapman, April 19; Chapman to Pinchot, June 2; Pinchot to Chapman, June 10, June 20;

Chapman to Pinchot, June 30, July 7, July 9; Pinchot to Chapman, July 13; Chapman to Pinchot, July 14; Pinchot to Graves, July 31; Pinchot to Chapman, Aug. 2; Graves to Pinchot, Sept. 7; Pinchot to Graves, Sept. 8; Chapman to Pinchot, Oct. 12; Pinchot to Chapman, Oct. 15, Oct. 17; Pinchot Papers, box 240.

33. "Demand for a Change in Policy of the American Forestry Association," *Journal of Forestry* 19, no. 6:661–64.

34. Graves to Pinchot, Sept. 7, 1921, Pinchot Papers, box 241; "Demand for Change," 662.

35. C. L. Pack, "To: Messrs. H. S. Graves, and the Gentlemen Who Joined Mr. Graves in Signing a Statement Dated April 20, 1921, Addressed to the Officers and Directors of the American Forestry Association, and Foreworded by Mr. Graves with Letter Dated May 21," Pinchot Papers, p. 1, box 554.

36. *Ibid.*, 2.

37. *Ibid.*

38. *Ibid.*, 3.

39. *Ibid.*, 2.

40. *Ibid.*, 3.

41. *Ibid.*, 3, 4.

42. *Ibid.*, 3.

43. *Ibid.*

44. From 1921: CLP to Pinchot, June 1; Ridsdale to Chapman, May 27; Pinchot to CLP, May 24; Pinchot Papers, box 243.

45. "Conference Report on American Forestry Association Matters," Pinchot Papers, box 241.

46. "Meeting of the Board of Directors of the American Forestry Association at New York City, August 30, 1921," *AFA Minutes*, p. 2, Forest History Society.

47. "Meeting of the Board of Directors of the American Forestry Association New York City, September 19, 1922," *AFA Annual Reports 1923–1932*, 1.

48. *Ibid.*

49. *Ibid.*

Chapter 14

1. "Meeting of the Board of Directors of the American Forestry Association at New York City, Dec. 2, 1919," Chapman Papers, box 41.

2. C. L. Pack, *The War Garden Victorious* (Philadelphia: Lippincott, 1919), 5, 6.

3. *Ibid.*, 6–7.

4. "Building Monument of 10 Million," *Lakewood Citizen,* undated, Pack Collection, SUNY-ESF, drawer 4.

5. C. L. Pack, *War Garden Victorious,* 9.

6. *Ibid.*, 4–8.

7. *Ibid.*, 7–8.

8. A. Pack, "From This Seed," 53.

9. C. L. Pack, *War Garden Victorious,* 8.

10. *Ibid.*, 9, 8. The heading "National Emergency Food Garden Commission" appears on the commission's stationery in 1917 in the following letters in the National Archives, Washington, D.C., RG 16: P. S. Ridsdale to Carl Vrooman, March 22, 1917; May 18, 1917; CLP to Vrooman, July 7, 1917. The new name,

"National War Garden Commission," appeared on the stationery at least as early as September 1918, as evidenced by a letter from Ridsdale to President Woodrow Wilson, Sept. 28, 1918; Woodrow Wilson Papers, Department of Maps, Micro-texts, and Newspapers, Cornell University Library, Ithaca, New York, microtext reel 369.

11. See note 10, above.

12. George S. Davis to David Franklin Houston, April 27, 1917, and E. B. Hul-ley to Newton D. Baker, April 9, 1917, in National Archives, Record Group 16, Washington, D.C., RG 16.

13. C. L. Pack, *War Garden Victorious*, 8.

14. *Ibid.*, 28.

15. *Ibid.*

16. A. Pack, "From This Seed," 53.

17. *War Garden Victorious*, 168.

18. *Ibid.*, 172.

19. *Ibid.*, 176, 23.

20. *Ibid.*, 21 and frontispiece; Poster: "Sow the Seeds of Victory: Plant Your Own Vegetables," Library of Congress, Dept. of Prints and Photographs, card catalog no. BU.S.F63.13.

21. *War Garden Victorious*, 21, 15, 128, 17; "From This Seed," 48.

22. C. L. Pack, *War Garden Victorious*, 18, 79–88.

23. *Ibid.*, 18, 30, 23.

24. *Ibid.*, 31.

25. *Ibid.*, 32, 16.

26. *Ibid.*, 16–17.

27. *Ibid.*

28. *Ibid.*, after p. 179.

29. "The Country Gentleman Charles L. Pack Nov. 19, 1917," one page of copy pertaining to CLP and the origins of the commission, Trinity College Archives, Hartford, Conn.; John R. McMahon, "The War Garden Campaign of 1917," *The Country Gentleman* 82, no. 45 (1917):1722.

30. McMahon, "War Garden Campaign," 17–22.

31. *Ibid.*, 35–36, 38.

32. *Ibid.*

33. "Food Gardens for Lakewood: The Old Slogan, 'Food F.O.B. the Kitchen Door,' Is Still Popular; Commission Organized to Help Unemployed," two-page press release, Pack Collection, SUNY-ESF, drawer 4.

34. "Charles Lathrop Pack," *National Cyclopedia of American Biography*, vol. 28, 125–26.

35. An album titled "Miscellaneous Letters from June 8, 1908 to Feb. 5, 1915" includes numerous letters acknowledging the receipt of *The War Garden Victori-ous*, beginning in April 1919; Pack Family Papers, Tucson.

36. A. Pack, "From This Seed," 30.

37. *Ibid.*

38. *Ibid.*, 31.

39. *Ibid.*, 32–33.

40. *Ibid.*, 34.

41. C. L. Pack, *Thomas Hatch*, 192, says Frances Pack died Nov. 17, 1917, but the

Nov. 23, 1917, entry of Arthur Pack's diary says "Grandmother passed away yesterday very suddenly and painlessly".

42. A. Pack diary, Feb. 19, 1919; C. L. Pack, *Thomas Hatch*, 169.

Chapter 15

1. Emanuel Fritz, interview with Elwood R. Maunder, Oral History Collection, p. 166, Forest History Society, Durham, N.C.

2. "The American Tree Association," in *Forestry Almanac* (Philadelphia: J. B. Lippincott Co., 1926), 117.

3. "American Tree Association," in *Encyclopedia of American Forest and Conservation History*, vol. 1, 21.

4. These titles are taken from letterhead on ATA stationery, such as CLP to Hugo Winkenwerder, May 12, 1926, Hugo Winkenwerder Correspondence, University of Washington Archives, College of Forest Resources Records, Seattle, box 5; and CLP to Winkenwerder, Nov. 25, 1930, Winkenwerder Correspondence, box 6; "Last Rites Today," fragment from Savage obituary, Pack Collection, SUNY-ESF, drawer 4. (Provided by Helen Huss, Lakewood, N.J.)

5. "Dr. Frank Crane's Daily Editorial: Trees," *Washington* (D.C.) *Times*, April 25, 1925; "Now Is the Time to Plant Trees," *Boston American*, April 28, 1925.

6. CLP to Henry Schmitz, Nov. 12, 1930, University of Minnesota Archives, Division of Forestry Papers.

7. A small sampling of news items includes: "Looking Fifty Years Ahead," *The Independent* (Wilkes-Barre, Pa.), July 25, 1925; "The Optimist," editorial, *Philadelphia Bulletin*, Jan. 23, 1926; "Tree Situation Needs Attention," *The Chronicle* (Spokane, Wash.), April 16, 1926; "Program for Flood Control Involving Forestry Is Sought," *Washington Post*, Sept. 25, 1927; "National Reforestation Neglected by Congress," *The Pioneer* (Johnson City, Kans.), June 30, 1932; "Another Gracious Act," *The News* (Detroit, Mich.), June 3, 1932; undated cartoon from the ATA, "Watch Out Uncle, It's Gonna Hit You," Pack Collection, SUNY-ESF, drawer 3; Charles Lathrop Pack, *Trees as Good Citizens*, (Philadelphia: J. B. Lippincott Co., 1922), 119.

8. Cartoon, "Uncle Sam Needs New Glasses," undated, University of Minnesota Archives, Division of Forestry Papers.

9. Ovid Butler, "A Foundation for the Forest," *American Forests* 59, no. 3, (1948):106.

10. "Oberlin Honors 'Son of Confucius' and for Forest Education Work, C. L. Pack," *Telegram* (Eyria, Ohio), June 14, 1926; Gill, unpublished biography, 25.

11. C. L. Pack, *Trees as Good Citizens*, 19.

12. C. L. Pack, *School Book of Forestry* (Philadelphia: J. B. Lippincott Co., 1922), introduction.

13. CLP to Henry Schmitz, March 10, 1926, April 2, 1934; University of Minnesota Archives, Division of Forestry Papers; "American Tree Association," *Encyclopedia of American Forest and Conservation History*, vol. 1, 21.

14. CLP to Schmitz, Oct. 6 and 8, 1928, University of Minnesota Archives, Division of Forestry Papers.

15. CLP to Albert R. Mann, May 15, 1930, Albert R. Mann Papers, Cornell Uni-

versity Library, Dept. of Manuscripts and Archives, Ithaca, N.Y., box 41, file 1929–30.

16. CLP to Mann, May 15, 1930, Mann Papers, box 41; CLP to Winkenwerder, June 27, 1930, Winkenwerder Correspondence, box 65; "Building Monument," *Lakewood Citizen*, undated, Pack Collection, SUNY-ESF, drawer 4; *George Washington Bicentennial Tree Planting* (Washington, D.C., publisher unknown, probably American Tree Association, 1932), 3; Russell T. Edwards to Winkenwerder, April 29, 1932, Winkenwerder Correspondence, box 7.

17. CLP to Hugh Baker, Jan. 11, 1932, Pack Collection, SUNY-ESF, drawer 1.

18. "Building Monument"; CLP to Baker, Jan. 11, 1932; "American Tree Association," *Forestry Almanac* (Baltimore: Dulany-Vernay Co., 1933), 159; "American Tree Association," *Encyclopedia of American Forest and Conservation History*, 21.

19. CLP to Baker, Feb. 1, 1932, Pack Collection, SUNY-ESF, drawer 1.

20. "American Tree Association," *Forestry Almanac*, 1933; "Bicentennial Tree-Planting," *Cincinnati Enquirer*, March 7, 1932; *George Washington Bicentennial Tree Planting*.

21. "Bicentennial Tree-Planting."

22. Elbert F. Baldwin, "World Wide Forestry Survey Is Urged," *Forestry News Digest Supplement*, June 1926; CLP to Henry Schmitz, July 3, 1926, University of Minnesota Archives.

23. "Forestry Legislative Survey Issued Today Shows Growing State Interest in Forestry," *Independent Times* (Streator, Ill.), July 27, 1926; CLP to Schmitz, Jan. 10, 1927, University of Minnesota Archives.

24. Schmitz to CLP, Aug. 3, 1926, University of Minnesota Archives.

25. I am grateful to Donald Theoe of Puyallup, Wash., who owns a complete set of the *Forestry News Digest* and provided information on years of publication and missing issues; Gill, unpublished biography, 23; *Forestry News Digest* extracts and samples: June 1926, June 1927, May 1928, June 1928, Nov. 1931, Oct. 1932, Jan. 1937, March 1937, Pack Collection, SUNY-ESF, drawer 2.

26. *Forestry News Digest*, June 1926, 1.

27. *Forestry News Digest*, March 1937, 3.

28. *Forestry News Digest*, March 1927, 5.

29. D. S. Jeffers, "Charted a Safe Course," *Forestry News Digest*, March 1937, 5.

30. Handwritten note, no salutation, signed RSK, attached to page 1 of January 1937 *Forestry News Digest*, in Ralph Sheldon Hosmer Papers, Dept. of Manuscripts and Archives, Cornell Univ. Library, 20/1/560, box 23.

31. CLP to Samuel N. Spring, March 24, 1936, Pack Collection, SUNY-ESF, drawer 4.

32. Chapman, "Has the American," 345.

33. Raphael Zon and Family Papers (1873–1956), Minnesota Historical Society, St. Paul.

Chapter 16

1. A. Pack, "From This Seed," 52–53.

2. *Ibid.*, 53.

3. *Ibid.*

4. *Ibid.*, foreword.

5. *Ibid.*, 48; A. Pack diary for 1919: March 11–12, 14, 22, 27, 28, 31; April 1–May 8 business trip in southern La.; March 20, 15; Aug. 29.

6. A. Pack diary for 1920; A. Pack, "From This Seed," 73–74, 49.

7. A. Pack, "From This Seed," 50.

8. *Ibid.*, 20; A. Pack diary, Oct. 13–25, 1920; A. Pack, "From This Seed," 55, 21.

9. A. Pack, "From This Seed," 51.

10. *Ibid.*, 52.

11. *Ibid.*, 52–53.

12. *The Pack Organizations*, booklet, no publisher, no date, Trinity College Archives; A. Pack, "From This Seed," 55.

13. Douglas S. Parker, "In Search of the Great White Heron: William Lovell Finley (1876–1953) and Wildlife Conservation in Oregon" (Ph.D. diss., Oregon State University, 1976), 58; A. Pack, "From This Seed," 57; Parker, 60; A. Pack, "From This Seed," 58; *Pack Organizations*, 12.

14. *Pack Organizations*, 12–14.

15. "American Nature Association," *Forestry Almanac 1926*, 129–30.

16. *Pack Organizations*, 11–12.

17. "American Nature Association, *Encyclopedia of American Forest and Conservation History*, vol. 1, 18.

18. A. Pack, "From This Seed," 53; "American Nature Association," 18.

19. A. Pack, "From This Seed," 56.

20. *Ibid.*, 79.

21. A. Pack, *Ghost Ranch*, 22–24, 27, 31.

22. *Ibid.*, 42–44; family tree, Pack Collection, SUNY-ESF, drawer 1 (provided by Virginia Townsend); A. Pack, *Ghost Ranch*, 46–48, 44.

23. A. Pack, *Ghost Ranch*, 89; "A Life of Service," *Arizona Daily Star* (Tucson), Dec. 9, 1975.

24. Carr, "Three Distinguished Conservationists," 8–9; "Noted Philanthropist Arthur N. Pack Dies; Museum Co-Founder," Pack Collection, SUNY-ESF, drawer 3; Carr, 9; "Arthur N. Pack," *Tucson Daily Citizen*, Dec. 9, 1975.

25. Frank A. Tinker, "A Museum Joins the Forest Service," *American Forests* 77, no. 5 (1971):33; William Carr, "Living Museums," *American Forests* 64, no. 10 (1958):19; A. Pack, *Ghost Ranch*, 106–10.

26. Tinker, "A Museum," 33; A. Pack, *Ghost Ranch*, 136–38.

27. A. Pack, *Ghost Ranch*, 117–18.

28. A. Pack, "From This Seed," 54.

Chapter 17

1. "Pack Gives $200,000 for Forestry School Foundation Fund," *The Michigan Daily*, Feb. 31, 1930; "School of Forestry Receives Large Gift," *Michigan Alumnus*, Feb. 22, 1930, 350.

2. A. Pack to Hugh P. Baker, Nov. 3, 1932, Pack Collection, SUNY-ESF, drawer 1, p. 1; *Pack Organizations*, 4; Tom Gill, untitled four-page manuscript describing Pack organizations, research, and publications, Gill Collection, box 1.

3. *Pack Organizations*, 4–5.

4. "The Harvard Forest," in the *Official Register of Harvard University, Report*

of the *President of Harvard College and Reports of Departments 1929–30* 28, no. 4, 188.

5. Ralph Sheldon Hosmer, *Forestry at Cornell: A Retrospect of Proposals, Developments, and Accomplishments in the Teaching of Professional Forestry at Cornell University* (Ithaca, N.Y., 1950), 30.

6. Philip W. Ayres, "The Charles Lathrop Pack Demonstration Forests," *The American Review of Reviews* 75, no. 5 (1927):514; "Public Demonstration Forest: Charles L. Pack's Gift to Yale," *The Christian Science Monitor,* Dec. 21, 1925, 1. Interview with David Smith, Yale professor of forestry, transcript, drawer 4, box 10; Smith to the author, July 27, 1989, drawer 1, both in the Pack Collection, SUNY-ESF.

7. *Pack Organizations,* 4–5.

8. Winkenwerder Correspondence, boxes 1, 5, 65, 66, and the Univ. of Wash. Archives Presidents' Office Records, box 122, contain correspondence between CLP and Winkenwerder from 1926–37 pertaining to the University of Wash. demonstration forest, as well as other forestry matters.

9. Henry Schmitz, *The Long Road Travelled* (Seattle, Wash.: Arboretum Foundation, 1973), 145–46.

10. A. Pack to Hugh Baker, Nov. 3, 1932, Pack Collection, SUNY-ESF, drawer 1; Raymond J. Hoyle, "The Middle Years," in George R. Armstrong and Marvin W. Krantz, *Forestry College: Essays on the Growth and Development of New York State's College of Forestry 1911–1961* (Buffalo, N.Y.: William J. Keller, Inc.), 49.

11. Schmitz, 146.

12. *Ibid.,* 149–50.

13. Gill, untitled four-page manuscript describing Pack organizations, Gill Collection, box 1; Liz Brown, "Forest of the Future: UW Forest Offers Living Laboratory," *The News Tribune,* Puyallup, Wash., Sept. 28, 1988, section E; interview with Stan Humann, transcript, Pack Collection, SUNY-ESF, drawer 1.

14. Liz Brown, "Forest of the Future."

15. Gill, "Show Windows of Forestry: The Charles Lathrop Pack Demonstration Forest in the Adirondacks," Pack Collection, SUNY-ESF, drawer 1; *Pack Organizations,* 5.

16. Nelson Courtland Brown, "Charles Lathrop Pack: An Appreciation," *American Review of Reviews* 75, no. 5, (1927):512.

17. Interview with Bruce Breitmeyer, manager, Charles Lathrop Pack Demonstration Forest, Warrensburg, N.Y., audiotape, Pack Collection, SUNY-ESF, box 10; conversations with Richard Schwab, forest properties manager, Pack Forest, Warrensburg; Clifford H. Foster and Burt P. Kirkland, "The Charles Lathrop Pack Demonstration Forest, Warrensburg, N.Y.: Results of Twenty Years of Intensive Forest Management" (Washington, D.C.: Charles Lathrop Pack Forestry Foundation, 1949), 7–8, 11, 15, 18.

18. Schwab to the author, Oct. 30, 1989, Pack Collection, SUNY-ESF, drawer 1, p. 2; "Some Notes on the Charles Lathrop Pack Forestry Foundation," Gill Collection, box 5, p. 2.

19. "Some Notes on the Charles Lathrop Pack Forestry Foundation," 2–3.

20. Untitled report of a meeting concerning demonstration forests in the Northeast, Gill Collection, box 8, p. 5; Brown, 512.

21. Brown to CLP, Feb. 11, 1927, Pack Collection, SUNY-ESF, drawer 1.

22. Untitled report of a meeting concerning demonstration forests in the Northeast, Gill Collection, box 8, p. 7; Gill, "Show Windows of Forestry;" news clips, including "Many to Study Forestry Work," "Excursion at Pack Demonstration Forest Will Be Conducted at State College Project May 3rd;" "U.W. Forest Draws Tourists, Visitors from All States: Experimental Station Donated by C. W. [*sic*] Pack Attracts Lumber Students from Many Parts of the World," "Ideal Lumbering Operations to Be Employed for the Education of Public," University of Washington Archives, College of Forest Resources Records, box 70; "Springfield Meeting—Pacific Northwest Section of Society of American Foresters, Charles Lathrop Pack Demonstration Forest, University of Washington, College of Forestry Friday and Saturday, May 2 and 3, 1930," Univ. of Wash. Archives, College of Forest Resources Records, box 65; Humann interview, 24–25.

23. Smith interview, p. 4.

24. Harry Burry, interview with Jackie Burns, Dec. 14, 1987, Pack Collection, SUNY-ESF, drawer 1.

25. Smith interview, 4.

26. Earl Stone interview with the author, 5, Pack Collection, SUNY-ESF, drawer 4; Edwin C. Jahn, "Research," in George R. Armstrong and Marvin W. Krantz, *Forestry College*, 240.

27. Richard Schwab interview, 1989, audiotape, Pack Collection, SUNY-ESF, box 10.

28. *Ibid.*

29. Gustav Robinson Gregory interview with the author, Pack Collection, SUNY-ESF, transcript (excerpts), drawer 4; audiotape, box 10; "First October Meeting, 1936," in *Regents Proceedings*, Bentley Historical Library, University of Michigan, 63.

30. "January Meeting, 1930," in *Regents Proceedings*, Bentley Historical Library, University of Michigan, 131.

31. *Ibid.*, 162.

32. Willett F. Ramsdell to CLP, May 7, 1937, Pack Collection, Denver.

33. Stephen Spurr to the author, June 6, 1989, Pack Collection, SUNY-ESF, drawer 2.

34. "Jan. Meeting, 1930," 163.

35. "Jan. Meeting, 1930," 161–62; *The University of Michigan: An Encyclopedic Survey*, vol. 2 (Ann Arbor: University of Michigan Press, 1953) 1115–16.

36. Gregory interview.

37. *Ibid.*

38. *Ibid.*

39. "Final Report on the Charles Lathrop Pack Project in Wild Land Utilization," Henry S. Graves Papers, Yale Univ. Library, Dept. of Manuscripts and Archives, box 35, p. 1.

40. *University of Michigan*, 1116.

41. "Final Report on the Charles Lathrop Pack Project in Wild Land Utilization," 4–5; Donald Theoe to the author, July 1989.

42. CLP to Samuel Dana, Sept. 18, 1926, Samuel T. Dana Papers, Bentley Historical Library, University of Michigan, box 1.

43. CLP to Dana, Sept. 4, 1926, Dana Papers, box 1, p. 1.

44. Dana to his wife ("Dearest"), Oct. 21, 1929, Dana Papers, box 1, pp. 1–2.

45. Hosmer, 30–31.

46. Gill, untitled four-page manuscript describing Pack organizations, p. 3; "Pack Prize to Be Offered This Year," memo from Schmitz, undated, for years 1926–1928; University of Minnesota Archives, Division of Forestry; "Pack Natural Resources Essay Contest," *Conservation Comments* 19, no. 23 (1988):2.

47. Hosmer, 30; "Cornell," Gill Collection, box 1.

48. "Cornell."

49. Hosmer, 40.

50. *Ibid.*, 49.

51. *Ibid.*, 49; Romell to A. Pack, May 11, 1934, Gill Collection, box 5.

52. Robert Chandler interview with the author, audiotape, Pack Collection, SUNY-ESF, box 10.

53. Susan J. Riha to the author, April 14, 1988, Pack Collection, SUNY-ESF, drawer 1, p. 1.

54. Fred Winch interview with the author, 1988, transcript, Pack Collection, SUNY-ESF, drawer 4.

55. *Ibid.*

56. Riha to the author, 2.

57. "Dear Katherine": Thomas Gill to Katherine [?], Sept. 28, 1936, two-page unsigned letter describing Gill's career, p. 1, and "Statement of Thomas H. Gill," p. 1, both in Pack Collection, SUNY-ESF, drawer 2, (provided by Edith Holscher, Gill's former secretary). "Death of Dr. Tom Gill, International Forestry Leader," May 22, 1972, Gill Collection, box 9, p. 1; "Statement of Rights Sold—Books by Tom Gill," Gill Collection, box 9; "Statement of Thomas H. Gill."

58. "Dear Katherine"; "Death of Dr. Tom Gill," 2.

Chapter 18

1. "Pack Gives $200,000 for Forestry School School Foundation Fund," *The Michigan Daily*, Feb. 31, 1930; *Pack Organizations*, 10.

2. Amelia R. Fry, "A Summary of the Career of Tom Gill, International Forester," interview with Gill, Oral History Collection, Forest History Society, Durham, N.C., 19–20.

3. *Ten Years of Fact Finding: A Review of the Accomplishments of the Charles Lathrop Pack Forestry Foundation*, (Washington, D.C.: The Charles Lathrop Pack Forestry Foundation, 1941), 1; "A Summary of the Career of Tom Gill," 19; *Ten Years*, 1.

4. *Ten Years*, 1, gives 1929, while Ellen C. Dowling, "The Charles Lathrop Pack Forestry Foundation," *Journal of Forestry* 44, no. 2 (1946):109, gives 1930.

5. Gill, "Charles Lathrop Pack Forestry Foundation," four-page manuscript, Gill Collection, box 4, p. 1.

6. "First Award by Pack Forest Education Board," University of Minnesota Archives, Division of Forestry.

7. *Ten Years*, 1–2.

8. *Ibid.*, 1; Ovid Butler, "A Foundation for the Forest," *American Forests* 54, no. 3 (1948):107.

9. *Ten Years*, 1; Graves, "Charles Lathrop Pack Forest Education Board Memorandum Regarding Past, Present and Future Policy," March 22, 1938, Gill Col-

lection, box 4, p. 1; Dowling, "The Charles Lathrop Pack Forestry Foundation," 108.

10. Gill, untitled four-page manuscript.

11. *Ten Years*, 1.

12. "Charles Lathrop Pack Forest Education Board Announcements of Fellowships in Forestry," University of Minnesota Archives, Division of Forestry, p. 1.

13. *Ibid.*, p. 2; "First Award by Pack Forest Education Board"; press release, "Charles Lathrop Pack Forest Education Board for Use at Once," University of Minnesota Archives, Division of Forestry.

14. *Ten Years*, 2.

15. *Ibid.*, 7–9.

16. *Ibid.*, 2.

17. *Ibid.*

18. *Ibid.*, 3.

19. *Ibid.*

20. *Pack Organizations*, 8.

21. Graves, "Charles Lathrop Pack Forest Education Board Memorandum," 1.

22. *Ten Years*, 4; Graves, "Charles Lathrop Pack Forest Education Board Memorandum," 1; Dowling, "The Charles Lathrop Pack Forestry Foundation," 108; *Ten Years*, 4; Graves, "Charles Lathrop Pack Forest Education Board Memorandum," 1.

23. Graves, "Charles Lathrop Pack Forest Education Board Memorandum," 7.

24. Dowling, "The Charles Lathrop Pack Forestry Foundation," 108; Butler, "Foundation for the Forest," 105, 126.

25. *Ten Years*, pp. 4–5.

26. *Ten Years*, 5; Dowling, "The Charles Lathrop Pack Forestry Foundation," 108; Butler, "Foundation for the Forest," 144.

27. Dowling, "The Charles Lathrop Pack Forestry Foundation," 109.

28. Townsend, note to the author, undated, Pack Collection, SUNY-ESF, drawer 4.

29. James B. Craig, "Forestry's Ambassador Without Portfolio," *American Forests* 66, no. 5 (1960):41; "Randolph Pack, Conservationist, Forestry Expert Who Headed Research Foundation Dies—Led Tree Association," *New York Times*, 26 Dec. 1956.

30. Craig, "Forestry's Ambassador," 41; Townsend interview, 1987.

31. "Pack, Randolph Dies"; Craig, "Forestry's Ambassador," 41.

32. Craig says that Gill started with the foundation in 1926, but he is mistaking the foundation for the trust. The foundation, established either in 1929 or 1930, took over the trust's work and used trust funds for new work, and Gill became the foundation forester once it was organized; Craig, 41.

33. Craig, 42; "Death of Dr. Tom Gill, International Forestry Leader," May 22, 1972, Gill Collection, box 9, p. 2.

34. "Tom Gill," one-page vita, Pack Collection, SUNY-ESF, drawer 2 (provided by E. Holscher).

35. "Randolph G. Pack," *American Forests* 63, no. 2 (1957):8; "Randolph G. Pack, 1890–1956," four-page manuscript, Gill Collection, box 4, p. 2; "Randolph G. Pack," *American Forests*, 8.

36. "Randolph G. Pack, 1890–1956," Gill Collection.

37. *Ibid.*

38. Townsend, note to author, undated, Pack Collection, SUNY-ESF, drawer 4; "The Pack Foundation," four-page manuscript, Gill Collection, box 5, 4.

39. Thomas Gill and Ellen C. Dowling, *The Forestry Directory* (Baltimore: Reese Press, 1943), 190; Thomas Gill, "Charles Lathrop Pack Forestry Foundation," four-page manuscript, Gill Collection, Forest History Society, Durham, N.C., box 4, 3.

40. In "Charles Lathrop Pack Forestry Foundation," Gill credits the foundation with endowing chairs at Michigan, Yale, and Cornell, which were actually founded by the trust, before the foundation was even created; Craig, 41, states that the Charles Lathrop Pack Forestry Foundation hired Gill as its secretary in 1926. Gill became the foundation secretary in 1930, when the organization was founded.

41. Gill and Dowling, *The Forestry Directory*, 189.

42. Craig, 41; Dowling, "The Charles Lathrop Pack Forestry Foundation," 109.

43. Fry, "Summary," 21.

44. Dowling, "The Charles Lathrop Pack Forestry Foundation," 109; Fry, "Summary," 38.

45. Jim O'Hearn (signed Jim, initialed JAO'H) to Gill, May 9, 1960, Gill Collection, box 1. O'Hearn was C. L. Pack's business manager.

Chapter 19

1. "To Urge a World Court, New York Branch of the League Asks to Be Incorporated," *New York Times,* May 13, 1915, p. 439f.; "The World's Court League," five-page document stipulating its purposes, Pack Collection, Denver.

2. Waldo Chamberlin, "League of Nations," *Encyclopedia Americana* (Danbury, Conn.: Americana Corp., 1980), vol. 17, 112; Howard J. Taubenfeld, "International Court of Justice," *Encyclopedia Americana,* vol. 15, 294.

3. "World Court Urged for Lasting Peace: Noted Men Attend Congress in Cleveland to Organize Practical Campaign," *New York Times,* May 13, 1915.

4. Rose, *Cleveland,* 731.

5. "Form World Court League: Organization Perfected at Lunch Given by John Hays Hammond," *New York Times,* Dec. 30, 1915.

6. Chas. Willard Young to CLP, March 27, 1917; CLP to Samuel T. Dutton, Jan. 2, 1919, Jan. 2, 1919, Feb. 8, 1919, Pack Collection, Denver.

7. Graves, "Effect of the War on the Forests of France," Graves Papers, box 46, pp. 2–3.

8. *Ibid.,* 2.

9. A. Pack, *Nature Magazine* 1, no. 1 (1923):35–38; "American Tree Seeds for Europe," *Nature Magazine,* 1, no. 6 (1923):58; Elbert F. Baldwin, "American Tree Seeds in Italy," *Nature Magazine* 1, no. 7 (1923):61–62; "Charles Lathrop Pack," *National Cyclopedia of American Biography,* 126; "American Trees in Europe," *American Review of Reviews* 93, no. 5 (1936):53–54.

10. Graves, "Effect of the War," 21–22.

11. T. S. Woolsey, Jr. to Lieut. Col. H. S. Graves, Jan. 13, 1919, Graves Papers, box 46.

12. "European Reforestation Fund," Chapman Papers, box 41.

13. A. Pack, "From This Seed," 48.

14. *Ibid.*

15. A. Pack diary, 1916.

16. "Hughes Who!" Pinchot Papers, box 489.

17. James J. Patchell to E. P. Earles, July 14, 1920; de Lancey Kountze to Stanley Washburn, July 14, 1920; Thomas W. Miller to Washburn, July 15, 1920; Thomas W. Miller to Washburn, Aug. 12, 1920; Washburn to CLP, Aug. 15, 1920; CLP to Miller, Aug. 20, 1920; all from Washburn Papers, box 4. Washburn to Ridsdale, Aug. 16, 1920, Washburn Papers, box 1.

18. Telegram from CLP to Washburn, 6:23 P.M., June 12, 1920, and telegram from CLP and Baldwin to Washburn, 8:05 P.M., June 12, 1920, Washburn Papers, box 4.

19. A sampling of correspondence regarding these publicity efforts includes Ridsdale to Washburn, March 15, 1920; Washburn to Ridsdale, Aug. 16, Aug. 30, 1920; Ridsdale to Washburn, Aug. 31, 1920; Washburn to Ridsdale, Sept. 2, Sept. 26, 1920; Ridsdale to Washburn, Sept. 27, 1920; all from Washburn Papers, box 1. CLP to Ridsdale, March 1, 1920; Washburn to CLP, Sept. 9, 1920; Washburn to Ridsdale, Sept. 9, 1920; all from Washburn Papers, box 4.

20. Washburn to the editor, *Home News,* Oct. 9, 1920, Washburn Papers, box 4.

21. CLP to George H. Nettleton, undated telegram, no salutation, beginning "The Harding and Coolidge Flying Squadron of New Jersey Closes . . ." Washburn Papers, box 4.

22. Undated telegram, no salutation, Washburn Papers, box 4.

23. Correspondence concerning their backing of Coolidge in 1924 includes: Washburn to CLP, March 25, March 7, 1924; Washburn to John Hays Hammond, March 9, 1924; Washburn to CLP, March 14, March 16; Washburn to CLP, telegram, March 19, 1924, and telegram, no printed date, but with the written notation "ca Mar. 1924?" Washburn Papers, box 2.

Documentation concerning Washburn's run for Congress includes: "Senator Elihu Root's Opinion of Stanley Washburn," newsclip; W. H. Savage, "Stanley Washburn, Republican Candidate for Congress, 3rd Congressional District: His Platform, the Objectives for Which He Strives"; newsclip, dateline Lakewood, N.J., Aug. 15 [1924], Washburn Papers, box 4; CLP to Walter Newton, Sept. 24, 1932; Newton to CLP, Sept. 29, 1932; CLP to Newton, Oct. 3, 1932; Newton to CLP, Oct. 6, 1932; CLP to Newton, Oct. 26, 1932; Newton to CLP, Oct. 29, 1932; CLP to Newton, Oct. 31, 1932, Herbert Hoover Presidential Library, West Branch, Ia., box 264.

24. "Certificate of Election," Pack Family Papers, Tucson.

25. CLP to Hoover, July 24, 1929, Hoover Library, box 164.

26. CLP to Newton, May 27, 1932, Hoover Library, box 264.

27. Newton to CLP, June 2, 1932, Hoover Library, box 264.

28. CLP to Hoover, July 24, 1929; Hoover to CLP, July 25, 1929, Hoover Library, box 164.

29. "Timber Conservation Board," *Encyclopedia of American Forest and Conservation History,* vol. 2, 647; "For Dr. Albert Shaw of the 'Review of Reviews,'" Hoover Library, box 164, p. 3; Ripley Bowman, "The United States Timber Con-

servation Board: Its Program and Its Progress," *Southern Lumberman* 144, no. 1817 (1931):88–89.

30. John H. Thorkelson, "The Great Depression," in *Encyclopedia Americana* (Danbury, Conn.: Americana Corp., 1980), vol. 13, 344; Alexander De Conde, "Herbert Hoover," in *Encyclopedia Americana,* vol. 14, 365.

31. A. Pack to Winkenwerder, Aug. 30, 1932, Winkenwerder Correspondence, box 66.

32. CLP to Newton, July 20, 1932; CLP to "Mr. President" [Hoover] Sept. 17, 1932, Hoover Library, box 164.

33. Edgar B. Nixon, *Franklin D. Roosevelt and Conservation, 1911–1945,* vol. 1, (Hyde Park, N.Y.: General Services Administration National Archives and Records Service, Franklin D. Roosevelt Library, 1957), 112.

34. "Reforestation as a Means of Emergency Employment: Is It Really Practical or Altogether Wise?" University of Washington College of Forest Resources Records, box 66; A. Pack to Hugh Baker, July 8, 1932, Pack Collection, SUNY-ESF, box 6; CLP to Schmitz, July 12, 1932, University of Minnesota Archives, Division of Forestry; Winkenwerder to A. Pack, July 14, 1932, University of Washington College of Forest Resources Records, box 66; Baker to A. Pack, July 14, 1932; A. Pack to Baker, July 16, 1932; Pack Collection, SUNY-ESF, box 6.

35. A. Pack to Baker, July 16, 1932, Pack Collection, SUNY-ESF, box 6.

36. "Forestry as an Unemployment Measure" and "Doctoring a Sick Nation," Hoover Library, box 164.

37. CLP to Newton, July 20, 1932, Hoover Library, box 164.

38. Washburn to Newton, July 25, 1932, Hoover Library, box 164.

39. *Ibid.*

40. *Ibid.*

41. *Ibid.*

42. Arthur M. Hyde to Newton, Hoover Library, box 164.

43. *Ibid.*

44. *Ibid.*

45. CLP to Newton, Sept. 12, 1932, Hoover Library, box 164.

46. *Ibid.;* "Forest Employment Survey Shows 70,000 Men for Year at Cost of $52,000,000," *Forestry News Digest,* Oct. 1932, 1–2.

47. CLP to Hoover, Sept. 17, 1932, Hoover Library, box 164, pp. 1–2.

48. "Forestry Statement For President Hoover—By Mr. Charles Lathrop Pack," Hoover Library, box 164.

49. Hoover to CLP, Sept. 20, 1932, Hoover Library, box 164.

50. CLP to Newton, Sept. 26, 1932, Hoover Library, box 164, p. 2.

51. "Forest Unemployment Survey Shows"; Newton to CLP, Sept. 27, 1932, and Newton to Hyde, Oct. 1, 1932, Hoover Library, box 164.

52. CLP to Newton, Oct. 26, 1932, Hoover Library, box 164.

Chapter 20

1. A. Pack, "From This Seed," 30.

2. CLP to Newton, Nov. 23, 1932, Hoover Library, box 264.

3. "Roosevelt Enlarges on Forestry Views," American Tree Association news sheet, Herbert Hoover Presidential Library, box 264.

4. CLP to Franklin D. Roosevelt, Nov. 21, 1932, Franklin D. Roosevelt Library, Governor's Collection, Hyde Park, N.Y., box 2.

5. FDR to CLP, Dec. 29, 1931, FDR Library, Governor's Collection, box 62.

6. Private Secretary to Gentlemen, Nov. 30, 1932; CLP to Guernsey T. Cross, Dec. 12, 1932; CLP to Cross, Dec. 13, 1932; Cross to CLP, Dec. 15, 1932; Cross to CLP, Dec. 16, 1932; CLP to Cross, Dec. 17, 1932; Cross to CLP, Dec. 22, 1932; FDR Library, Governor's Collection, box 2.

7. CLP to Schmitz, Jan. 24, 1933, University of Minnesota Archives, Division of Forestry.

8. CLP to FDR, Feb. 20, 1933, FDR Library, President's Personal File, box 191.

9. *Ibid.*

10. "Jobs on Trees," Feb. 14, 1933. *Republican-News* (Kananakee, Ill.)

11. FDR to CLP, April 1, 1933, FDR Library, President's Personal File, box 191.

12. Ridsdale to Stephen T. Early, April 15, 1933, FDR Library, President's Personal File, box 191.

13. M. A. Le Hand to CLP, March 11, 1933, FDR Library, President's Personal File, box 191.

14. Dana, *Forest and Range Policy*, 249.

15. CLP to Winkenwerder, May 13, 1933; "From Charles Lathrop Pack," May 10, 1933, Winkenwerder Correspondence, box 65.

16. CLP to Winkenwerder, May 13, 1933, Winkenwerder Correspondence, box 65.

17. CLP to Schmitz, Nov. 14, 1933, University of Minnesota Archives, Division of Forestry.

18. CLP to Spring, Feb. 27, 1934, University of Minnesota Archives, Division of Forestry.

19. CLP to Winkenwerder, June 21, 1933, Winkenwerder Correspondence, box 65.

20. Schmitz to CLP, May 14, 1935,

21. CLP to Schmitz, Feb. 7, 1934, University of Minnesota Archives, Division of Forestry.

22. CLP to Schmitz, Nov. 14, 1933, University of Minnesota Archives, Division of Forestry.

23. CLP to Jeffers, Sept. 30, 1933, University of Washington Archives, College of Forest Resources Records, box 65; CLP to Winkenwerder, Aug. 7, 1933, Winkenwerder Correspondence, box 65.

24. CLP to Schmitz, June 27, 1933, University of Minnesota Archives, Division of Forestry.

25. CLP to Winkenwerder, Aug. 22, 1933, Winkenwerder Correspondence, box 65.

26. *Ibid.*

27. *Evening Leader* (Lowell, Mass.), Aug. 20, 1935.

28. "Leaving CCC Camps," *The Banner* (Asheville, Tenn.), Aug. 19, 1935.

29. "The CCC Issue," *Providence* [R.I.] *Journal*, Aug. 17, 1935.

30. "President Roosevelt, in Statement for the *Digest,* Says Future of Ameri-

cans and Forests Interlock," *Forestry News Digest*, Jan. 1936; "People Linked by Roosevelt with Forests," *Capital Journal* (Salem, Ore.), Jan. 9, 1936.

31. CLP to Winkenwerder, Aug. 22, 1933, Winkenwerder Correspondence, box 65.

32. CLP to Winkenwerder, Aug. 9, 1933, Winkenwerder Correspondence, box 65.

33. Barrett G. Potter, "Civilian Conservation Corps," in *Encyclopedia of American Forest and Conservation History*, vol. 1, 82.

34. Dana, 250; *NACCCA* [National Association of CCC Alumni] *Journal* (St. Louis, Mo.) 11, no. 12 (1988):18; Dana, 250.

35. Dana, 249.

36. "Franklin Delano Roosevelt," *Encyclopedia Americana* (Danbury, Conn.: Americana Corp., 1980), vol. 23, 768; CLP to Winkenwerder, undated, but appears with August 1933 correspondence, Winkenwerder Correspondence, box 65.

37. C. L. Pack, "Auditing the CCC Ledger," *Review of Reviews and World's Work* 89, no. 1, (1934):28.

38. *Ibid.*

39. Dana, *Forest and Range Policy*, 249; Harold Titus, "Will We Make the Same Mistakes Again?" *The Saturday Evening Post* 219, no. 11 (1944):19, 93.

40. Dana, 249–50.

41. Winkenwerder to CLP, Aug. 31, 1933, Winkenwerder Correspondence, box 65.

42. CLP to Winkenwerder, Aug. 31, 1933, Winkenwerder Correspondence, box 65.

43. Winkenwerder to CLP, Sept. 16, 1933, Winkenwerder Correspondence, box 65.

44. Winkenwerder to CLP, May 1, 1935, Winkenwerder Correspondence, box 65.

Chapter 21

1. Telegram, William Savage to Schmitz, June 14, 1937, University of Minnesota Archives, Division of Forestry; "Charles Pack Is Dead; War Gardens Man," *New York Times*, June 15, 1937; "Charles Lathrop Pack," *Dictionary of American Biography*, 508.

2. CLP to Winkenwerder, Jan. 26, 1937, Winkenwerder Correspondence, box 65.

3. Savage to Winkenwerder, June 20, 1936; Savage to Professor Meyer, Feb. 23, 1937; Savage to Winkenwerder, April 2, 1937, Winkenwerder Correspondence, box 65.

4. Helen Huss to Winkenwerder, Jan. 27, 1937, Winkenwerder Correspondence, box 65.

5. Pack interview, p. 14.

6. "Charles Lathrop Pack Dies in New York: Brief Illness Fatal to World's No. 1 Forester & Town's Benefactor," *Lakewood* (N.J.) *Times*, June 14, 1937.

7. *St. Mary Academy 1898–1973.*

8. Carl Bannwart to CLP, May 5, 1927, Pack Collection, SUNY-ESF, drawer 3 (facsimile provided by Virginia Townsend).

9. C. B. Waldron to CLP, May 4, 1927, Pack Collection, SUNY-ESF, drawer 3 (facsimile provided by Virginia Townsend).

10. James Henry Darlington to CLP, April 12, 1927, Pack Collection, SUNY-ESF, drawer 3 (facsimile provided by Virginia Townsend).

11. E. T. Meredith to CLP, May 3, 1927; Frank Crane to CLP, April 25, 1927; Katherin Claberger to CLP, May 3, 1927; Harold S. Buttenheim to CLP, May 6, 1927; Theodore E. Burton to CLP, April 28, 1927, all in Pack Collection, SUNY-ESF, drawer 3 (facsimiles provided by Virginia Townsend). J. Carrier, Director General of Waters and Forests, French Ministry of Agriculture, Pack Collection, SUNY-ESF, scrapbook.

12. "A Septuagenarian Lover of Trees," *New York Times,* editorial section, April 15, 1927.

13. C. A. Schenck to CLP, May 5, 1937, Pack Collection, Denver.

14. Pinchot to CLP, 1927, Pinchot Papers, container 280; Pinchot to CLP, May 5, 1937, Pinchot Papers, box 357.

15. "Heirs of Pack Are Pledged to Conservation," *New York Herald-Tribune,* June 22, 1937.

16. Joan Burns interview, drawer 1, pp. 3–4, 7, 11; Patsy Norfleet Degener interview, drawer 2, 8; Albert Manus interview, drawer 2, pp. 2–5; Townsend to the author, Nov. 8, 1989, drawer 4, p. 1. all in Pack Collection, SUNY-ESF.

17. Gill, "Charles Lathrop Pack, 1857–1937," *Journal of Forestry* 35, no. 7 (1937):623.

Chapter 22

1. Last will and testament of Charles Lathrop Pack, Surrogate's Office, Ocean County, N.J., p. 31.

2. *Ibid.,* 32.

3. *Ibid.,* 33–34.

4. Gill to Arthur Pack, May 23, 1961, Gill Collection, box 5; "The Pack Foundation," Gill Collection, box 5, p. 3.

5. "American Tree Association," *Encyclopedia of American Forest and Conservation History,* vol. 1, 21.

6. The *Nature Magazine* masthead lists Arthur Pack as president emeritus of the ANA from May 1946 through December 1950, and Richard W. Westwood as president of the ANA during these years; "American Nature Association," *Encyclopedia of American Forest and Conservation History,* vol. 1, 18.

7. Note from Townsend, Pack Collection, SUNY-ESF, drawer 4.

8. Luther Halsey Gulick, *American Forest Policy* (New York: Duell, Sloan and Pierce, 1951). In *Forest and Range Policy* Dana mentions briefly the American Tree Association in connection with its publishing a report on the McSweeney-McNary act in 1926, and Greeley in *Forests and Men* mentions the ATA listing 2,950 county and community forests in the United States; however, neither author mentions Charles Lathrop Pack.

Sources

Archives and Collected Papers

Chapman, Herman H. Papers. Sterling Memorial Library, Yale Unversity, New Haven, Connecticut. Boxes 20, 41.

Dana, Samuel Trask. Papers. Bentley Historical Library, University of Michigan, Ann Arbor. Box 1.

Garfield, James R. Papers. Library of Congress, Washington, D.C. Boxes 117, 118, 148.

Gill, Thomas Harvey. Collection. Forest History Society, Durham, North Carolina. Boxes 1, 2, 4, 5, 8, 9.

Graves, Henry S. Papers. Department of Manuscripts and Archives, Yale University Library, New Haven, Connecticut. Box 46.

Hoover, Herbert. Papers. Herbert Hoover Presidential Library. West Branch, Iowa. Boxes 164, 264.

Hosmer, Ralph Sheldon. Papers. Department of Manuscripts and Archives, Cornell University Library, Ithaca, New York. Box 23.

Mann, Albert R. Papers. Department of manuscripts and Archives, Cornell University Library, Ithaca, New York. Box 41.

Pack, Charles Lathrop. Family Papers, Manuscript number 640. Arizona Historical Society, Tucson, Arizona.

Pack, Charles Lathrop. Papers and collected materials. Charles Lathrop Pack Collection. Terence J. Hoverter Archives, State University of New York College of Environmental Science and Forestry, (SUNY-ESF), Syracuse. Drawers 1–4, boxes 1, 6, 8, 9, 10.

Pack, Charles Lathrop. Papers. Charles Lathrop Pack Collection. Western History Department, Denver Public Library, Denver, Colorado.

Pinchot, Gifford. Papers. Manuscript Division, Library of Congress, Washington, D.C. Boxes 169, 182, 199, 240, 241, 243, 357, 482, 489, 514, 554. Container 280.

Roosevelt, Franklin Delano. Franklin Delano Roosevelt Library. Hyde Park, New York. Governor's Collection, boxes 2, 62; President's Personal File, box 191.

Schenk, C. A. Papers. Forest history Society, Durham, North Carolina.

Schenk; C. A. Papers. North Carolina State University Archives, Raleigh.

Schmitz, Henry. University of Minnesota Archives, Division of Forestry. Minneapolis.

Washburn, Stanley. Papers. Library of Congress, Washington, D.C. Boxes 1, 4.

Winkenwerder, Hugo. Correspondence. College of Forest Resources Records, University of Washington Archives, Seattle. Boxes 1, 5, 6, 65, 66, 70.

Winkenwerder, Hugo. Correspondence. President's Office Records, University of Washington Archives, Seattle. Box 122.

Zon, Raphael. Family Papers. Minnesota Historical Society. St. Paul.

Interviews and Letters to the Author

Copies of the letters and transcripts or audiotapes of the interviews are stored in the Charles Lathrop Pack Collection, Terence J. Hoverter Archives, State University of New York College of Environmental Science and Forestry, Syracuse, New York.

Boggs, Elizabeth. Interview with author, 1988. Transcript, drawer 1.

Chandler, Robert. Interview with author, 1988. Audiotape, box 10.

Gregory, Gustav Robinson. Interview with the author, 1988. Written excerpts, drawer 4; audiotape, box 10.

Hammond, Dorothea. Interview with the author, 1989. Transcript, drawer 1.

Hibben, Eleanor Brown Pack. Interview with the author, 1988. Transcript, drawer 2.

Humann, Stan. Interview with the author, 1989. Transcript, drawer 1.

Liddell, Eleanor Pack. Interview with the author, 1988. Transcript, drawer 2; audiotape, box 11.

Pack, Phoebe Finley. Interview with author and Virginia Lathrop (Pack) Townsend, 1988. Transcript, drawer 4.

Pullen, Muriel. Interview with the author, 1988. Transcript, drawer 4.

Riha, Susan J. Letter to the author, April 14, 1988, drawer 1.

Schwab, Richard. Interview with the author, 1989. Notes, drawer 1; audiotape, box 10.

Smith, David. Interview with the author, 1988. Transcript, drawer 1; audiotapes, box 10.

Stone, Earl. Interview with the author. 1988. Transcript, drawer 4.

Tarver, John. Interview with the author, 1988. Audiotapes, box 10.

Townsend, Virginia Lathrop (Pack). Interviews with the author, 1987 and 1988. Audiotapes, box 10.

Townsend, Virginia Lathrop (Pack). Notes and letters, drawer 4.

Winch, Fred. Interview with the author, 1988. Transcript, drawer 4.

Select Bibliography

Alburn, Wilfred Henry, and Miriam Russell Alburn. *This Cleveland of Ours.* 2 vols. Cleveland: S. J. Clarke Publishing Company, 1933.

"American Nature Association." *Forestry Almanac,* pp. 129–30. Philadelphia: J. B. Lippincott Co., 1926.

"American Tree Association." *Forestry Almanac,* pp. 52–55. Philadelphia: J. B. Lippincott Co., 1926.

Armstrong, George R., and Marvin W. Krantz. *Forestry College: Essays on the Growth and Development of New York State's College of Forestry, 1911–1961.* Buffalo: William J. Keller, Inc., 1961.

Avery, Elroy McKendree. *A History of Cleveland and Its Environs.* Vol. 3. New York: Lewis Publishing Company, 1918.

Ayres, Philip W. "The Charles Lathrop Pack Demonstration Forests." *The American Review of Reviews* 75, no. 5 (1927):513–15.

Brown, Nelson Courtland. "Charles Lathrop Pack: An Appreciation." *The American Review of Reviews* 75, no. 5 (1927):511–13.

Burns, Anna C. "Louisiana Forests." *Encyclopedia of American Forest and Conservation History,* vol. 1, 363–64.

Butler, Ovid. "A Foundation for the Forest." *American Forests* 54, no. 3 (1948):105–6, 126–44.

Carr, William. "Three Distinguished Conservationists." *American Forests* 82, no. 6, (1976):8–9.

Chapman, Herman Haupt. "The American Forestry Association Versus Charles Lathrop Pack." Unpublished article. Pinchot Papers. Manuscript Division, Library of Congress, Washington, D.C., box 240.

Chapman, Herman Haupt. "Has the American Forestry Association Losts Its Former Usefulness? Reflections of a Life Director." *Journal of Forestry* 19 (1921). Eight-part series. Parts 1, 2, no. 3, 285–94; parts 3–5, no. 4, 327–53. Parts 6–8, no. 5, 449–65.

Clepper, Henry. "American Forestry Association." *Encyclopedia of American Forest and Conservation History,* vol. 1, 16–18.

Clepper, Henry. "Crusade for Conservation: The Centennial History of the American Forestry Association." *American Forests* 81, no. 10 (1975).

"CLP Materials: Recollections of Charles Lathrop Pack." Pack Collection, Denver.

Cox, Thomas R. "Lumberman's Frontier." *Encyclopedia of American Forest and Conservation History,* vol. 1, pp. 385–89.

Craig, James B. "Forestry's Ambassador Without Portfolio." *American Forests* 66, no. 5, (1960):21.

Dana, Samuel Trask. *Forest and Range Policy.* New York: McGraw-hill, 1956.

"Demand for a Change in Policy of the American Forestry Association." *Journal of Forestry* 19, no. 6 (1921):661–64.

Dowling, Ellen C. "The Charles Lathrop Pack Forestry Foundation." *Journal of Forestry* 44, no. 2 (1946):108.

Dumond, Neva. *Thumb Diggings: Adventures into Michigan's Thumb Area.* Lexington, Mich.: privately published, 1962.

Encyclopedia of American Forest and Conservation History. New York: Macmillan, 1983.

Garfield, Harry A. *The Cleveland Trust Company: A History.* Privately printed, no date. Pack Collection, SUNY-ESF, drawer 1 (provided by the AmeriTrust Corp., Cleveland, Ohio).

"George Pack Story." Unpublished. Produced by Sanilac County Historical Society, Port Sanilac, Michigan. Pack Collection, SUNY-ESF, drawer 4.

Gill, Thomas H. "Charles Lathrop Pack Forestry Foundation." Four-page manuscript. Gill Collection, Forest History Society, Durham, North Carolina. Box 4.

Gill, Thomas H. Untitled, four-page manuscript describing the Pack organizations, research, and projects. Gill Collection. Forest History Society, Durham, North Carolina. Box 1.

Gill, Thomas H. "Show Windows of Forestry: The Charles Lathrop Pack Demonstration Forest in the Adirondacks." Pack Collection, SUNY-ESF, drawer 1.

Gill, Thomas H. Unpublished biography of Charles Lathrop Pack. Gill Collection, Forest History Society, Durham, N.C.

Gill, Thomas H., and Ellen C. Dowling. *The Forestry Directory*. Baltimore: Reese Press, 1943.

Gillis, Peter, and Thomas R. Roach. *Lost Initiatives: Canada's Forest Industries, Forest Policy and Forest Conservation*. New York: Greenwood Press, 1986.

Graves, Henry S. "Charles Lathrop Pack Forest Education Board Memo Regarding Past, Present & Future Policy," March 22, 1938. Gill Collection, box 4.

Graves, Henry S. "Editorial Comment: The American Forestry Association Turns a New Leaf." *Journal of Forestry* 19, no. 3, (1921):315.

Gray, Gary Craven. "Conservation Movement." *Encyclopedia of American Forest and Conservation History*, vol. 1, 105–13.

Greeley, William B. *Forests and Men*. Garden City, N.Y.: Doubleday, 1951.

Harbor Beach Centennial 1882–1982. Pamphlet [1982]. Pack Collection, SUNY-ESF, drawer 4. (Provided by Marilyn L. Hebner, Port Huron, Michigan.)

History of Iosco County. Iosco County Historical Society. East Tawas, Mich., no date.

History of Lake Huron Shore, with Illustrations and Biographical Sketches of Some of Its Prominent Men and Pioneers. Chicago: H. R. Page, 1883.

Hosmer, Ralph Sheldon. *Forestry at Cornell: A Retrospect of Proposals, Developments, and Accomplishments in the Teaching of Professional Forestry at Cornell University*. Ithaca, N.Y., 1950.

Hatch, Alice Gertrude. Diary for the years 1879, 1880, 1885. Pack Family Papers, Tucson.

Kerr, Ed. "History of Forestry in Louisiana," in Kerr, *Tales of the Louisiana Forests*, 1–26. Baton Rouge, Claitor's Publishing. (There is no copyright date for this book, but Claitor's says it is at least five years old, as of 1989.)

Lakewood in the Pines: A Backward Glance. Lakewood, N.J.: Lakewood Heritage Commission, 1987.

Lawrence, Joseph Collins. "British Columbia." *Encyclopedia Britannica Macropedia*, vol. 3. Chicago: Encyclopedia Britannica, 1983, 296–301.

Lower, A. R. M. *The North American Assault on the Canadian Forest*. Toronto: The Ryerson Press, 1938.

Mason, Philip. *Michigan Historical Commission: Lumbering Era in Michigan History, 1860–1900*. Lansing: Michigan Historical Commission, 1956.

Mayor, Archer H. *Southern Timberman: The Legacy of William Buchanan*. Athens: The University of Georgia Press, 1988.

McMahon, John R. "The War Garden Campaign of 1917." *The Country Gentleman* 82, no. 45 (1917):1722–23, 1747.

Mellick, Hazel. "A City Is Born," in *A Wind Gone Down: West-Running Brook*, 25–27. Lansing: Michigan Department of State, History Division, 1978.

Miller, Jane, and Madeline Felker. "The George Pack Story." Produced under the auspices of the Sanilac County Historical Society, Port Sanilac, Mich., 1988. Pack Collection, SUNY-ESF, drawer 4.

Morrow, James B. "Cleveland Man War Gardener's General." *Cleveland Plain Dealer*, Sept. 13, 1917.

Morrow, James B. "No Sentiment, Just Plain Common Sense Made Him the First Active Worker for Forest Conservation." *Sunday Plain Dealer,* Jan. 5, 1913. Editorial and drama section, 3.

Nixon, Edgar B. *Franklin D. Roosevelt and Conservation 1911–1945.* Hyde Park, N.Y.: General Services Administration National Archives and Records Service, Franklin D. Roosevelt Library, 1957.

"Notes from Mrs. McNary in Asheville." Pack Collection, Denver.

"Notes from CLP." Pack Collection, Denver.

Pack, Arthur Newton. Diary. The years 1911, 1914, 1915, 1916, 1919, Pack Family Papers, Tucson; 1920, property of Margaret Pack McKinley, Santa Fe, N.M.

Pack, Arthur Newton. "From This Seed." Unpublished autobiography. Undated. Pack Collection, State University of New York College of Environmental Science and Forestry, Syracuse. drawer 1. (Provided by Virginia Lathrop [Pack] Townsend.)

Pack, Arthur Newton. *We Called It Ghost Ranch.* Albuquiu, N.M.: Ghost Ranch Conference Center, 1979.

"Pack, Charles Lathrop." *Dictionary of American Biography.* Vol. 1, sup. 2. New York: Charles Scribner's Sons, 1958.

"Pack, Charles Lathrop." *National Cyclopedia of American Biograpy.* Vol. 28. New York: James T. White, 1940.

Pack, Charles Lathrop. "Auditing the CCC Ledger." *Review of Reviews and World's Work,* 89, no 1, (1934).

Pack, Charles Lathrop. Diary for April to August 1878. Pack Family Papers, Tucson.

Pack, Charles Lathrop. *The School Book of Forestry.* Philadelphia: J. B. Lippincott Co., 1922.

Pack, Charles Lathrop. *Thomas Hatch of Barnstable and Some of His Descendants.* Newark, N.J.: The Society of Colonial Wars in the State of New Jersey, 1930.

Pack, Charles Lathrop. *Trees as Good Citizens.* Philadelphi: J. B. Lippincott Co., 1922.

Pack, Charles Lathrop. *The War Garden Victorious.* Philadelphia: J. B. Lippincott Co., 1919.

"Randolph G. Pack." *American Forests* 63, no. 2 (1957):8.

"Randolph G. Pack, 1890–1956." Four-page manuscript. Gill Collection, box 4.

"Pack, Randolph," in *Who Was Who,* vol. 3, 659. Chicago: Marquis-Who's Who Inc., 1960.

The Pack Organizations. Booklet. No publisher. No date. Trinity College Archives, Hartford, Conn.

Parker, Douglas S. "In Search of the Great White Heron: William Lovell Finley (1876–1953) and Wildlife Conservation in Oregon," B. A. thesis, Oregon State University, 1976.

Phillips, Charles J. "Charles Lathrop Pack: Forester, Economist, Philatelist." *Stamps* 1, no. 4 (1932):117–18.

Pinchot, Gifford. *Breaking New Ground.* New York: Harcourt, Brace, 1947.

Portrait and Biographical Album of Huron County. Chicago: Chapman Brothers, 1884. Reprint. Sebewaing, Mich.: Red Flannel Underwear Press, 1976.

Rollins, Philip A. *The Butt of the Log of the Sinnemahoning: Being the Record of a Trip to New Orleans in Jan. 1905.* Privately printed, undated. Pack Collection, SUNY-ESF, drawer 2. (Provided by Virginia Townsend.)

Rose, William Ganson. *Cleveland, The Making of a City.* Cleveland: World Publishing Co., 1950.

Sanilac County [Mich.] Historical Society. *Portrait and Biographical Album of Sanilac County.* Chicago: Chapman Brothers, 1884.

Schmitz, Henry. *The Long Road Travelled.* Seattle, Wash.: Arboretum Foundation, 1973.

Solomon, Harry R. "Historical Sketch of Oscoda and Au Sable," in *Homecoming Week on the Sable.* Evansville, Indiana: Unigraph, Inc., 1979.

Stokes, George Alwin. "Lumbering in Southwest Louisiana: A Study of the Industry as a Culturo-Geographic Factor." Ph.D. diss., Louisiana State University, 1954.

Ten Years of Fact Finding: A Review of the Accomplishments of the Charles Lathrop Pack Forestry Foundation. Washington, D.C.: The Charles Lathrop Pack Forestry Foundation, 1941.

Thornton, Neil. *Along the Historic River Aux Sables.* Tawas City, Michigan: Printer's Devil, 1987.

Tinker, Frank A. "A Museum Joins the Forest Service." *American Forests* 77, no. 5 (1971):32–35.

Van Tassel, David D., and John J. Grabowski, eds. *The Encyclopedia of Cleveland History.* Bloomington: Indiana University Press, in association with Case Western Reserve University, 1987.

"Verona." An unpublished, uncredited article on file with the Bad Axe Public Library, Bad Axe, Mich. (Submitted by Helen M. Kerr.)

Whitford, H. N., and Roland D. Craig. *Forests of British Columbia.* Ottawa: Commission of Conservation, Canada Committee on Forests, 1918.

Index

Essay prizes, Charles L. Pack Foundation establishes, 218–19
Euclid Avenue, Cleveland, Oh., as business district, 38–40
Euclid Avenue National Bank, 44
Europe: Charles L. Pack's tour of in 1874, 16; in 1878, 22–25, 23; forest management in, xv–xvi
European Reforestation Fund, American Forestry Association's, 238
Everett, Henry A., 44

Far East Forestry Commission, 231
Farman, Frances ("Phoebe"), 6, 7. See also Pack, Frances (Charles L. Pack's mother)
Farman, Samuel Ward, 6
Fellowships: Charles L. Pack establishes at Cornell, 219; through Pack Forest Education Board, 226
Fernow, Bernhardt, 89, 162
Fertilization practices, 220
Finley, Phoebe, 201. See also Pack, Phoebe Finley
Finley, William Lovell, 199
Fire control systems, xv
First Presbyterian Church (Lakewood, N.J.), 266, 269
Fisher, Irving, 171
Flagg, James Montgomery, 175
Flying Squadron, 240–41
Ford, Henry, 66, 179
Ford Foundation, 215
Forest Act of 1912 (Canada), 129
Forest conservation, Charles L. Pack's early interest in, 25; history of, 81–82; and sawmill owners, 229. See also Conservation; Nature conservation
Forest economics, study of, 215
"Forest Employment Survey," 248
Forest management, in Europe, xv–xvi
Forest Poetic, The, distribution of, 145
Forest Resource Economics (Gregory), 215
Forestry, FDR on importance of, 258–59
Forestry Almanac, 190
"Forestry As An Unemployment Measure" (C. L. Pack), 244
Forestry Directory, 190
Forestry Legislative Survey, 190, 191
Forestry News Digest, 191, 206, 221, 256; Charles L. Pack and, 264
Forest Primer, The (C. L. Pack), xvii; Civil Conservation Corps edition of, 262; marketing of, 188
Forests, wartime devastation of, 237
Forest soils, university chair at Cornell in, 219–21

Forest Soils Society of America, 220
Formosa, forestry policy for, 230, 231
Fort Gratiot, Mich., 5
Foster, Cliff, 212
Fowler, Gary W., 216
Frank, Bernard, 227
Fritz, Emanuel, 182
"From This Seed" (Arthur Pack), 197
Fuller, Georgia, 116. See also Pack, Georgia Fuller

Gardening, Charles L. Pack's zeal for, 70–72
Garfield, Harry Augustus, 44, 46–47, 115
Garfield, James A., 38
Garfield, James Rudolph, 44–45, 78, 90, 170; and waterpower fight, 105, 106
Gaskill, Alfred, 136, 137, 140; on Charles L. Pack's propaganda, 143–44; resigns from American Forestry Association, 149
George Willis Pack Land and Lumber Company, 118
George Willis Pack Forestry Foundation, 212–16, 218
George Willis Pack Professor of Forest Land Management, 213–16
Georgian Court, 70
Ghost Ranch, 201
Ghost Ranch Museum, 202, 203, 271
Gill, Thomas, as Pack Forestry Foundation secretary, 225; in the Phillippines, 231; and Randolph Pack, 230–31; tropical forests, survey of, 221. See also Biography (unpublished) of Charles L. Pack (Gill)
Goff, Frederick H., 169
Good Pine Lumber Company, 32
Goodyear, Frank H., 128–29
Gordon Pasha (Lois Lake), 129
Gould, George Jay, 70
Gould, Jay, 32, 74
Gowanlock, R. K., 119, 161
Grant Timber and Manufacturing Company, 3, 161
Graves, Henry S., 157–58, 166; and Charles L. Pack, 223–24; heads Pack Forest Education Board, 226; reforestation idea of, 237–38; on wartime forests, 237
Great Smoky Mountains National Park, 260
Great Southern Lumber Company, 34
Greeley, Arthur W., 99
Greeley, William B., 8, 35, 90, 152, 159, 162
Gregory, Gustav Robinson, 215–16
Grim, William Rhoads (W. R.), 123

Townsend, Jim (Charles L. Pack's great-grandson), *268*
Townsend, Virginia Pack (Charles L. Pack's granddaughter), *268*
Tree-planting, as custom, 19; and Washington Bicentennial, 189–90
Trees as Good Citizens (C. L. Pack), 187–88
Tree seeds, shipped to Europe, 143, 198, 237
Trinity College (Hartford, CT), 179–80
Tropical Plant Research Foundation, 221
Trout Creek Lumber Company, 32
Tucson, Ariz., Arthur Pack family in, 201–3
Typhoid fever, 3

Union Club of Cleveland, 170
United Nations : Food and Agriculture Organization of, 215, 230, 231; forestry division of, 231; Scientific Conference on Conservation and Utilization of Resources, 230, 231
U. S. Forest Service, 141
University of California, 218
University of Michigan, 218; forest conservation chair at, *xviii;* and George Willis Pack Forestry Foundation, 212–16, 218; honorary degree of, to Randolph, 231; School of Natural Resources of, 218; Wild Land Utilization Professorship in, 216
University of Minnesota, 218
University of Tübingen, 25
University of Washington, 218; demonstration forests at, 205, 206–9
Unpublished biography of Charles L. Pack (Gill). *See* Biography (unpublished) of Charles L. Pack (Gill)

Vanderbilt, George W., 82; Charles L. Pack and, 83–84
Vanderbilt Hotel, Charles L. Pack's suite at, 55
Verrees, J. Paul, 175, 176
Victory gardens, *xvii–xviii,* 142
Vrooman, Carl, 171, 172

Wagener, W. W., 227
Waldron, C. B., 266–67
War gardens, impact of, 176–77. *See also* National War Garden Commission
War Garden Victorious, The (Pack), 168, 180
Warrensburg, N.Y., 209

Warrensburg Pack Forest, 209, 212
Washburn, Stanley, 74, 139; and 1920 Republican campaign, 239–41; and forestry unemployment measure, 244–45
Washington Bicentennial Tree Planting Association, 189–90
Washington (state) Conservation Association, 97
Washington Township, Mich., 4
Watermelons, Charles L. Pack's failed venture with, 15–16
Water Power Act (1920), 112
Waterpower monopolists, 96–97
Weddell, Peter M., 40
Weeks Act of 1911, 134
Wells, Maxine, 232
Wells, Philip P., 154, 155
Western Reserve Trust Company, 47
Westwood, Richard W., 184, 271
Weyerhauser, Frederick, 82, 84
White, Edwin, 212
White, John Barber, 35, 123, 136
White, Rollin H., 38
White pine: in demonstration forests, 209, 212; as heat sensitive, 28–29; Michigan's, 4, 8, 11, 27
Williams College, 115, 117
Wilson, Woodrow, 238, 239
Winch, Fred E., 220
Winkenwerder, Hugo, 187, 194, 206, 226, 235; and Civilian Conservation Corps, 254–57, 259, 260, 262–63; and Charles L. Pack, 264
Wood, Leonard, 239
Woods, John Lund, 5, 6, 44, 78
Woods & Company, 6, 20
Woods, Perry & Company, 43
Woolsey, T. S., Jr., 238
World Court Congress, 142, 236
World Court League, 142, 233, 235
World Forestry Congress (1926), 190; Third (1949), 231; Fourth (1954), 231
World War I, Charles L. Pack and, 142

Yale Forest (Yale-Myers Forest), 205. *See also* Keene Forest
Yale School of Forestry, 205
Yale University, 88, 218
Yellowstone National Park Timberland Reserve, 82

Zon, Raphael, 194, 226